Foreword by **JONI MITCHELL**

BUFFY
SAINTE-MARIE

THE AUTHORIZED
BIOGRAPHY

ANDREA
WARNER

GREYSTONE BOOKS
Vancouver/Berkeley

This book is dedicated to
Indigenous women, girls, and Two-Spirited people—
yesterday, today, tomorrow.
We see you, we honor you, we love you.
Thank you.

First paperback edition 2021

21 22 23 24 25   5 4 3 2 1

Greystone Books Ltd.
greystonebooks.com

Cataloguing data available from Library and Archives Canada
ISBN 978-1-77164-729-8 (pbk.)
ISBN 978-1-77164-358-0 (cloth)
ISBN 978-1-77164-359-7 (epub)

Editing by Jennifer Croll
Copyediting by Susan Safyan
Proofreading by Jennifer Stewart
Cover design by Will Brown
Text design by Nayeli Jimenez
Cover photograph courtesy of Buffy Sainte-Marie
Printed and bound in Canada on ancient-forest-friendly paper by Friesens

Permission for all lyrics quoted in this book provided by Buffy Sainte-Marie.

Greystone Books gratefully acknowledges the Musqueam, Squamish, and Tsleil-Waututh peoples on whose land our office is located.

Greystone Books thanks the Canada Council for the Arts, the British Columbia Arts Council, the Province of British Columbia through the Book Publishing Tax Credit, and the Government of Canada for supporting our publishing activities.

Canadä

BRITISH COLUMBIA | BRITISH COLUMBIA ARTS COUNCIL
An agency of the Province of British Columbia

Canada Council   Conseil des arts
for the Arts   du Canada

TABLE OF CONTENTS

FOREWORD

BY JONI MITCHELL

WHEN I STARTED out in the sixties there weren't many women writing music, but Buffy Sainte-Marie was an exception to the rule. Whenever Buffy came through town I went down to the coffee house to hear her play. Her songs were so smart, so well-crafted, and her performances were stunning. She was different from the stereotypical music industry old boys' club. When I moved to Toronto to pursue music, I stopped at the Mariposa Folk Festival on the way to see Buffy perform. A year later, I played that same festival, so you could say I followed in Buffy's footsteps.

Buffy really helped me at the beginning: before I was well-known, she performed songs I wrote, bringing them to a wider audience, and she played my tape for anyone who would listen. Over the years since, Buffy and I have maintained a long-distance mutual respect. We have ties to Saskatchewan, but we share more than just a home: we both write songs with emotion, songs with a message. And to this day, we both walk our own path.

I've watched Buffy's long career with admiration, and I'm honored to write this foreword to her authorized biography. Buffy Sainte-Marie is one of folk music's unsung heroes, and her inspirational life is a story that deserves to be read.

JONI MITCHELL, JUNE 2018

PROLOGUE

IT'S ALMOST MIDNIGHT in Woodstock, New York. Less than an hour ago, a line of about 150 people stretched the length of the theater's foyer and bar, fans clutching everything from old vinyl and CDs to posters literally just torn off the wall, all waiting for their moment of communion with Buffy Sainte-Marie.

She's spent her whole life hearing compliments from people about how much they loved her set at Woodstock back in the day. It makes her laugh every time. Tonight is actually Buffy Sainte-Marie's first-ever Woodstock performance. She was never at the famous counterculture music festival that became one of the defining moments of the sixties. In fact, Sainte-Marie, the woman who wrote "Universal Soldier," one of the most provocative and relevant protest anthems of the twentieth century, was never even *invited* to Woodstock.

It wasn't the first time, and it wouldn't be the last, that Sainte-Marie wasn't asked to the party. During her years in show business, she has lived simultaneously in the spotlight alongside musical giants such as Bob Dylan and Joan Baez and also very much at fame's outer limits on the edges and precipices of the music industry. Although she wasn't always in the headlines, Sainte-Marie has been creating, challenging, and questioning during a career that has spanned more than fifty years. While history books and museums and governments and pop culture seemed intent on erasing Indigenous people, she persisted, and she's spent decades amplifying Indigenous voices, experiences, and resistance.

Through it all, she's been blacklisted by two American presidential administrations, and she's taken long breaks, some accidental and some chosen. She's lived most of her life way up in the mountains of Hawai'i, intentionally tucked away on a little farm. She's as intensely private about her family and personal relationships as she is about her home, which is a self-created paradise with space for her studio. She spends a lot of time with her animals and in the garden, with dirt on her skin and neck-deep in nature. When she leaves home to go out on tour, she misses her cat; appropriately, the first new friend she makes here in Woodstock is a black-and-white kitty.

Short tours are Sainte-Marie's preference. Long stretches on the road away from her home are too hard; she needs time to recharge, rest, and be out of the spotlight. The Woodstock stop is the second on a quick, three-day, East-Coast tour. Sainte-Marie has some connections to the venue, the historic and rustic Bearsville Theater, the brainchild of famed entrepreneur and music manager Albert Grossman, whose clients included Bob Dylan, Janis Joplin, The Band, and many more—and who is apparently buried out back. He founded a recording studio in this space in 1969; the theater was an extension of his dream, but he died suddenly in 1986 before he could make it a reality. Sally Grossman, Albert's wife, established the theater in 1989.

Sally has an enormous bouquet of flowers delivered to Sainte-Marie's green room, and when she stops in to say hello, the two women embrace, though Sainte-Marie says she never knew Sally very well. In many ways, Albert and Sally Grossman were at the center of "the scene," but Sainte-Marie never was.

In part, this was by her own design. She's a self-described hermit and Goody Two-Shoes. Some people think she's a snob, but she's an artist with a mission quite different from the one pursued by musicians chasing the rock 'n' roll trifecta of money, fame, and sex. She sees the worst parts of show business as the manifestation of greed and an abuse of power—an extension of entrepreneurial colonialism, a system that reinforces a hierarchy of bullies. Sainte-Marie uses the words "bullying," "racketeer-ing," and "colonialism" almost interchangeably, since each thrives on hierarchy and fear, power and control, competition and toxic machismo.

The upside of show business for Buffy Sainte-Marie? Plane tickets. They have opened up the world to her in ways she could only dream of as a child. Those plane tickets have signified free-dom and learning to Sainte-Marie ever since the release of her groundbreaking 1964 debut album, *It's My Way!* There was no life map or blueprint for a Cree woman adopted out of Canada and raised by a mostly white family in Massachusetts. She was a self-taught, musical wunderkind brandishing a mouth bow and finding her voice in the stylings of French chanteuse Édith Piaf and flamenco artist Carmen Amaya. She pursued an education intending to be a philosopher in India or a teacher on a reserve. She never planned to become a famous singer-songwriter at the age of twenty-three, or even to be playing shows more than fifty years later.

She believes in the power and intrinsic value of music—and it's evident not just in the way she reflects light onstage, but in how she shares her gifts and how those gifts are received. The audience members cheer at the opening chords of their favorite songs—they know all the words—are raucous and rowdy when they're ready to rise up, and reverent in the softer moments. She might be more famous in Canada than the U.S., but even the American venue managers offer up the same observation every night: the lineup to meet Sainte-Marie and her band after the show is the longest they've ever seen.

Her fans are young and old, and they're not just looking for autographs (though they definitely want them). They're carrying their truest selves into this moment. Every Sainte-Marie record is a soundtrack to some revelation; her songs were their anthems, mirrors, and life-preservers, containing the tenderness of new love, a personal discovery or reckoning, their celebrations and losses, and moments of resistance and courage.

It's a steady stream of gratitude and affection, in both tentative and effusive displays, by people who have grown up with her, were shaped by the bend of a lyric or found solace in the curve of a melody. At one show, there's even a woman whose name is also Buffy. She has come with her mother and stood in line for almost an hour to meet her namesake face-to-face. Others are new fans, called to action by her 2016 Juno Award– and 2015 Polaris Music Prize–winning album *Power in the Blood* and let loose into a back catalog of fifty-plus years of music that's richer, deeper, and more daring than that of many of her peers.

As the line dwindles, a Lakota woman in full regalia emerges. She carries a large, folded piece of fabric that looks like a blanket. A man brings out a small video camera. The Lakota woman is a Water Defender who has traveled all the way from Standing Rock, South Dakota, to Sainte-Marie's concert. The Lakota Water Defender makes a short speech to the forty or so people who remain, fans and venue staff, about resistance and what's happening in America, and shares her experiences on the front lines. She's also brought the original Lakota flag dating from the

1876 Lakota and Cheyenne defeat of General Custer, and she asks Sainte-Marie to conduct a special flag ceremony with her.

The energy in the room is charged with solemnity as well as a fierce rush of emotion. It's the heaviness of the history—how unrelentingly cyclical and unchanging it seems that Indigenous people must still fight so hard for their land rights and human rights. It's the living history of this Lakota woman who's still resisting, advocating not just for her people, the environment, and the land, but for everyone's futures. After the Water Defender speaks, Sainte-Marie offers up a few words, heartfelt and powerful. Then they bow their heads to one another and offer prayers. Time seems to slow down. The two women embrace.

The unexpected act of solidarity, protest, and ceremony is an overwhelming experience, eye-opening and educational and emotional, but also a little surreal. Everyone in the room seems to catch each other's gaze at the same time, sharing the unspoken words between witnesses: *Did I really just see that? Did that really just happen?*

"That was nice, wasn't it?" Sainte-Marie says afterwards, once almost everyone else has left. She's not downplaying the significance of the experience; this is her humility at work, a grounded and low-key combination of wonder, gratitude, and delight with the world.

It's after midnight, her first time in Woodstock, and she's just held a 140-year-old flag in her hands from a time when Indigenous people defeated their colonizers. It might feel surreal to everyone else in the place, but it's a pretty regular night in the life of Buffy Sainte-Marie.

CHAPTER 1

SUFFER THE LITTLE CHILDREN

THERE'S NO OFFICIAL record of Buffy Sainte-Marie's birth, not really. At least not a satisfactory and decisive one that answers questions before they're asked, grounded in a family lineage with all the gifts and baggage that accompany that kind of belonging.

She was born with the given name Beverly, mostly likely in 1941, on or around February 20th, and probably on a reserve called Piapot in the Qu'Appelle Valley, Saskatchewan. She is Cree, and to be born Cree in the 1940s in Canada was to be a person who was not always counted, at least not in a formal and legal fashion. Birth records from the time, particularly on reserves, were spotty, and there are countless reports of records being lost or destroyed. The children who, like Buffy Sainte-Marie, were adopted or taken had their birth stories erased, stolen by people whose motivations were rooted in misconceptions and who thought their whiteness and their faith made them superior. Chelsea Vowel, a Métis writer and educator from the Plains Cree–speaking community of Lac Ste. Anne, Alberta, who publishes under the name âpihtawikosisân, refers to processes like this as "adoption as cultural annihilation."[1]

The combination of religious hubris and colonizer supremacy shaped the belief that Indigenous people needed to adapt to white society, and while many Indigenous children were sent to residential schools, others were taken from their parents and adopted into white homes. Sainte-Marie was adopted out of her reserve—for reasons that are still unclear, muddied by time and a lack of accurate records—by Albert and Winifred Sainte-Marie, a mechanic and a newspaper copy editor, respectively. They were a modest, visibly white family (though Winifred identified as part Mi'kmaq) who for much of Sainte-Marie's childhood lived in a trailer by Sebago Lake in Maine and in North Reading and Wakefield, Massachusetts.

Sainte-Marie discovered a love and natural talent for the piano and composition when she was just three years old, waiting out her older brother's lessons. "All he wanted to do was play baseball, but for a few months somebody made him take piano lessons, poor thing," she says. "But I would listen to him practice his lesson, and I couldn't wait for him to get gone and leave and go play baseball so that I could take over the piano and play not only his whole lesson by ear, but what I really wanted to play, which was anything in my head."

A teacher advised against music lessons for Sainte-Marie, thinking it would discourage her natural abilities, so she began to improvise music to an illustrated book of Christmas songs and poems. "I'd sit there at my piano and I'd either be making up stories in my head and playing to them, or I'd be looking at the pictures in the book and making the music be the characters," she recalls. "I was expressing the emotions of the pictures and making up little-kid stories. And actually, I was scoring in my head these books of nursery rhymes."

Sainte-Marie identifies as "musically dyslexic," a condition she learned about from a Berklee College of Music professor in the 1990s. It's similar to dyscalculia, an inability to use symbols in arithmetical calculations. She can't read music, but she can accurately write down the music she hears in her head—she just can't read it back the next day. Every note she's ever played, arranged, composed, or produced is by ear and memory, gut and feel.

"All I've been able to do is improvise because I never took any lessons," she explains. "I don't read [music], and I was never boxed in that way. But I was kind of ashamed of the way I played when I was a kid. So I wouldn't play for people. I played all the time at home, but I kind of thought it was low-rent amateur-y because it didn't have a store price tag on it."

Janice Murphy Palumbo, Sainte-Marie's childhood best friend, remembers being a little jealous of her pal Beverly's musical talents, even as a kid. "She could sit down at the piano and just play anything," Palumbo says with a laugh. "I had taken lessons, and I was awful. I always felt awkward. I just couldn't be bothered if I couldn't be an expert right off the bat. [Beverly] would come over and sit there at the old-fashioned upright and play anything by ear, and my parents loved her."

Sainte-Marie and Palumbo's families were both on the lower end of middle-class. The friends walked to school together, rode horses once a year, and went to ballroom dancing classes like the other kids did. "I never heard her say a bad word about anyone in my entire life, ever in all the years," Palumbo says. "She just always had that sweet smile on her face. And you know, [she was] just a nice, nice girl." Sainte-Marie's Indigenous ancestry didn't come up much, but Palumbo says that what people in Wakefield held against her was her family's lower-middle-class status. "It was a very cliquey, snotty town," Palumbo says. "It was right down the middle; we were on the right side of town, but we didn't have the money that the other [kids] had to do things."

Palumbo remembers that girls, in particular, were very cold and ignored them both. "We were in Girl Scouts, up at the higher end of town, with the beautiful homes and all, and I remember one day the girls saying their mothers didn't want them to associate with Beverly," she recalls, acknowledging that this could have been where racism started to manifest more directly. "I remember going home and telling my mother that Karen and Sue and Nancy's mothers didn't like Beverly. My mother was furious. She loved her. She was a nice kid, she played piano beautifully, and she was a good, loyal friend. But that's when I remember the distinction."

Sainte-Marie's own relationship to her town and her family was complicated. Ideally, home represents idyllic basics— belonging, safety, love—but that wasn't her experience. She didn't know who she was or where she came from, and there were few people who looked like her in the predominantly white Wakefield. Her existence provoked questions that no one knew how to ask, and it only made her more isolated and vulnerable.

"At various stages of my life, I refused to believe that my mother was not my true biological mother," Sainte-Marie says. "I was told that I was adopted. I was told that I was just born on the 'wrong side of the blanket.' In other words, one of my parents was my parent and one wasn't. I was told that we were part-Indian, but nobody knew anything about it, and when I grew up, I could find out about it if I was interested, which worked out very well. I had this identity question, but it wasn't something that was haunting me or getting at me until far later in my life."

The fact that she was adopted wasn't openly acknowledged in Sainte-Marie's earliest years, but her older brother used that information to bully her when she was very little. Gradually, by listening to what was said and what wasn't between family members, Sainte-Marie understood that she was both adopted and Indigenous. Winifred didn't talk much about the former, but she wholly embraced the latter and encouraged her daughter to find out everything she could about the world, including Indigenous culture and the real history of Indigenous people, not just the sanitized North American version that persisted in school books.

Sainte-Marie now laughingly calls the town where she went to school "Javex, USA" because it was a white colonial town where everyone was either Catholic or Protestant. There were a few Jewish people, but there wasn't much diversity aside from that, and there was little education or awareness about what being Indigenous meant. Sainte-Marie can't recall knowing another person of color in her small town. "I didn't know any Black people. There was one family who was Puerto Rican, and everybody was always reminding you that they weren't really Black; they were Puerto Rican. I look back on that town not with negativity in that way, but with understanding of what their ignorance was like, because I was living right in it."

However, it was alienating. With her dark hair and tan skin, Sainte-Marie was already visibly identifiable as an outsider. She was small for her age and often a target of neighborhood bullies, beaten up by boys and older girls. "There *were* reservations in Maine that you wouldn't hear about, but for the most part, people didn't mention reservations or Indians or anything except in the same way that they would mention the Salem Witch Trials, the Boston Tea Party—in other words, like historical references [that were] all over now." She was told in school that "Indians didn't exist," yet relatives in her mother's family expressed pride that they were "part-Indian." Sainte-Marie laughs. "That's the way they would put it." Today, it's not a word she cares for, but she says she's "used 'Indian' all my life so it doesn't bother me as much." Her family's addition of the word "part" reminds her of a joke that her friend, Oneida-Mohawk-Cree comedian/

writer Charlie Hill told her later in life: "'Oh, yeah, yeah, we're Indians, but we don't really practice it, you know?' As if it's being a lapsed Catholic or something!"

While Sainte-Marie knew she was Indigenous, she didn't have a lot of information about what that meant. School books told her that people who looked like her no longer existed, but she knew that wasn't true—she was proof of that. Encouraged by her mother to ask questions and do her own research about what it meant to be Indigenous, Sainte-Marie would ride her bike four miles around the lake to visit the only other visibly Native American person near her town, a Narragansett man named Leonard Bayrd. (The Narragansett are an Algonquin tribe from Rhode Island.) Bayrd, whom Sainte-Marie describes as "really nice," ran a trading post in the town stocked with his own handicrafts and was also the mailman. Sainte-Marie would spend hours visiting him and his wife, just feeling safe in their company, listening to his stories and asking questions. Sainte-Marie says there was "no Indian agenda." Bayrd was welcoming and helped provide some shape to Sainte-Marie's earliest education about their shared Indigeneity in a world that worked hard to make them invisible. "Nobody believed in his tribe either," Sainte-Marie says. "We were invisible. Native American people were invisible."

Bayrd was proud of his beadwork, which Sainte-Marie says appeared in Hollywood films, and she loved to bead alongside him. He couldn't give her answers about her identity, but he could give her a sense of reality beyond the narrow parameters society provided. "He couldn't help me out with knowing who I'm related to and who I'm not, but that has always been just something that's part of my life," Sainte-Marie explains.

When she was a child, "it wasn't talked about that I looked different. But my brother told me; he let me know in no uncertain terms that my mom was not my mom and that I didn't belong in that family." Sainte-Marie heard it over and over. Every time, Winifred would tell her young daughter some variation of "He's mistaken."

She took refuge inside her mother's hasty reassurances. It was one of the first pieces of psychological armor Sainte-Marie learned to put on. "I loved my mother so much, I just wanted her to be my mother, and I didn't know what was correct," Sainte-Marie says. Every time Sainte-Marie went to her mother to talk about things her brother said and did to her, Winifred brushed it off as teasing. Winifred didn't know that what she thought was teasing was actually the groundwork for something much darker and more predatory.

Sainte-Marie was abused for years by both her older brother and an older male relative who did not live in the house. The mistreatment from her brother expanded from verbal and psychological bullying to physical and sexual abuse. "And, you know, I'm no dummy. Later on, I would think about it and, as a little girl I was being—my brain was being—influenced and operated on by a boy who was five-and-a-half years older than me. Do you know what a ten-year-old can do to a five-year-old— to the body and self-esteem of a five-year-old? To their psyche and confidence? What a boy going through puberty can do to a little unprotected girl? It's a very, very big problem for little girls who are in a situation like that."

Unfortunately, her brother wasn't her only problem. "I had the other side of pedophilia [too], coming from someone else much older, a grown-up in the family who was not a bully, just a horny old man," Sainte-Marie says. The older relative didn't live in her home, and she didn't have to see him frequently, but the sexual abuse lasted for years. "I've read some things where somebody accused of pedophilia will say, 'The kid liked it.' Okay.

That one [justification] gets kicked out right away. Children are born with sexuality. Things feel good. Sexual abuse of an innocent child imprints a confusing unequal relationship imbalance. There are things that the public doesn't know about child abuse, and it's not about how far he stuck it in. It's about power and control over girls. Pretty nasty, isn't it?" The effects of the abuse she experienced lasted in both expected and unexpected ways. "Prematurely sexualizing children is about bullying and emotional exploitation. It cripples children so that they are never really truly comfortable with another person at that level, and sometimes at many other levels," Sainte-Marie says.

Palumbo didn't know exactly what was going on with her friend, but she had her suspicions. "Her brother was a total creep," Palumbo says. "I can remember one time, I stayed overnight at her house and he came into the bedroom and tried to get me to put on roller skates. And I kept falling down and falling down because you can't put roller skates on a hardwood floor and not trip and fall and all that. He got the biggest kick out of it. He was bad." She also vividly recalls one of the last times she and Sainte-Marie hung out, when they were thirteen or fourteen. "It was probably before we went to high school, and she came to my house, up in my bedroom," Palumbo says. "I remember her having a crazy, scared look on her face and talking about things that I really didn't understand, and she was—it was like she was terrified. I didn't know how to handle it. I think she was being abused. I don't know for certain. I just didn't know what to do. We were innocent back then. I couldn't have been much of a good friend, but I just didn't know anything."

During the abuse, Sainte-Marie would shut down, and sometimes she would pass out. She says she felt an overwhelming need to disappear. She was "disassociating," she explains, though she didn't know the word for it at the time. "I just thought that's the way people were treated, and what you had to do was just get tough and endure it." She retreated because she didn't know how else to stay safe. "I didn't have any idea of it being just plain wrong," Sainte-Marie says.

Sainte-Marie credits her mother with helping to protect her vulnerability despite the trauma. "My mom didn't know the details of what my brother was doing to me that made me cry, and she had no idea there was a problem in the other case. But she would see me crying or upset or traumatized and she would say, 'What? Have they been picking on you again?' So I thought that's what sexual abuse was called. And what you were supposed to do when somebody was 'picking on you' was to get a thicker skin, don't worry about it. 'When you grow up, it won't be like this. As you get older, you'll be able to cope better with people's "bad manners."' Fuck. But we were talking about two different things, and she didn't know it. If we'd been talking about it using the words 'sexual abuse' today, she would not have had the same dismissive attitude."

To escape, Sainte-Marie took refuge in music and nature, two halves of her that subconsciously worked towards wholeness. "I had a real need for privacy and isolation as a child. I wasn't only some traumatized, scared little kid hiding under the bed—which I was—but I was also this other person who had an inner world that was really, really good. It really was." She played for hours in the woods, made up songs, and she adored animals. "I was by myself, and that was good. I was happy. There was a cat and a dog, and eventually I had some rabbits, although my brother abused them, too. Animals—that's where I would put my love, and so I wasn't unhappy; I was having a good time in my solitude. I was the recluse who needed to think about it, who needed to turn shit into Shinola [a popular shoe polish]. I needed to be able to turn lemons into lemonade. I needed to because I had something inside me that was really, really interesting—to myself!"

In Maine, her family's trailer was in the middle of the woods next to Sebago Lake state park. "I slept in a jungle hammock—oh, it was my little world." When the family relocated to Wakefield, Massachusetts, nature continued to be central to Sainte-Marie's happiness. "My uncle Eddie had a farm in the next town. There was a lake down the street [from my school] and woods right next to my house," she says. "So I was always really comfortable in the woods. I was happy that I was happy, and I knew it consciously. It was beautiful."

In the process of turning inward, she found strength and solace. "I had no music teacher saying, 'Yes, you played that very well.' I had nobody hearing my stories. It wasn't like I was doing it for some praise from a music teacher or for my parents or anything. It was just between me and the Creator. I have a real solid sense of creativity; the Creator and the whole creation being one continually evolving thing: nature, and everything in it, all of us." Creating and nurturing and inventing gave her a sense of control and safety and stability, and it helped her heal herself in the moment, though as a child, she thought of it as having fun. Sainte-Marie had an innate understanding of how to keep her inner spirit safe, no matter what was going on, and she couched her creativity in this instinctive and self-protective generosity and warmth. Her childlike hope never gave out, and it helped her cultivate kindness in creativity.

CHAPTER 2

QU'APPELLE VALLEY, SASKATCHEWAN

T**HE MID-1950s**—when Buffy Sainte-Marie was in junior high and high school—were lonely times for her, and for a while, she wanted desperately to fit in. She often walked to school by herself. Mornings weren't easy. "It was weird getting ready to go to school, putting up with my older brother's bullying—he always picked on my looks—and trying to look okay like all the other teens," Sainte-Marie says. "I tried to lighten my hair, piled on the usual makeup, but really, I just didn't fit in. I had an occasional friend but had kind of given up on being part of the crowd. My interests weren't the same as theirs. It didn't occur to me that maybe I was smart and lucky to be [on the] outside, but now I think maybe I was."

Within both the upper and lower classes there were pecking orders, she says, complete with social dramas that didn't include her. She had attended grade school with the "snobby kids" when they were all little—"I found out a few years ago that the snob mothers didn't like me much," she says—but by her junior year, she was entirely on her own.

"I wasn't equivalent to a goth or any other courageous high-school counterculture queen you might imagine," Sainte-Marie admits. "I was defeated, limp, a nobody, non-existent except in my own head, probably clinically depressed, and invisible during high school hours." But after school, it was like an entirely different world, and she particularly loved the winter season. "I'd drop my books at home, grab my skates, go down the hill to the lake, and skate until dark, hearing Tchaikovsky in my head... as well as Elvis, Fats Domino, Little Richard, Jerry Lee, LaVern Baker, and Chuck Berry. I don't know if anybody else was skating to 'Maybelline' in their heads, but I was—it always felt right. Even though I was alone, I was happy." Even when she got home late, she'd find her mother waiting for her. "It'd be dark by the time I skated to shore, chipped my frozen loafers out of the snow, and trudged up the hill to walk home, usually in the starlight. Sometimes I was so cold my mother would make me put my feet on a towel at the oven door. She was a great mom." These happy memories stand out in sharp relief against the miseries of high school; Sainte-Marie was looking for escape wherever she could find it.

Around this time, she became known as "Buffy"—the nickname came from a high school friend, Pete Duston—and it stuck. She loved learning but found the classroom a limited place, and so she didn't get great grades. And because she didn't read music, she didn't connect with structured offerings like the school band. She was content retreating into her own music.

Happy to have escaped piano lessons, Sainte-Marie was nonetheless a huge fan of classical composers, of both symphonies and opera. She liked the fact that many of the greats were also natural musicians, self-taught like herself. "You know who my first crush was? Tchaikovsky!" She laughs. It's not every little kid growing up in the 1950s who falls hard for a long-dead Russian composer, but she wasn't really a typical child. Coping with years of secret sexual abuse, she was also coming into her own sexuality, like every other teenage girl; the safest place in which to explore those emerging feelings was with a deceased, tortured genius who both inspired and stirred her.

Pyotr Ilyich Tchaikovsky was one of the greatest composers of the nineteenth century. He wrote the music for some
of the most popular ballets of all time, including *The Nut-
cracker* and *Swan Lake,* which are still among Sainte-Marie's
favorites. He suffered greatly from depression, and she identified with his suffering. He also had a host of complicated
relationships with women and men, and historians believe he
was gay.[2] Tchaikovsky's personal struggles can be heard in his
compositions, rife with the beauty of escape, echoes of which
found their way into some of Sainte-Marie's own compositions.
Thanks to the music in her head, Sainte-Marie, like Tchaikovsky,
could be the architect of a more nuanced world than the one
in which she lived. Tchaikovsky's life offered a shadow-map for
her, both creatively and romantically; her tender heart would
gravitate towards difficult or broken men throughout much of
her life. "I believed I was the one who could have saved him,"
Sainte-Marie remembers. "And even now, when I go to ballet
class, I'm still in it for the music."

She taught herself to play guitar as a teenager. Without
formal instruction, she tuned the strings uniquely for each
song she made up, thinking that's what she was supposed to
do. She didn't know it at the time, but her alternative tunings
were more in keeping with the African-American gospel and
blues artists of the 1920s and 1930s, rather than the classical
Spanish tunings most mainstream guitarists used. When she
discovered this, she dug into those artists more deeply, and it
dovetailed perfectly with some of the other sounds that inspired
her. Sainte-Marie loved blues, soul, rock, and early R&B, and
like most teens at the time, she was obsessed with Elvis's early
records and with rockabilly. "When I was a teenager and he
came along—I mean, that was it for me!" Sainte-Marie laughs.
"It was over. I *loved* him, I just loved him. There was nobody like
that in my town."

Winifred urged her daughter to think seriously about college. No one on either side of Sainte-Marie's family had ever gone to college. Her father, Albert (called Smokey by his friends), was a mechanic by trade and a hunter and fisherman in his spare time. Winifred (called Winnie by her friends) was a voracious reader and longed to travel. She was a proofreader and a copy editor for newspapers and publishing companies, positions she earned without formal training because she had no money for school. "Self-educated to the max," Winnie's love of learning became the through-line of her daughter's life.

"She's still one of the smartest people I've ever known," Sainte-Marie says. "She put things together in a self-taught way. Although she never said so, I could read between the lines and learn that formal methods of doing things were not the only way." That's how Winnie approached everything from Indigenous history and identity to humanity and philosophy. Winnie encouraged her daughter's interest in exploring anything and everything—music, philosophy, veterinary care, as well as her Indigenous identity, preparing her to go beyond the history books that skewed Eurocentric. Winnie also taught her daughter about the importance of giving back, and she was particularly interested in the teachings of Mahatma Gandhi and in making the world a better place amidst overwhelming odds. "Even though my family did not belong to any organization or churches or anything like that, I did grow up with a big picture of the world, the troubles in the world, and that some people tried to make things better," Sainte-Marie says. Winnie wanted her daughter to have every opportunity to learn, grow, and possibly change the world.

When it came time to apply to college, the University of Massachusetts at Amherst accepted Sainte-Marie's application two weeks before the fall semester started. Winnie told her daughter that she could drop out and come home any time she wanted, and that lack of pressure made it easy for Sainte-Marie to give university studies a try. Sainte-Marie said goodbye to her family and entered college on a trial basis.

But Sainte-Marie loved UMass and everything it represented at the time. "In those days, as college freshmen, we were told that the reason you went to college or a liberal arts state university was because college was broadening," Sainte-Marie recalls. "They don't even use that word anymore. We were going to learn basics from which we were then going to build our lives. Now it's just a meal ticket—you go to college to get a stamp of approval so you can go and work in somebody's plantation, making money for them. That sounds like the army to me. But so many people have gone through college for a meal ticket, including in the creative arts, that today few people consider that there's an intrinsic benefit to learning about a lot of things. An education in the field you really love grows your head. Just to bathe in expanding your knowledge base, learning stuff every day, is an incredible privilege, without thinking of turning it into a product for somebody to sell. The true motivation for art has been, I bet, the same since the caveman: it's beautiful, it's satisfying on a personal level, and because it's personal, not everybody will get it."

At university, she saw students from all over the world and real diversity. Sainte-Marie was no longer the only person of color in a tiny town. Some things stayed the same, of course, as she observed a collision of perspectives and encountered gendered expectations. "I was around a lot of girls who had gone to college because their parents said, 'You go to college, you become a teacher, you catch a husband.' I was around some girls who were not big thinkers at all," Sainte-Marie recalls with a laugh. But she was also exposed to fellow students who were brimming with ideas around justice, civil rights, and the burgeoning protest movements. However, Sainte-Marie says, almost no one at the time talked about Indigenous issues.

Sainte-Marie started university during a pivotal time in America, particularly for civil rights. It was 1958, twenty years before the American Indian Religious Freedom Act would be passed on August 11, 1978. Hippies were still a few years away, but the beatniks had arrived in coffee houses with an emphasis on critical thinking and poetry, and a significant cultural shift was beginning. McCarthyism—Senator Joseph McCarthy's campaign against American Communists or left-wing sympathizers, during which thousands lost jobs, some were imprisoned, and other Red Scare targets were driven to suicide—was in decline by 1956, but there was plenty of lingering anti-Communist sentiment and Red Scare rhetoric driving major decisions in the U.S. and internationally. There was already an American presence in Vietnam that would escalate dramatically in the mid-sixties. The first two years of the decade saw not only the Cuban Missile Crisis, but the construction of the Berlin Wall.

Ideological conflicts were just one aspect of the political and social climate. The African-American Civil Rights Movement was trying to end segregation and advocating for human and constitutional rights, freedoms, and equality for Black people. Public schools were desegregated in 1954, though segregation itself was not officially banned by the Civil Rights Act until 1964. Simultaneously, treatment of Native Americans was, arguably, getting worse; the years between 1953 and 1968 became known as the "termination era," when 109 Indigenous bands and tribes were suddenly terminated and found themselves stripped of the right to govern their own people.[3] The Indian Relocation Act of 1956 displaced Indigenous people from their lands into urban areas under the guise of integration and assimilation, though Indigenous people saw it as an attempt to control and exploit their natural resource–rich lands. It went as poorly, and cruelly, as it sounds, resulting in hundreds of thousands of Indigenous people being displaced from their reservations and communities over several decades. The "relocated" were promised jobs, housing, and training once they'd moved to urban centers, but the reality was vastly different. There were very few jobs or training opportunities, communities were broken up, and families were torn from their homes.[4]

Around 1961, Sainte-Marie traveled to Washington, D.C. She can't quite recall the purpose of the trip, but it was there that she met members of a new group called the National Indian Youth Council, including Thelma Stiffarm and Walter Funmaker. The NIYC was composed primarily of Indigenous law students, and for Sainte-Marie, the group offered her the chance to meet people who were a lot like her: young, college-educated, politically charged, and ready to make a change. "I was hearing from individuals whose stories were somewhat similar to mine in that they had grown up in abuse," Sainte-Marie says. "And in having to deny that the abuse even was abuse, since it was basically colonialism—you were gettin' it from the church or the mayor or whoever's biggest in the pecking order or something: 'It's obviously right and you're wrong.' So I was finding out that there was that, and I was finding out that they had problems in other communities too. Some of the people had grown up on the rez and others did not. Some of them, who'd grown up on one rez, were different than those who'd grown up on another rez. Some had been adopted out, and some had gone to residential schools."

Her involvement in the NIYC also revealed the ways in which her reality as an Indigenous person differed from that of other

Indigenous people. "All of a sudden, I was spending time with Indian people of my own age from all different backgrounds, and they had western accents," Sainte-Marie laughs. "That was a first for me. I had never imagined that kind of 'cowboys and Indians' cowboy accent." Her new friends were smart, progressive, and like-minded young people who had founded NIYC in 1961 after splitting from more conservative tribal leaders.

"They were becoming lawyers, they were becoming educated, they were becoming real activists," Sainte-Marie says. "Not so much street activists but activists who were getting master's degrees in law. They were really doing significant work that was very different from mine, but we connected." Sainte-Marie traveled with NIYC co-founders Clyde Warrior and Mel Thom around Ponca City, Oklahoma. It was an eye-opening experience for the East Coast–raised college student. "There were signs in windows: 'Help wanted, Indians need not apply,' and it was kind of like a joke," she remembers. "We went into a restaurant in a small town to get something to eat. The other people had real knives and forks, and they gave us picnic ware. We also saw a house, it was either for sale or for rent, and the sign said, 'No Indians.' You know, day after day, these signs were there. I had not seen that before I hung around with these people who were from intensely Native American backgrounds."

When she returned to UMass, Sainte-Marie continued to explore Indigeneity but had to grapple with not only the horrifying historical effects of colonization, but also the present-day ramifications—and none of her non-Indigenous student peers seemed to know or care about the plight of Indigenous people. But her love of philosophy helped confirm her lifelong belief that there was a bigger picture, and UMass offered an entire discipline that invited her to think more deeply about the world, to imagine the unimaginable. "Studying philosophy and the way philosophers think was as intriguing to me as listening to somebody else's music," Sainte-Marie says. "But it was still me in the driver's seat. That is, I was learning how other philosophers think, not learning how to think like them or because of them. It was a first-person identification with that part of the brain."

Sainte-Marie adored the "bigger thinkers" from India, as well as most Asian philosophy, particularly the early writings and subsequent translations of the Tao Te Ching and the Upanishads. She declared her major in Oriental Philosophy and Religion with a minor in teaching. Because her major could not be completed only at UMass, she qualified for a cooperative program that UMass shared with Smith, Mount Holyoke, and Amherst colleges. This enabled her to take classes at two Seven Sisters colleges while enrolled at the more affordable UMass. She participated in studies in Buddhism and Hinduism at Smith, took Christianity seminars with Jesuits at Mount Holyoke, and did Bible Studies and Drama at Amherst College, which was a men's school at the time. She held the Eastern philosophers in the highest esteem but wasn't fond of Western philosophers such as Kierkegaard and Kant. She wasn't interested in semantics and the implied "superiority" of Western philosophy. "That drives me crazy, the term 'Western' philosophy. It's one of my pet peeves. As if it's impolite and rude to say 'white' people. You can say Black people, you can say Indigenous people, but when you refer to white people, you say Westerners. I live in Hawai'i. West of me is China. I used to live in California; west of me was Hawai'i. 'Westerners' is so British—can we please say it's obsolete and incorrect? Like the word 'Indian': we use it, but ugh. I'm much more bothered by the use of the word 'Westerners' as a code for white people."

Still, at the start of her philosophy studies, she fell briefly in love with every Greek philosopher she came across. "Every one of them became my hero for a few weeks, and then I'd read the next one and I'd see what was wonderful about the way they thought, and then I'd be in love with that," she says. "I guess I fell in love with thinking in its limitless manifestations." Studying philosophy broadened both Sainte-Marie's intellectual horizons and her understanding of her interior world. "I came to understand myself in a bigger way, and at the same time I was understanding the universe in a way that I had guessed at, as a child. The more I have experienced in my life, the more that [those experiences] confirmed much of my basic feelings from childhood."

Studying philosophy and world religions reinforced her church-less spirituality as well as the connection she'd always felt between herself and something bigger: the earth, animals, ancestors, and life itself. She has always been in love with human potential, and she believes there's something beyond this world, even if she doesn't know what. Ultimately, it's creativity itself that is holy to Sainte-Marie. "The Creator, creativity, the creation: it's all perfectly natural," she says. "Creativity is some kind of internal gift from the Creator, at least in my experience. We're made in the image of the Creator: that's our green light for creativity. We create our songs, our families, our countries. We are *supposed* to be discovering and developing new ideas all the time, I think, not dragging our feet and living in some ancient past." And to her, almost everything is a creative act—dropping money in a busker's hat, fundraising for somebody to go to college, spending some extra time with a dog or cat, or even offering someone a smile. "Creative compassion doesn't have to be something huge and political like what Gandhi did," she says. "I love what the Dalai Lama says: 'You always have the best, most effective tool for peace with you, and that's your smile.'"

Sainte-Marie considered these ideas as she honed her persuasive writing voice. During her time in college, Sainte-Marie met students from around the globe. It wasn't exactly a *Wizard of Oz* shift from black-and-white to glorious Technicolor, but her studies and peers confirmed something she'd always suspected and hoped for: there was so much more to the world than what she'd known when she was growing up. Sainte-Marie was thrilled by her conversations with fellow students about art, philosophy, protest, activism, ethics, and morality; these were the kind of consciousness-expanding exchanges that could revolutionize the world. And it wasn't just the students, but the teachers, too, who encouraged intellectual and creative engagement. "I was with these incredible professors from all over the world, and they were talking about things that were really almost not of this world, and I was just loving it."

Sainte-Marie continued to write songs as well as term papers. It wasn't easy for her to share her music widely at first. She believed in the messages of her songs, but it was hard to break the patterns of her young life and push herself out of solitude and into the spotlight.

"My parents weren't social; my mom didn't belong to any groups," she says. "I had flunked Girl Scouts! I didn't belong to any clubs. In college, several sororities rushed me, but I didn't even go. I wanted to be by myself. I was coming out of childhood trauma. I didn't like living very much. My music was so personal. I would play it for some people who would enjoy it, but it wasn't like I was playing on a big stage, and it wasn't like I was part of a band. The only way I had the courage to get out onstage at all was because I believed in the content of the songs. I was like a journalist reading the news."

Sainte-Marie took a risk and stepped outside her solitude, playing her songs for the women in her UMass dorm, and with the encouragement of her house mother and college friends, began to perform in small local coffee houses before venturing to bigger city coffee houses and later, a bar in Springfield, Massachusetts. In 1960, Sainte-Marie had no idea that she would become a professional singer. Rather, she was like many of her peers on campus: a student, a musician, and a writer. "A few students had guitars and some had even formed a little folk music club called the Pioneer Valley Folk Society," she says. "It wasn't unusual for students to hang out and share a song. I was doing that with Taj Mahal in the stairwells of the University of Massachusetts. He was a very hot musician even then, and the echo [in the stairwell] was fantastic. But there wasn't any audience. It was real music, just for the love of playing the music."

Famed American blues musician Henry Saint Clair Fredericks, who performs as Taj Mahal, was a year younger than Sainte-Marie. He was also self-taught, politically active, and took creative cues and inspiration from all over the world. Mahal remembers reading a newspaper and seeing a picture of "this engaging-looking young woman" who was named Beverly Sainte-Marie. The photo showed her playing at the local coffee house and identified her as a student at UMass. Mahal was intrigued, and when he enrolled at the university later that year, he set out to try and find her.

"It didn't happen," Mahal remembers with a laugh. But he made friends with a group of male students who hung out in the music room, playing for the women students. "One day, I was coming out of the music room and, what do you know, in comes Buffy with a big coat and a book bag and a guitar and God knows what all else," Mahal says. "She was trying to make it upstairs, and [it was a] perfect opportunity for me to help out. She said, 'Oh, you're the guy I've been hearing about,' or something, and I told her I had seen an article on her in a newspaper. She says,

'You want to play?' and I said, 'Sure!' I went and got my guitar and we sat down and we strummed whatever chord came to our minds, and it turned out we were perfectly in tune. It was the most amazing thing in the world."

Mahal and Sainte-Marie have been friends ever since, and Sainte-Marie is also friends with his wife, Inshirah Mahal. Eventually the two families became neighbors in Hawai'i where they both raised their children. Sainte-Marie's son Cody and Mahal's son, Ahmen Mahal, have been best friends since they were little and were even roommates in college, and Sainte-Marie says that Mahal's daughters, Deva, Nani, and Zoe, are all unique, extraordinary, powerful singers. More than forty years later, the old friends recorded together for the first time when Mahal played piano on Sainte-Marie's song, "I Bet My Heart on You," for her 2008 record *Running for the Drum*.

Even though it was Sainte-Marie's looks that originally caught Mahal's eye, once they'd met and played together, he discovered that he loved the self-taught guitar tunings she used, which were evocative of the blues greats that inspired him. He was also knocked out when he heard her sing. "When she played music, you could get excited, you know, and she had this great, interesting voice, a beautiful, vast vibrato."

Sainte-Marie's wide-ranging, cross-cultural musical tastes in college were the reason her voice was so distinctive and interesting. (She knows that some people can't stand to listen to her, and she's fine with that.) She credits three main vocal influences that she's pretty sure Joan Baez or Judy Collins would not have had—or if they did, it didn't come through in their singing. "One was the music of India; nobody listened to that in the early sixties," Sainte-Marie says. She was ahead of the curve, embracing Indian musical influences well before the Beatles headed there in 1968. "I was singing all these quarter tones and getting away with it because nobody was around to tell me not to. I never worked with a band, so I didn't have that self-critic thing going on."

Her other two influences were vocalists. French chanteuse Édith Piaf was a massive star in her own right, but her passionate vibrato didn't really have a place in the North American folk scene. When the house mother of Sainte-Marie's UMass dorm played her Piaf's music in 1958, she felt a jolt go through her whole body. And when she discovered Carmen Amaya, around the same time, she experienced the same sense of electricity. "Carmen Amaya was a flamenco dancer who's also the most outrageous singer you've ever heard in your entire life," Sainte-Marie says. "She sings her guts out. The two of them sang with the kind of passion that I just inhaled like air. It was just totally natural for me to sing with passion, and again, nobody told me not to. If I'd been a flamenco performer or a chanteuse in Paris, maybe everybody would have understood. But it was quite unusual to sing with that kind of passion in the USA," Sainte-Marie laughs. "I just let 'er rip."

Sainte-Marie's teenage love of rock and R&B hadn't dissipated, however, and when she could, she'd make the trek by train to New York to attend DJ Alan Freed's live rock 'n' roll shows to watch performances by Chuck Berry, Little Richard, Fats Domino, Jerry Lee Lewis, LaVern Baker, the Platters, and other great artists of their time. It was at one of Freed's shows that she discovered Jo Ann Campbell, often the only solo woman on the bill. Sainte-Marie remembers being floored by the singer.

"Her clothes were like a southern belle's—except, forget the hoop skirt and cross that with Las Vegas," she says. "She used to wear these gowns with trains and sparkles and beautiful colors. I'd go on a train from Maine to New York—and that'd take all day—just to see my heroes who I'd heard on the radio, and all of a sudden here comes this woman who looked like every little girl wanted to look, you know—it was just a real surprise and a revelation. I'd be sitting in the audience, and to see someone wearing those clothes, someone I could identify with as a musician, and I'd never even heard of her? It affected me in a lot of ways. I saw that there weren't many women [in the music industry]. I learned that visuals were part of a show. I didn't think too much about it, but the music that I loved was so important to me. I inhaled it all. But in my town, I couldn't tell anybody."

At the time, Sainte-Marie kept her rock and R&B musical influences to herself. Not many people in Maine or Massachusetts were listening to musicians like Lottie Kimbrough or Bukka White, hugely influential blues artists who never got the name recognition they deserved. In the late 1960s, British artists like Eric Clapton and a host of American rock musicians would make it popular to reference Delta blues guitarists. But when Sainte-Marie began to toe the edge of the folk scene, she found that the music was a little vanilla. In the early 1960s, "Bob Dylan was not famous yet. Joan Baez was just getting to be well known. Pete Seeger was well known. But basically, we had just finished with the Highwaymen and the Four Freshmen, the preppy boys' groups. Nobody even mentioned Fats Domino anymore. It was like, 'That R&B stuff is yesterday; this is—ta-da—folk music!' but it was mostly Euro-American folk music. I became aware that in music, there were all kinds of cliques."

In her senior year of college, Sainte-Marie was teaching first grade in Greenfield, Massachusetts, as part of earning her teacher's degree. It also marked the beginning, she says, of her rebellious streak. "I was very Goody Two-Shoes in college. I didn't drink or throw paint all over the walls or any of those stupid things. But I did have a clandestine rabbit in my room!"

She doesn't fully remember how she ended up with the rabbit, but she kept it in the first-grade classroom with the kids during the week, and on the weekend, she'd sneak it into her college dorm room. She already loved animals, but what she didn't anticipate was how much she would grow to love the kids. "It almost turned me off teaching because I missed the kids so much," Sainte-Marie remembers. "When the year was out, I thought, 'Oh, my gosh!' I had never looked at teachers from that point of view. You learn to love the kids so much and then you miss them, and I never got to see any of them again."

But Sainte-Marie's other interests were also taking her away from teaching. Her musicianship and songwriting evolved as she played in public more frequently and honed her performing skills. She also immersed herself in Indigenous education and activism, and she was passionate about fueling her songs with the realities of Indigenous people, culture, and the consequences of colonization. She realized that teaching on a reservation would just be another way to have her hands tied since she'd be constrained by the parameters set by the Bureau of Indian Affairs school system, and she thought that she could do more for Indigenous people by operating outside the system. After graduation, she was able to spend more time playing on the college coffee-bar circuit as well and eventually, her music led her to Toronto's burgeoning Yorkville folk scene to play shows there and explore the country.

"In the USA, I never learned very much about Canada," she says. "It's very hard to give Canadians a picture of how it was for American students or Americans in general. Canada was just 'our neighbor to the north.' And when you look at the map in an American school, you have this big United States and then you have this thing at the top of the page that makes Canada look like a little horizontal skinny country to the north. 'What's up there?' 'Oh, I don't know, Canada. It's up there by Montana or something? And they speak French.' So it was really a loony tunes view of Canada."

She played gigs and spent time at the new Friendship Centre on Spadina, which is now the Native Canadian Centre of Toronto. She didn't know anyone; she'd just show up and hang out, talk to interesting people, and exchange thoughts and ideas, just like she did at school. Among Sainte-Marie's new Toronto friends was Elizabeth Samson, who would go on to be a producer of the CBC program *Our Native Land*. She also met Wilfred Pelletier (sometimes spelled Peltier), a Wikwemikong-born philosopher, writer, and educator who, like Sainte-Marie, was interested in embracing Indigenous education as an alternative to the dominant colonial narrative.

Sainte-Marie told Samson and Pelletier that she had been born to an Indigenous family in Saskatchewan. Samson and Pelletier believed that she could be the daughter of their friend Emile Piapot, the grandson of Chief Piapot of the Piapot Reserve, and his wife Clara Starblanket, daughter of the famed Chief Star Blanket of the File Hills Reserve in Saskatchewan's Qu'Appelle Valley. Emile and Clara had reportedly had a daughter taken from the reserve around the time Sainte-Marie was born. Sainte-Marie went to a powwow that Piapot was at in Ontario, and the two were introduced. They spoke at length, and he invited her to come to the Piapot Reserve. She accepted the invitation and flew in a few months later to meet Emile's wife, Clara, and the rest of their large family. She stayed for several weeks and kept going back. She'd found another place to call home.

Around 1964, Sainte-Marie was officially adopted into the Piapot family, as is the cultural custom, and was given the Cree name Medicine Bird Singing. "But we never have known whether I'm a [biological] relative or not," Sainte-Marie says. "I wrestled with that for a while." It wasn't until she was pregnant with her son in 1976 that she truly came to terms with her dual identities. "The conclusion that I finally came to is that I had been lucky to have two families," she says. "I had a family that had raised me and another who have been my family for my entire adult life. In each of those families, I may or may not be a blood relative. I have never known, and sometimes it bothered me a lot. But finally I accepted that I was lucky: I've had two families whom I loved in various ways. With my first family, I had a lot of issues with the men who were bullies and pedophiles. And with my second family, there was nothing like that; they were always good to me. So I had issues as a child, and some of them had to do with race or identity, but most really had to do with love and the way people treat each other."

She recalls how some media assumed that she went to a reserve, had an "epiphany," and became an activist for Indigenous people, but that wasn't the case. "My activism had been building over the years, through my mom, through my own interests, through chance things that would happen," she says. "It wasn't an all-of-a-sudden change; it's been with me since I was a kid. It's the kind of things that I'd been talking about with Leonard Bayrd. I knew that reservations existed—and I knew that the colonial rap was a crock. Nobody was ever, ever, ever giving me activism lessons. There was no such thing; it just didn't exist."

Sainte-Marie now recognizes that her natural inclination to learn about her identity and challenge the stereotypes and perceptions of Indigenous people was a form of activism, but it was never confrontational. She calls it "if only you knew" activism, which means never shaming the listener but rather offering up information and alternatives. As her songwriting style emerged, this "if only you knew" activism coalesced with her love of philosophy, at least when it came to protest songs. "Because I've never come from anger, I think my message has been clearer," Sainte-Marie says. "Protest songs have to be more than just emotional, 'angry' Indian songs or angry anti-war songs—they're not effective. It's okay to do that, but anger itself is not necessarily effective in making change, which is what I really wanted to do."

Buffy Sainte-Marie on surviving abuse

I think that talent and our natural talents, our hunches, our intuitions, they're really very important survival tools. We ignore them to our detriment; we've been so talked out of them, we've been disempowered. Not deliberately. I'm not talking about, "Ooh, the evils of colonialism. They want to tie our hands." No, I'm talking about how our moms sent us to first grade and hid our crayons and wouldn't let us play the piano anymore. Now that didn't happen to me, but if it had, I wouldn't be talking to you today. [Laughs] I would have died.

Buy your kids some toy drums, a little xylophone, a cheap ukulele to play with like toys. Buy your kids nice paper for their drawings, encourage them, buy them some nice little art supplies. Not so that you can make a product that will impress Auntie Sue or make a living but because it's fun and because the kid gets to express herself and make something that she felt like making that day. Our whole lives are happening now. They're not happening when you're twenty-one and have to get a job, they're happening now. We're not taught to treasure the gifts of nature that we're born with. Instead we squash them and we become bean counters and I think we smother our children's talents. It's the lucky ones who get to hang onto it because it's nourishing for your whole life.

CHAPTER 3

UNIVERSAL SOLDIER

AFTER LEAVING UMASS in 1962, Sainte-Marie found herself playing music full-time. She was having success playing on the coffee-house and college circuits, as well as in some small clubs. That same year—two years before the Gulf of Tonkin Resolution justified, at least legally and politically, America's escalated involvement in Vietnam—Sainte-Marie was sitting in the San Francisco airport. She was booked to play some shows and was en route to Toronto from Mexico. It was late at night when she noticed wounded soldiers being deplaned. She asked a medic where they had been and he confirmed: Vietnam. He gave her a first-hand account of what was happening there, and it horrified her.

Before the twenty-four-hour news cycle and Twitter and citizen journalists and Facebook live-streaming, it was easier for those in power to control what shape a news story took. If the American government wanted to maintain the fiction that the U.S. was not escalating its involvement or suffering casualties in Vietnam, they could, and with few challenges. The American media wasn't reporting on much of what was actually happening in Vietnam, and there were few American journalists on the front lines in the early 1960s. But young activists were hearing about the brutality and violence, and word began to spread that victory was not nearly as close as promised. People like Sainte-Marie, who were lucky enough to travel around the country, could hear first- and secondhand accounts and witness the actual fallout with their own eyes.

As soon as she arrived at the Purple Onion coffeehouse in Toronto's Yorkville neighborhood, she settled down in the building's basement and finished writing what she had started in the San Francisco airport and on the plane ride to Toronto. She didn't want this new song to be simply accurate; she wanted it to be "factually bulletproof." Sainte-Marie had been too much of a "good college girl" to let anger skew her writing, and she knew how to convince cranky professors to give her an A. "Like anybody else who's had a lot of education, now and then I'd have a professor who didn't like me. Therefore, the paper you write for that guy had to be really A++. That's what I tried to do in those songs. I tried to give people information that they couldn't get anywhere else, and I thought I'd have one shot at it, so that's what I did."

That song, "Universal Soldier," was later viewed, in part, as an exposé of the perceived cover-up by the American government about the extent of their involvement in Vietnam. It's also a searing indictment of war itself, of greed, and our complicity in the war machine. Every verse is full of fire:

And he's fighting for Canada,
he's fighting for France,
he's fighting for the U.S.A.,
and he's fighting for the Russians
and he's fighting for Japan,
and he thinks we'll put an end to war this way.

Sainte-Marie's critique is generous and self-reflective, and her suggestions are clear. When she sings, her frustration is palpable, but there's also vulnerability in her demands. She's imploring every listener to consider their own complicity, to challenge the so-called inevitability of war, and instead find another way.

> *And he knows he shouldn't kill*
> *and he knows he always will*
> *kill you for me my friend and me for you.*

Sainte-Marie's condemnation of war lasted just two minutes and seventeen seconds, and though it was concise, it was also powerful. By traveling around the country performing the song, she was essentially warning people about what was happening in Vietnam before most fully realized the extent of the conflict. In many ways, "Universal Soldier" was another instance of Sainte-Marie being ahead of her time. She was leaning into a future that was still a few years away, when anti-war sentiment and hippie culture would be at an all-time high, and protesters would fill the streets, clashing with cops and the national guard, demanding that America withdraw its troops from Vietnam and put an end to a seemingly endless war.

"Some people say, 'Oh, how did you know? You were years ahead of your time with this song or that song?' But it's not like that; it's not as though you have a crystal ball," Sainte-Marie says. "I had a lot of airplane tickets and a very creative mind and a need to find what was good about the world, and that involved facing what wasn't so hot about it, too."

By 1962, Sainte-Marie was immersed in the troubadour life, doing coffee-house gigs and concerts. She headed to New York's Greenwich Village, the hub of the emerging folk scene, where young artists and intellectuals filled up small, crowded coffee houses with rows of wooden chairs and tiny tables, all eyes on whoever was up onstage singing or sharing their poetry.

Soon after, Sainte-Marie moved to New York to pursue music more seriously. With a university friend she shared a tiny apartment in a five-floor walk-up on Perry Street in the West Village, which she calls "an easy hike to the coffee houses where the streets were full of people from everywhere." Over the next few years, Sainte-Marie also lived on Sullivan Street and on Thomson Street, right by Washington Square. "The neighborhoods in Greenwich Village were adorable, very innocent by today's standards," Sainte-Marie says. "Italian coffee houses, secondhand anything-you-want, small, well-lit streets, and Izzy Young's Folklore Center store. I always felt safe in New York. I didn't expect to stay long, and I loved it, especially the crowds of people, most of them on a pretty good trip, especially people just out of high school and college. On Perry Street, I played my guitar and wrote songs on the fire escape. When I made some money singing, I found an apartment on Sullivan Street, and traveled in and out of New York mostly on the bus with my guitar and a small suitcase."

Right from the start, she got a sense of something big bubbling under the surface. "Early on, there were a lot of artists and musicians and some consciousness-raising on social issues," Sainte-Marie recalls. "Eventually entrepreneurs smelled money, and as hippies replaced beatniks, the student populations filled the streets shoulder-to-shoulder with grown-up tourists from out of town. There was a pre–Renaissance Fair atmosphere, and some real Woody Guthrie worship."

The folk scene was flourishing, and Sainte-Marie found herself sharing stages and spaces, exchanging ideas with, and observing established artists and future superstars. She first met Bob Dylan at a famous venue called Gerde's Folk City in Greenwich Village. "First time I played, there was an open-mic night when anybody could play, so I did. People liked it a lot;

they were a little shocked by my songs like 'Universal Soldier' and 'Now That the Buffalo's Gone,' as hard protest that made sense, and songs about Native American issues were pretty unique—but that's what was so great about the coffee-house days and the early folk music era: diversity. Bob Dylan heard me that night or some other night, chatted me up and told me to go see Sam Hood at the Gaslight where I played many times after that."[5]

The Gaslight was a basement venue, dark and cramped and intimate, with wood-paneled walls and a low ceiling. It opened in 1958 and was home to beat poets like Allen Ginsberg and Hugh Romney (later known as Wavy Gravy), but eventually became one of folk music's main performance hubs. In 1963, influential *New York Times* music critic Robert Shelton saw Sainte-Marie there and raved that she was "one of the most promising new talents on the folk scene."[6] *Time* called her "the most intriguing young folk singer to emerge in many a moon."[7] Soon, Vanguard Records came calling to offer her a deal.

The label, co-founded in 1950 by brothers Maynard and Seymour Solomon, was initially focused on classical music, but wanted to grow its business and released a series of jazz recordings, eventually moving into folk and blues as well. They proved that they were on the right side of the growing counterculture, releasing records by blacklisted acts such as African-American actor and singer Paul Robeson and the Weavers, a folk group that included Pete Seeger and Lee Hays. Vanguard had released Joan Baez's self-titled debut album in 1960, and she quickly became one of the few prominent women artists in the burgeoning folk scene, which, in turn, helped establish the label as part of the cornerstone of the new folk movement. (In 1963, Baez was the star in both her career and her relationship—and her boyfriend was Bob Dylan.)

While Vanguard Records pursued her, Sainte-Marie took it all in stride. She was admittedly naïve when it came to show business. When they asked her if she had a lawyer, she said no. "I felt conflicted," Sainte-Marie says, recalling the day she signed the record deal, "knowing zero about contracts or business, and actually not knowing a lawyer." Vanguard encouraged her to use their legal counsel, a decision she would come to regret.

Sainte-Marie was motivated by a sense of urgency: she figured that she had just one chance to say everything she needed to say, since she assumed she'd put out a record and then leave to pursue her studies in India. More than fifty years later and millions of flight miles logged, India is one of the few places she's still never been. "I thought I was going someplace else, that my life and my path was to continue studying in India. I didn't know if it was going to work... and I never envisioned a 'career' in show business," she says. "I really thought I was a guest."

That spirit echoes throughout Sainte-Marie's debut album, 1964's *It's My Way!* It's the sound of an artist who wants to leave it all on the record and has nothing to lose. There is arguably no more politically and socially charged, incisive, demanding, exciting, or relevant record of the folk era. By 1964, student activists had developed a sense of outrage about Vietnam and the Civil Rights Movement, and they were turning their anger towards oppressive policies, racism, and marginalization of minorities into action on college campuses across the United States. Students were building solidarity with other progressives, and that political momentum spilled over into coffee houses and protest marches. But though Sainte-Marie cared about Vietnam and the Civil Rights Movement, she knew that if she didn't focus on Indigenous rights, at least in her own music, no one else would.

"In an expanding atmosphere of hippie chic and wannabes in the cities, I was at Indigenous places where there wasn't anybody there except people who were 'stuck' with being Indian," Sainte-Marie says. "And what I mean by that is, they were Indigenous 24/7, not wannabes selling the latest fad. Some people were 'Indians in their last life,' and now they sold T-shirts, right? They sold sweat-lodge ceremonies or some kind of thing with fringes. Then there's another group of people who are part-Indian or cocktail-party Indians. They're Indian when it's convenient. But beyond this, there are actually real living, breathing, Indigenous people of the Americas who are stuck with being Indian from the day they're born until the day they die—morning, noon, and night and whatever is going on in their social life. They don't put it on and take it off. And traveling around the way I've been able to do, those differences quickly became obvious. I've been around all of these. I do appreciate the help of anybody from anywhere who loves our cultures and wants to help alleviate poverty and landlessness in Indian country. I'm extremely privileged to know many solid traditional people of all ages still committed to sustaining both our rights and our cultures. It's hard to see the beautiful uniqueness of our elders and the old ways suffer or diminish or fade away."

It's My Way!'s album cover was a beautiful departure from other folk records of the time with its rich, warm color palette. It features Sainte-Marie with her head bent slightly, eyes downcast, her shiny, dark hair hanging in curtains on either side of her face, with a fringe of bangs that's just a tiny bit crooked. Just below her chin she holds a mouth bow (a traditional stringed instrument fashioned from a curved stick connected with string), which became one of her signatures. Fifty-plus years later, it's still a striking image.

She remembers recording *It's My Way!* standing in the

ballroom in the Manhattan Towers hotel where Vanguard had built its studio, an immense space with high ceilings and a wooden floor. "I'm all by myself here, and way down there, [the producers are] in a room that they have fitted out to be a control room, and I don't know what I'm doing. I sing a song several times and they chose—it wasn't very good what they chose." Her fans disagreed, and by 1965, *Life* magazine reported her annual earnings as more than $100,000 from record sales and touring.[8] Audiences were enthralled by the sheer force and power that twenty-three-year-old Sainte-Marie brought to her debut.

Consider the opening track, "Now That the Buffalo's Gone." Imagine beginning a record with a protest song that packs an ambitious and emotional survey of colonial history and a plaintive demand for Native American rights into just two minutes and forty-six seconds. When she wrote "Can you remember the times that you've held your head high/and told all your friends of your Indian claim," it was an invitation. The lines are deliberately addressed to a "proud good lady, proud good man." "Not 'you racist son of a bitch,'" Sainte-Marie says. "Because I knew these people; I'd grown up around these people. They were very proud to be 'part Indian,' even though they didn't know anything about it. I invited them to join in, become more knowledgeable. I didn't want to push them away. And all through that song it's including the listener as part of the solution. Yes, it's laying the thing right smack in their laps, but it's not humiliating or offending people."

Sainte-Marie's friend and Steppenwolf lead singer John Kay still remembers the first time he heard her sing it. "I get very emotional about certain things when they connect deeply with me, and I just burst into tears of rage," Kay says. "It was such a spot-on indictment of justice denied."

"Now That the Buffalo's Gone" moves from gentle insistence to thunderous desperation. The guitar rolls in over and over at varying intensities—between a few rocks tumbling down a dusty canyon and the crushing weight of a landslide. Sainte-Marie's voice shifts, too. There's a sweetness to her beseeching, and as her message intensifies, she pulls her vibrato up from the depths, the lower register of her vocals like a reluctant growl from the earth's core. The song is about the building of Kinzua Dam in upper New York State on the Seneca Indian Reservation, an action taken against the Indigenous people's wishes. "There were several alternative sites, but politicians, contractors, and a lot of money were involved, and somehow America chose to break the oldest treaty in the congressional archives—the Pickering Treaty [the Treaty of Canandaigua] made during George Washington's administration—and flood the Senecas out of their home," Sainte-Marie says. Beyond the specifics of that particular issue, Sainte-Marie knew that the song represented the experience of many Indigenous nations that continued to be similarly threatened and exploited. "Up until then, there hadn't been any songs addressing Indian issues in this way," she recalls. "All the public had ever heard was Hank Williams's song 'Kaw-Liga (Was a Wooden Indian),' and 'Ten Little Indians.' Peter LaFarge wrote a few, but they didn't get much attention."

The song's remarkable clarity extends throughout *It's My Way!* It presents Sainte-Marie's vision of music as a medium for love and protest, for addressing inequality, systemic racism, and the horrors of colonialism. Sainte-Marie was recognized as an outspoken, public, Indigenous woman who refused to conform or be silent—whose very existence was a politicized form of resistance.

She faced far more barriers to success than many of her folk peers, yet Sainte-Marie stayed true to her guts and her grit. Side one of *It's My Way!* begins with "Now That the Buffalo's Gone," includes "Cod'ine," and ends with "Universal Soldier." Over the course of seven songs, Sainte-Marie covered an expanse of musical terrain that few artists will touch in their entire careers: folk, traditional, gospel, rock, blues, and a little country. Side two went deeper and darker, but also included the playful "Cripple Creek," where she showcased the versatility and vibrancy of the mouth bow, and ended with the titular song, which is frenzied and phenomenal, a compelling closer. Full of agency, her voice cracks across certain words and lifts others up under a shimmery, deep vibrato. In the lines "Put down the story of what I say/you're bound for glory/all on your own one day," she takes back her narrative while empowering her listeners to go out and discover their own.

The exclamation point that separates the song from the album title is its own genius. It reads as powerful and purposeful, an act of defiant intention. It feels like Sainte-Marie is modeling something akin to bravery and a sense of daring, a different way of thinking. But some thought that exclamation point was too provocative. "People who never listened to the song—journalists who were interviewing me on the radio or over the phone—thought that I was real pushy and that I was, like, six feet tall," Sainte-Marie remembers, laughing. "They always thought I was big. A lot of people are very, very surprised that I'm little—because I'm loud."

She says some listeners interpreted the album title as if Frank Sinatra was saying it, with the emphasis on the "my." "You know, 'Us wise guys, we've got it covered, we've got it cornered. It's *my* way, and by God, I'm going to stick it to you. I did it *my* way, you motherfuckers.' No! *It's My Way!* was about, 'This is my path. Discover your own. They're out there. The paths to wonderfulness, to effectiveness, to joy, to living are generated everywhere! They're coming from inside you. Project your path outward from where you are inside yourself.'"

It's My Way! is also a reference to dharma and Hinduism, a major area of interest for her within philosophy, but so many people have misinterpreted the title over the years that Sainte-Marie was sometimes sad about it. "I thought I was going to make one record and continue to India," she says. "I recorded 'It's My Way' and put it on that album, and it sounded like a pretty good title, but I didn't think I was going to last beyond that."

The song "It's My Way" was specific, right from the opening declaration: "I'm cutting my own way." As she flirted with the fringes of show business, planning to go to India, she couldn't shake the image of cutting a path through the wilderness. "It's one of my most deliberate songs. I was so new and just out of college. Maybe I'm kind of pedal-to-the metal on this point, but I really meant that I was cutting my own way. I had lived in Maine, and I was raised near a lake, so I'm real familiar with hacking a trail and going through a meadow by a different way. I kind of had this image of a machete—of a farmer's tool, not a machete from a horror movie—cutting a path through a big field of tall grasses or through wilderness."

One of the most striking elements of the album is its emotional intensity. It manifests not only in the melody, composition, and lyrics, but in Sainte-Marie's vocal performance as well. "Some of my songs are super emotional; not only the love songs but some of the songs about oppression," she explains. "I mean, they're painful, and the sound of my voice changes, too, like it would if I'm having a conversation with a friend. I don't know if it happens to all singers; maybe singers who are trained and taught to be aware of things wouldn't become as emotional, but I sure do. Sometimes I'll just be crying in songs. It's not something you do for the audience; it can't be anticipated, but every now and then, a song will just get the better of me. And you can feel a voice break and things happen to a voice."

Sainte-Marie's audiences responded to her evocative performances and the passionate abandon in her voice whether she was playing in a small space to a hundred people or in a large outdoor show to a few thousand. Those who loved her—who understood the thunder in her vibrato and the spark in her words—cried and gave standing ovations at the end of her shows. Even the critics were captivated, including the *New York Times'* Robert Shelton, who had written so glowingly of her the previous year. His brief review of *It's My Way!* wasn't without criticism—he begins by calling the record one of the most "confounding" he's heard "in a long while"—but he raved about her "soulful, rich alto voice and ... compelling intensity."[9]

"When I was first singing, I wasn't thinking about pitch or timing," Sainte-Marie says. "I was only thinking about the content of the song, including the emotional content. A song had to really make sense for me to want to give it to my audience." And her audiences responded in kind: over the coming years, her professional performance highlights would include a 1966 outdoor show for 4,200 fans in New York,[10] a ten-minute standing ovation in 1967 at the New York Philharmonic, and a triumphant solo show in 1968 at Carnegie Hall.

CHAPTER 4

IT'S MY WAY

T'S MY WAY! was a creative triumph, but the record wasn't a huge commercial success—it sold well but didn't chart, and it didn't make Sainte-Marie a household name. However, it did catapult her to a level of success that made her enough money to ensure a lifetime of relative freedom and cemented her position as one of the most important folk songwriters of the 1960s, even if she wasn't one of the most famous. With "Universal Soldier," "Now That the Buffalo's Gone," "Cod'ine," and the title track, *It's My Way!* was a bona fide triumph.

And Sainte-Marie kind of hated it.

"I was just heartbroken with my first album," she says, putting on a slightly vengeful, funny voice. "But it sold and it's still selling, so maybe I shouldn't have an opinion, I guess!" Sainte-Marie had no say in the process of selecting which takes Vanguard used, but she believes that if she'd been consulted, it would have been a better record, one that was in tune, beautiful as well as tragic. "They were going for 'if it bleeds, it leads,' and they wanted it to sound like it was bleeding," she says. "I can't get anybody to agree with me on this point, and most people will say, 'No, no, no.'"

There's a cruel irony to the fact that the album is so decisively titled, and yet Sainte-Marie felt so excluded from the decision-making process. This background doesn't diminish the importance of *It's My Way!*—if anything, it reaffirms the challenges facing many new artists, particularly a racialized young woman who wanted to make a brilliant, bold, utterly confident debut. "The only thing that matters to the business side of show business is money," Sainte-Marie says. "If it sells, it doesn't matter—it can be a turd in the basket. What I always come back to is: this old world is very young, but some things don't change. Jesus threw the money changers out of the temple for some very good reasons."

Sainte-Marie's cynicism about the business part of show business is born out of her own first-hand experiences. It also stems from talking to other artists and witnessing some spectacular disasters. "There's no telling how many records they [the music industry] have destroyed, but everybody I know, every artist who I've ever talked to, has had a similar dilemma in trying to get their baby born intact," Sainte-Marie says. "Maynard Solomon [Vanguard's co-founder] was saying that he was producing me, but actually, he was editing me."

Sainte-Marie wasn't thrilled with the final outcome of *It's My Way!* or the next few records that followed, primarily because of her vocal performance. "I wish that I had been able to choose the takes because Vanguard had a certain perception of me, I think, and really wanted to rub it in," she says. "In my first couple of records, whoever was choosing the takes wanted me to sound like I was kind of old and dying. I think they imagined that maybe I was a junkie or they probably thought that I was going to be a young casualty."

It's possible that Vanguard thought it was best to steer hard into the harsh tragedy of "Cod'ine" without understanding the real hell Sainte-Marie experienced in order to write it. "Cod'ine" was written in despair but also in anger. It wasn't the explosive, fiery kind that burns up and burns out. Nor was it the kind of anger that scorches the earth, necessary for regrowth and renewal. "Cod'ine" conveyed something deeper. It was world-weary and from the bone, leaden with exhaustion and frustration and the resentment that comes from decades of survival and trauma, oppression, and violation. As Sainte-Marie sang it, it's not surprising that some of the people at the record label may have thought they were dealing with a young person active in her addiction. She was twenty-three when she first recorded the song, but she sounds ninety in some parts. Even though there's a performative element to the original 1964 recording, the wildness of her vulnerability and her broken howls are chilling.

The song comes from Sainte-Marie's brief addiction to opioids. "I was assaulted in the sixties—well, I think of it as assault—by a doctor," Sainte-Marie says. "It was the only time I had been involved with opiates. I was given them against my will by a doctor who [later] went to jail for turning young women out, you know, into prostitutes. He went to jail. Not because of me, but I heard [about it] later."

The opiates were administered to supposedly help manage an ongoing cough she experienced following a bronchial infection. In Florida, a clinic doctor prescribed her shots and pills that Sainte-Marie thought were vitamin B12 and antibiotics. She received the shots for a few weeks, and then she set out to drive to Atlanta with some friends. Sainte-Marie wasn't feeling well and figured she was still sick, so she stopped at a drugstore to get a refill. The pharmacist looked at the prescription and told her that he didn't think she was sick—she was strung out and going through withdrawal. She was stunned, and in the days that followed, she continued to struggle through withdrawal. It was hell, she remembers, and a shocking violation of consent:

according to Sainte-Marie, the doctor prescribed the opiates without telling her what they were. She alleges that he did this to her on purpose and for personal gain, hoping to get her and other young women addicted so he could exploit them.

There's a pained authenticity in the earthquake of her voice as she sings "Cod'ine," the aftershocks of her vibrato almost swallowing words whole as she bellows, "An' it's real, one more time." Yet "Cod'ine" wasn't meant, as some critics interpreted it, as a contribution to the anti-hippie, anti-drug, reefer-madness panic-song canon. She wrote it as a means of processing her experience and offering a personal warning; there was nothing glamorous or rock 'n' roll or cool about addiction. Some of her peers laughed at the notion of being addicted to something as "tame" as codeine, but an opiate is an opiate, and there are deadly consequences to its addictiveness as well as its relative availability.

The producers at Vanguard who'd mistaken her for a drug addict misunderstood her in other ways too. Not only had they steered her towards vocal performances that were not up to her own live performance standards, they failed to trust their young artist's instincts about where she should be marketed. While her peer group in New York liked it, she is still disappointed that there was no push and no strategy to get it into the hands of not only music industry types, students, and art-y counter-culture activists in major cities like L.A. and London, but also to the places that could most benefit from it, such as her two "homes."

"It didn't get to the boonies, and it didn't get to Indian country," Sainte-Marie says, referring to any reservation or land occupied and self-governed by Indigenous people. Now, the term is more of an Indigenous colloquialism to refer to any area primarily inhabited by Indigenous people. Sainte-Marie wanted a wider audience for *It's My Way!* because she believed in the songs and that the information needed to be out in the world.

Despite Sainte-Marie's misgivings, *It's My Way!* experienced continued success. She frequently played on the road, got rave reviews for her performances, and grew her audience one show at a time—which is still her approach to this day.

When Sainte-Marie is onstage, she's transfixing. When she opens her mouth to sing and the words spill over you, they tuck inside every hollow, even the ones you didn't know you had. The sensation is a visceral one. It can be unsettling and unnerving to be temporarily subsumed. But it can also be the greatest experience of your life. John Kay still remembers the first time he saw Sainte-Marie play live. It was in the summer of 1964, and he was visiting Toronto's Yorkville neighborhood. Kay himself wasn't in a band yet—he was a year away from joining the Canadian rock band the Sparrows, and three years away from forming Steppenwolf.

"That was the first time that I heard Buffy live," Kay says. "I got her first album, *It's My Way!*, and I was just totally bowled over. In fact, the reason why I went and got the album is because Buffy's stage persona and the intensity of her performance and the passion with which she sang the songs—particularly 'It's My Way' and 'Now That the Buffalo's Gone' and 'Cod'ine'— just knocked me out. At this juncture, we had heard Joan Baez, we had Judy Collins, but these were all females that were very restrained, shall we say, in their vocal delivery. Buffy was like this whirlwind of intensity—she gave you goose bumps."

As her fame grew and she attracted new audiences, she took full advantage of the airplane tickets that could bring her to Indigenous areas and communities, and she often built in time to visit the Piapots and meet other young Indigenous activists wherever she'd play. She consciously capitalized on the success of *It's My Way!* to bring attention to Indigenous people and talk about broken treaties, exploitation, unfair treatment, and genocide. And she knew only too well that while she was using her privilege and success to talk about Indigenous rights, other musicians—mostly men—were recording her songs and turning them into hits.

Sainte-Marie had been singing "Universal Soldier" for a few years, and it featured prominently on the tracklist for *It's My Way!* The Highwaymen had recorded it too, but the song didn't become a hit until 1965—though not for Sainte-Marie. Folk singer Donovan Philips Leitch, who recorded as Donovan, started performing in 1964. Hyped sometimes as the British Bob Dylan, Donovan heard Sainte-Marie sing "Universal Soldier" live in London, England, and decided to cover it. He released his version in 1965, and it charted both in the U.K. (at number five) and in the U.S. (number fifty-three on *Billboard*). Suddenly, everyone was talking about "Universal Soldier" as if Donovan had written it. When he covered "Cod'ine" shortly thereafter, Sainte-Marie's authorship was erased yet again. To this day, there are numerous websites that credit him as the songwriter and it's blatant sexism that, fifty years later, this is still a common misconception.

"I still have people insist that Donovan wrote 'Universal Soldier' and 'Cod'ine,'" Sainte-Marie says. "I've had people actually confront me about it." Donovan's success could be attributed to the inherent "authority" that society gives to men's words, the weight they carry, unlike women who apparently speak in dandelion fluff and helium balloons, not bricks of gold. Sainte-Marie's songwriting, her infiltration of the "boys' club" mentality of show business and the folk music scene, precedes the women's liberation movement by a number of years. While this isn't an issue unique to Sainte-Marie and Donovan, it's easy to identify two major ways in which he has been lauded by the music industry while Sainte-Marie's contributions have been ignored. In 2012, Donovan was inducted into the Rock and Roll Hall of Fame, and in 2014, he was inducted into the Songwriters Hall of Fame—neither of which have recognized Sainte-Marie.

It's even more galling considering how hard Sainte-Marie had to work to get the rights back to "Universal Soldier." One night at the Gaslight, Sainte-Marie signed away her publishing rights to the song for one dollar. In John Einarson's book, *Four Strong Winds: Ian and Sylvia*,[11] Sainte-Marie recalls that it was the night the Highwaymen heard her perform "Universal Soldier." She got off stage and went to join them, and they told her they planned to record her song. They asked her who the publisher was, and she responded "What's that?" Pianist and musical supervisor Elmer Jared Gordon was sitting with them and offered to "help," drawing up a contract on the spot. She signed away the rights to "Universal Soldier," happy that somebody was going to help spread its message to an audience she never felt she would reach. "I didn't know what I was doing," Sainte-Marie sighs. "Basically I had already made up my mind that I was okay as a loner. I was never going to be part of a group. I was never going to have a big career in show business." (It took her ten years and $25,000 to buy the song's rights back.)

That outsider feeling remained even when *It's My Way!* hit in the U.K. Sainte-Marie went to England, Scotland, Ireland, and Wales on a tour with Julie Felix, Reverend Gary Davis, Ramblin' Jack Elliott, and a then-unknown Paul Simon. They were in England, and she was the headliner at the famous Royal Albert Hall—Simon was just starting out—and all she really remembers is that he was quite reserved. She was surprised when her name came up in his 2016 biography, *Homeward Bound: The Life of Paul Simon.*[12] According to the biography, Simon was determined to flip the order of the show so that he was the headliner, with Sainte-Marie opening for him—even though she was the established star and Simon was just starting out. "The book says that Paul was just determined that he was going to headline the show, and the concert producer was saying that was absolutely ridiculous," she recalls. "[Paul] wasn't well known yet, he wasn't a star, he had no respect, and he was just trying to claw his way up like a businessman. I only found out about it a few months ago in that book. I didn't even know that was going on at the time!" She laughs. "That's how unimportant it was to me."

While some artists were jealous of Sainte-Marie's burgeoning fame and prominence, others could see a whole new world of possibility with Sainte-Marie in the spotlight. Denise Kaufman was a fan of Sainte-Marie's before they became close friends more than forty years ago. In the mid-sixties, Kaufman co-founded Ace of Cups, widely considered to be San Francisco's first all-woman rock band. Sainte-Marie reaffirmed what kind of artist Kaufman wanted to be.

"There was a dearth of women who touched my heart, but Buffy did," Kaufman says. "A lot of people that were into music at the time were really into Joan Baez. And I appreciated Joan's voice and I appreciated her activism, but I wanted to believe that the person singing was the person who wrote the song. It sort of always bothered me. When I first heard Buffy, it was like, you know, she *was* her songs. She wrote them, which was much more of an inspiration to me. She's so real, and it cut me to the core when I first heard her. Just that a woman could be that strong and also that tender. She transmitted so much in her voice. Her beauty and her look opened up so much because there weren't people around singing who looked like her and who sang about what she sang about. She was my hero."

CHAPTER 5

COD'INE

SAINTE-MARIE LIKED THE performance part of show business, but not its colonial vaudeville roots. Particularly since the business side of those roots were—and are—so often tied to exploitation, a recurring theme and frequent subject of condemnation throughout *It's My Way!* When the album came out, she was young and trying her best to navigate the industry and her growing fame, but she was also wary of men, many of whom seemed hardwired for predatory behavior. And then, in 1964, vulnerable and alone, she ended up falling for a vagabond artist.

"I had a boyfriend who was a painter—he was also a son of a bitch, but he was a really good painter," she says. Ramon Indius Alvarez wanted nothing to do with galleries or commercial art, and he and Sainte-Marie bonded over their shared approach to artistic practice. She wanted to escape the spotlight and he wanted to paint, so they headed to Spain for a few months. Sainte-Marie hoped to see and hear great flamenco and finish writing her ambitious song, "My Country 'Tis of Thy People You're Dying," the almost seven-minute-long epic that appeared on her 1966 album, *Little Wheel Spin and Spin.*

"I wanted to finish this song, and my boyfriend wanted to paint, so that's what we did," she remembers. "We got a house in Formentera and lived there for a while in isolation." Alvarez was tall and handsome, with a sharp, square jaw and a brooding, smug expression. He appeared in a *Life* magazine spread with her in 1965, looming like an attractive undertaker.[13] In 1966, Sainte-Marie put her money into buying an old farmhouse in Maine and gave up her New York apartment. In an early 1967 interview with the journal *Status & Diplomat*, Sainte-Marie talked about her two favorite people: Leonard Cohen, "boyish and charming, who looks like a prince looking for his kingdom"; and Alvarez, "who is austere and is a painter of charm and talent and good looks."[14]

It sounded good, but it wasn't. "He was beautiful, very striking looking, but like a vampire. And that's how he acted too. He was not a kind person," Sainte-Marie says. "As a matter of fact, a few years ago, I ran into one of his other girlfriends. I didn't know he had other girlfriends but he did, and she didn't know he had other girlfriends, but she found out he was with me too. He was a bully, and he beat us both up. He was a bad guy."

In 1967, Sainte-Marie fled the abusive relationship and headed back to New York. With nowhere else to stay, she booked into the Chelsea Hotel. The landmark New York hotel was home to many influential artists over the years, particularly in the sixties and seventies, including Leonard Cohen and Joni Mitchell, as well as Sainte-Marie's hero, Édith Piaf.

"I don't think the Chelsea was a big deal at that time," Sainte-Marie says. "I think it maybe got famous in retrospect? To me, it was just a place to stay now and then. You needed a place to stay for a week or two, there was the Hotel Earle, the Gramercy Park, the Chelsea—whoever had a room. I didn't hang out much socially, and it wasn't till years later I found out that a lot of famous artists had had the same idea. I just kind of hid, wrote songs, and would journal stuff about my world."

The 1960s New York music community was, in many ways, a microcosm of the larger counterculture, and the Chelsea was a common intersection for many artists, with a vibrant social scene that offered almost the exact opposite of Sainte-Marie's usual preference for the periphery. But the Chelsea had a compelling magnetism, a built-in if transient community, and it was close to everything. Cohen immortalized it in his poem, "Chelsea Hotel #2," which he later admitted was about Janis Joplin, who famously adapted Sainte-Marie's song, "Cod'ine."

Sainte-Marie, a self-described teetotaler, is still somewhat amused that the two most famous and infamous covers of "Cod'ine" are by Joplin and Courtney Love, women whose phenomenal musical talents were often eclipsed by their addictions. Joplin credited Sainte-Marie with the song, but she re-wrote most of the lyrics. In Joplin's version, there are more allusions to death throughout, but her delivery is less wrought. There's little of Sainte-Marie's angst in Joplin's vocals, more like a defiant resignation, even as she sings about how the drug will kill her because that's the "bargain" they made. Joplin debuted her cover in 1965. Five years later, she would be dead of an accidental heroin overdose at the age of twenty-seven. Courtney Love's 2010 cover was released on a Japanese version of Hole's album *Nobody's Daughter*. It's an amalgamation of Sainte-Marie's original and Joplin's revision, and appropriately, Love's vocals suggest a similar duality—pained and defiant—but also the snarled, disaffected, painted-on cynicism that Love so often utilizes to detract from her vulnerability.

Most "Cod'ine" covers miss the anchoring perspective from which Sainte-Marie wrote the song. She was bearing witness to the initial ripples of the eventual seismic shift from coffee-house culture to bar culture, a move that would cause, in Sainte-Marie's experience, irreparable damage to the most effective aspects of the growing counterculture. "Coffee houses offered an atmosphere for young people to be together and have a safe place to go and hear music that was actually about themselves and their peers—that was us, the songwriters," Sainte-Marie says. "Coffee houses were really something special. People who are sitting in a coffee house drinking coffee and talking, they're thinking, not boozing. They're sharing political perspectives and artistic perspectives, and it was quite beautiful."

The natural community organizing that happened in these spaces was a powerful foil to what Sainte-Marie saw reflected in the exploitative and oppressive tactics going on in the outside world. Coffee houses were home to those who sought to reinforce demands for civil rights for African-Americans, Indigenous people, women, and other minority groups. People weren't yet using the word "decolonize," but that's what they were doing. They were, mostly unconsciously, putting into practice Indigenous philosophies about life in a circle, which was idealistically less about "me" and more about "us." Coffee houses of the early sixties had also been a hotbed of world music, creativity, and collaboration.

According to Sainte-Marie, those early days in the folk scene were also pretty innocent. "It's the difference between a bar crowd and a coffee-house crowd," she says. "They come to listen, not just to get drunk, get laid, and go home. It was a healthy environment." But as more of the music industry began to operate within these spaces, coffee didn't offer up the same profit margin as alcohol. As liquor licenses were obtained and booze began to flow, the age restrictions changed and the more meaningful conversations—and their resulting activism—dried up. "Things changed," she remembers. "A lot of artists got involved with alcohol and heroin who before were not. I think that the whole coffee house movement was euthanized. I think it was put to sleep deliberately." Silencing dissent and the uprising youth movement was one aim, but so was making a profit, and the way to get more money was to get people away from coffee and turn them on to booze. When coffee houses became bars, the shift was dramatic. The greed that Sainte-Marie had already identified as a foundation of colonialism was about to rip a hole in the patchwork youth movement slowly organizing itself between acoustic sets and caffeine fixes. And although she was part of the folk scene, Sainte-Marie never felt like she belonged, particularly socially, once the scene evolved into bars. Still, she continued to play on the same stages as a rotating cast of now-famous faces. Sainte-Marie wasn't part of the big-money management stables that Albert Grossman and David Geffen ran, but she still refers to their clients in a way that's both intimate and matter-of-fact. "Joni," "Neil," and "Leonard" are real people in her story; they are famous and influential enough to not need the specificity of a surname.

"Bob Dylan I knew a little tiny bit just as an acquaintance, and we've had a couple of conversations, but not much that lasted very long, so, no, we didn't really know each other back in the day," Sainte-Marie says. "But what a writer—I always liked him; still do. We spent some time together in Australia a few years ago, and it was fun talking about this and that, and we laughed a lot. Tom Paxton I met a couple of times at multi-artist concerts where you'd see people and you'd say, 'Hi,' and 'Oh, I like your new song.' And once I did a workshop with Kris Kristofferson."

She didn't know Joan Baez very well, though they met once at a big weekend festival in California, and she's pretty sure she never even met Judy Collins. "When I was first starting to play in Greenwich Village, I wasn't really a part of a social scene [because] I don't drink," she says. "I was scared of men. I wasn't comfortable after the show going out with a bunch of guys and drinking in a bar, which a lot of people did—certainly all the guys did and several of the girls. I didn't, so I missed a lot of those business and social opportunities."

But she did love using whatever clout she had to help other young artists she believed in. Sainte-Marie carried Joni Mitchell's demo tape in her purse for months, trying to get record industry people excited about the young singer-songwriter, but they didn't want to hear her. Sainte-Marie still doesn't know why there was so much resistance to Mitchell at first. She saw nothing but success ahead for the up-and-comer. "It wasn't just her music," Sainte-Marie says. "It was also her persona. Admittedly, I liked that she was from Saskatchewan. And I liked her point of view; she had a unique musical point of view. I thought she was beautiful and had a real shot at attracting a bigger audience than usually will follow a smart person.

"I thought she would probably attract people who, even if they didn't understand her, would find her charming and beautiful. So I thought she had a chance. And she was a woman. She was not owned and operated by a corporation at that point. I mean, who knows what Joan Baez and Judy Collins were about? I don't know because I don't know either of those people, but Joni came from a place that I could understand, and she wasn't getting a shot. Joan Baez and Judy, they already had the toughest management in the business. And Joni [at that point] had nothing."

But soon Mitchell had two of the most powerful men in the music industry managing her career: Elliot Roberts, who was just starting out and would become Neil Young's manager, and Roberts's business partner, record executive David Geffen. Mitchell's transition from fledgling folkie to superstar songwriter was swift, and her move to California solidified her celebrity status. "Elliot really was nice. I always liked him,"

Sainte-Marie remembers. "But between Elliot and David Geffen—I mean, these are two extremely sharp machetes. These are true sharks. These guys will do anything for the art of the deal, for their artists. It was very, very different from Phil Ochs's career or my career, or the careers of ninety-nine percent of the talented artists in show business."

Sainte-Marie didn't just carry her new friends' tapes around with her, playing them for record executives; she also chose to cover their songs, giving them a financial boost as well. Sainte-Marie covered several of Mitchell's songs on her earlier records both because she loved them and because she wanted to help Mitchell, a then-emerging artist, get her music out into the world. She also set Leonard Cohen's "God Is Alive, Magic Is Afoot" to music, and that song opens her 1969 experimental electronic album, *Illuminations*. Members of Crazy Horse, Neil Young's band, played on her 1971 record, *She Used to Wanna Be a Ballerina*, and she also covered his classic song "Helpless" on that record, as well as Cohen's "Bells."

"It sounds like friendship," Sainte-Marie says, "but it was more about admiring craft than anything. Actually, I think Neil disliked me. Joni and Leonard were hanging out, but I wasn't hanging out in that intimate kind of level with anybody. Joni and Crosby, Stills and Nash—they're all real, true friends and buddies and peers to each other. I didn't know anyone. Well, I knew Leonard a little bit." She carried his tape in her purse for a while too, hoping to help his songs reach the right ears. "We hung out and had coffee and talked a little bit, but it's not as though there was bromance or romance. There was neither one. Not because I wouldn't have liked to or he wouldn't have liked to, but no, it just wasn't there."

Today, Sainte-Marie's name is often associated with Neil Young, Joni Mitchell, and Leonard Cohen, as they are four of

Canada's most important songwriters, but she doesn't see it that way. Sainte-Marie had positioned herself outside the center of the folk movement—though arguably, her refusal to fall in line with the commodification of resistance kept her true to folk's authentic core. Sainte-Marie was selling records, but she wasn't a money-making machine. She was famous and rich (enough, for her), and without ruthless management behind her, she could opt out to a certain extent. "I didn't have a shark in my corner. I wasn't being commodified, and I don't know whether that's a plus or minus," she says. "I don't know whether I dodged the bullet or whether I missed the point entirely. Now and then I think about it. There's a difference between being an artist and a careerist. And all careerists will claim to be artists, right? It's 'bad' to be a careerist," she says with a laugh. "Neil and Joni and Leonard—I don't think of them as a group. I think of Neil and Joni because of the California social scene; they were much more [a part of] a real circle than I was. I really don't know about Leonard. But three out of four of the people you mentioned lived in L.A., right at the fulcrum of 'le showbiz.' Where was Buffy? Did she have a $100,000-a-year publicist to keep her current? I don't think so!"

She's also heard stories of musicians who were milked dry by agents or producers and then dumped or dismissed or shelved. Sainte-Marie knows firsthand how tough show business can be on artists, though she can't help but challenge some of what she's been reading about in their biographies, particularly the musicians who started in folk music like her. They began from a similar place of social consciousness and working-class activism, but many ended up phenomenally famous and were ultimately sheltered by that privilege.

"Joni had two of the world's giant sharks shepherding her career. [In her biography], she complains about show business, and her complaints are—they may be accurate, but they're not the same kinds of complaints that most of us have had. Bruce Springsteen too—he's got complaints and stuff, but basically, they're protected by this huge colonial career system, and you can complain if your colonial shark is not keeping up with somebody else's colonial shark. But none of them really come out and complain about [the bigger picture]. They just don't seem to identify it. Neil [Young] too. These are very intelligent, intuitive, talented people, but for some reason, there's a bigger picture that just doesn't seem to show up in show business very often."

The "bigger picture" to which Sainte-Marie refers is colonialism and the systemic greed, inequality, and injustice within and outside of the music industry. "Colonialism doesn't just bleed Indigenous people; eventually, it bleeds everybody except the jerks who're running the racket," she says. "What's wrong with the world is not just a series of little, momentary bad guys," she continues. "It's a system that goes back to before the Old Testament and needs to evolve from where it is now to something better. I think we go about it by fits and starts. Artists can help a lot and sometimes do—but I don't understand why they stop. What happened to Bob Dylan's sense of outrage? 'Masters of War,' or 'With God on Our Side.' What happens? How does it go away? For me, it hasn't gone away. And I don't understand how somebody can be that smart, talented, rich, famous, and in the perfect position without continuing to want to make change."

Sainte-Marie suggests that a greed for commercial success is something that many aspiring artists learn from their business-minded families or friends. Or they might learn it in music school, where the emphasis is on careerism as opposed to art. "I think a lot of musicians are chasing some template for a hit [single]," she says. "They learn a formula—established by entrepreneurs rather than artists—that's supposed to make you rich, famous, successful, and fulfilled, and sometimes it works. The first three might be correct, but fulfilled, I don't know. It depends on who you ask. I'm a biblioholic, and I read a lot of musician's biographies, mostly by and about men, and I see with hindsight how different my life and career have been from theirs. For me it was never about 'getting a hit' or 'getting pussy' or 'getting famous.' It wasn't about 'the Get.'"

Without those commercial or carnal motivations, Sainte-Marie's artistry was unencumbered, and she could make the music she wanted to. About half the songs on *It's My Way!* have upside-down tuning, and Sainte-Marie says the other half are inside out. This is the way she's made all of her records, but in the mid-sixties, amidst the popular sounds of Tom Paxton, Judy Collins, and Joan Baez, all of whom used Spanish tuning, Sainte-Marie stood out. "Being 'unique' was not popular when I was coming along," Sainte-Marie says wryly. "There was a lot of preppy college-boy influence like the Kingston Trio, and Woody Guthrie three-chord vanilla songs, some of which told a good story but didn't have a lot of edge musically."

It's hard not to notice that white artists, contemporaries of Sainte-Marie, such as Bob Dylan and Joni Mitchell, had praise heaped upon them for their "unique" approaches to music and alternate tunings. These artists continue to get credit while Sainte-Marie has been repeatedly erased, and in part, that's because they also had high-priced managers in their corners to ensure their success. "Bob Dylan was uniquely developing a style based on Woody Guthrie and Cisco Houston and some of those other sound-like-an-old-man ways," Sainte-Marie says. "I'm a big fan; I can't say a bad word against [Dylan]. I think he's a brilliant writer, and his career, his life, his fame and everything—I know some people who know him very well, and whatever you say about all of that, just getting super, super,

super famous, whatever that does to a person, I can't comment on that. But I really think that he was the best of all of us. And I'm not sure that Joni [Mitchell] ever paid much attention to any of the blues people who had played in unique tunings before she did or if she stumbled upon them the same way I and others have done. But I'm self-taught, tuned my guitars all weird from the start, and didn't know any better."

Sainte-Marie was deep inside the folk scene in 1965 when her song, "Until It's Time for You to Go," became a hit for Bobby Darin and so many other artists and propelled her into the spotlight. As her visibility increased, so too did the reach of her message, her advocacy for Indigenous rights. But it seemed like it was always two steps forward, one step back. She believed she was being pushed to the outer edges because she didn't have a shark-like manager behind her, and she observed that there was a sort of fraternity at work in the music industry. From Sainte-Marie's vantage point, there was an upper echelon created and occupied by people like Bob Dylan's manager, Albert Grossman, and Clive Davis, who signed Janis Joplin, that would never be available to her. In part she was right, though there were other forces at work that attempted to suppress Sainte-Marie's voice. She didn't know how to belong to the world of businessmen or politicians, so she went by instinct and did the best she could. She was too self-taught, too centered within herself, and too naïve about show business to acquiesce in order to get ahead. And Sainte-Marie had other goals. She wanted to help change the world.

"When I wrote 'Universal Soldier,' I was real serious about it," she says. "The heartbreak behind some of those perspectives is real. It comes from something that I am experiencing. With songs of meaning that have a certain kind of political clout, I'm hoping to reach people."

By the time the hippie movement was cresting, her peers in the folk movement seemed to move on from the concerns that drove their protests, but Sainte-Marie couldn't. Her investment was a long-term one. Just because she personally had "made it" in the early 1960s, that didn't mean her work was done.

"I was still a Native American person with identity questions, and I saw bellies full of nothing but poverty on a lot of reservations and urban Indian slums, and it was all being ignored, even snickered at, by showbiz folks who simply didn't know or care enough to help," Sainte-Marie says. "My life is what was informing my songs. A lot of artists, I think they achieve some status in the music business and then they start to build their bank account and their houses and their cars because their dreams have come true. But my dreams were different—and were not coming true at all."

When many of the New York–based folk artists packed up and headed west for California, Sainte-Marie opted to go further: Hawai'i. "When I started to make it, I didn't move to Laurel Canyon and hang out and do coke with the lawyers. That's what everybody else did, I guess—at least, I'm hearing about it in their memoirs. I didn't do that. I totally blew it." She laughs because she's joking, but she knew other people, including some of her more show biz–minded peers, were probably thinking that at the time. "I didn't hang out. I didn't kiss the ring. I didn't sleep with the right people. I didn't have a social life or family friendships or affairs. I didn't do any of that. What did I do? I moved to Hawai'i. I went from bad to worse. I was a semi-recluse."

At the time, she felt burnt-out and over-exposed. "I was too visible and too famous, and it wasn't fun anymore; that's when I moved to Hawai'i," Sainte-Marie says. "I've never been one to go out after the show anyway, as in 'Now the real show starts,' you know, 'Let's get it on and party and have our picture taken.' I'm an entertainer, and I love that. It's fun—lights, camera, action, clothes, you know, makeup, autographs, it's all fun—but there's something more than that behind it."

It began as a Hawai'ian vacation. Sainte-Marie didn't intend to fall in love, but she did—both with the place and with a young surfer five years her junior named Dewain Kamaikalani Bugbee. The pair married in the fall of 1967, and according to a 1970 *New York Times* interview with Sainte-Marie, they split their time between her two farms in Hawai'i and in Maine.[15] Bugbee tried to acclimate to life on the road but didn't like it, and although his name appears in some archival interviews and photos, the pair guarded their privacy. They divorced in 1971, but Sainte-Marie had made Hawai'i her permanent home.

She remembers when she first decided to move to Hawai'i in 1967 and all of the people who let her know that it would be career suicide. "I didn't care—you kidding me? To my credit and to my detriment—I mean, some people just say, 'Oh, she was just a snob,'" Sainte-Marie laughs. "And there might be something to that."

Buffy Sainte-Marie
on uncertainty

Discrepancies are something that I've lived with since I was very little. I had an undeniable, irrefutable view of what the world said was so, and it was fine. I was fine with it. But I learned early on that what was "absolutely" true was not necessarily true for me. And I think it's always drawn me to loners and to people who are creative. Think of the creative process of songwriting. On Tuesday the song doesn't exist. You cannot prove that it exists. But on Wednesday, all of a sudden, something exists that didn't exist yesterday. A lot of things that have happened to me are not true on Tuesday but by Wednesday, the world is different. And this is a huge concept for me. It reinforces my sense of health and well-being and sanity because of the way my life has been with airplane tickets and my non-9-to-5, five-days-a-week, weekends off—I don't live that kind of life. I have a different life and I just became comfortable eventually with, you know what, it's okay not to know because the future hasn't happened yet.

CHAPTER 6

MY COUNTRY 'TIS OF THY PEOPLE YOU'RE DYING

WHEN *BILLBOARD* MAGAZINE named Sainte-Marie the best new artist of 1964, it was more than just a thrilling honor for an emerging musician.[16] It was a disruption in the ecosystem of the mainstream music industry. *It's My Way!* wasn't a chart-topper nor was it a "conventional" folk record, but it was a powerful work made by a Cree woman who thoroughly and proudly centered Indigenous identity at its core, whose voice rattled the moon and the status quo, and who refused to capitulate to popular stereotypes and clichés of Indigeneity. With each record that followed, Sainte-Marie expanded her message, increasing awareness, and making the invisible visible.

There was little Indigenous representation in pop culture and the media in the mid-twentieth century aside from the stock characterization of "the noble savage," and although a few Indigenous actors had careers—like Mohawk Canadian Jay Silverheels, who played Tonto in the *Lone Ranger* series on TV and in films until about 1960—non-Indigenous actors were usually cast to play Indigenous roles. (In the 1955 film *The Far Horizons*, for example, Donna Reed was cast as Sacagawea, the Lemhi Shoshone woman known for assisting the Lewis and Clark Expedition. In 2011, *Time* named *The Far Horizons* one of the top ten most historically misleading films.[17])

But Sainte-Marie modeled a different Indigenous reality than that perpetuated by the entertainment industry. "When I say I'm a journalist, I don't mean that I had stories coming out my pen: I mean, I had stories going in my eyes and ears for years that built to a body of interest," Sainte-Marie says. "With 'Now That the Buffalo's Gone,' I wanted people to know how important an issue it was, and I wanted them to understand it. The Seneca Reservation was flooded for a bunch of businessmen, and the oldest treaty in the congressional archives was broken. I wasn't thinking about whether I was sharp or flat—it was what the song was about, and the emotion of it is just plain built-in because that's just how I felt about the issue."

The song had put Indigenous rights in the spotlight, and her position behind the mic had amplified her image as a potential leader in the growing peace movement. Other activists and leaders noticed her influence and respected the ways in which she approached the work: hands-on, effective, and all about the movements and the people, not her ego. Sargent Shriver, the husband of Eunice Kennedy, brother-in-law of President John F. Kennedy, and first director of the Peace Corps, founded an outreach program for poor and rural students called Outward Bound in 1965. Sainte-Marie was invited to Washington, D.C., to participate in the federally funded program. Through Outward Bound, she became more deeply enmeshed with the National Indian Youth Council. Sainte-Marie and other young Indigenous activists stood up to established energy corporations like the Rockefellers' Standard Oil (which has profited enormously since the 1800s from convincing Indigenous people to sign away their lands) and demanded accountability from the Bureau of Indian Affairs, which seemed to essentially legislate exploitation of the very people they were supposed to be looking after.

"The Bureau of Indian Affairs used to be the War Department; it was not set up as, 'Oh, goody, now there's an agency to help the Indians!'" Sainte-Marie says. "That's what people thought on the East Coast where I was raised. 'The Bureau of Indian Affairs looks after them. Isn't that nice? And they don't pay taxes.' [Laughs] I don't know where they got that Disney perspective, but that's not the way it was. The Bureau of Indian Affairs was set up to solve the government's problem, not our problem."

She's quite critical of "the racketeers," as she calls the big business operatives, crooked politicians, and lawyers who exploit Indigenous communities—parts of the colonial systems that collude in predatory practices. But Sainte-Marie still operates from a place of empathy rather than rage or scorn. "When I wrote 'Now That the Buffalo's Gone,' I wasn't singing about Indians as victims so much as about the unknowledgeable colonials, the unwitting predators who support this corrupt system of contractors and politicians and 'businessmen' who pride themselves on perfecting the art of the deal."

The life-broadening experience she got through Outward Bound and her meetings with like-minded young Indigenous activists couldn't have come at a better time. "I was perfectly ripe for learning and for sharing," Sainte-Marie says. "Working with people who came from a different facet of the same jewel—we were of the same stuff, but we were reflecting things from different angles. These were not like grassroots elders who hardly spoke English and who *National Geographic* would take a picture of; it wasn't like that. No, these were vibrant college students who had had it up to *here* with colonialism. None of us called it 'colonialism' back then, and we didn't know what to do about it on the big scale, but we were willing to confront it as we ran across it in our lives."

Sainte-Marie confronted colonialism in her activism and with her music. On her 1965 album, *Many a Mile*, she covered several British traditional folk songs, but her originals were deeply rooted in her activism and core beliefs, including "Welcome, Welcome Emigrante" and "The Piney Wood Hills." She didn't always get the credit she deserved as a songwriter, but Sainte-Marie was accumulating professional power. She continued to use the spotlight to talk about Indigenous issues and alternative conflict resolution, but she also began to push her sound away from coffee-house acoustic. Her rapidly expanding sonic universe became more apparent on her third album, 1966's *Little Wheel Spin and Spin*, which featured electric guitar by Bruce Langhorne and set the stage for further sampling across genres.

"You were supposed to stick to Pete Seeger and that kind of genre," Sainte-Marie remembers, referencing the total acoustic devotion of the early folk scene and the fans who went apoplectic when Bob Dylan "went electric" at the Newport Folk Festival in 1965. "I thought it was stupid for everybody to go up in arms. I thought he was great! It just didn't make sense to me. But that's how audiences and the business are sometimes."

Little Wheel featured her near-seven-minute epic, "My Country 'Tis of Thy People You're Dying," a devastating account of Indigenous reality in America that took down the stereotypes and clichés perpetrated by Hollywood, the government and racketeers, and the media. It also pointedly called out Canada's residential school system, which, starting in 1884, made it mandatory for Indigenous children to attend and live at government-funded, church-run schools where the goal was assimilation and cultural eradication. The last residential school in Canada was closed in 1996. It's estimated that more than 150,000 Indigenous children spanning multiple generations were ripped from their homes and communities and put into residential schools rife with systemic physical and sexual abuse, mental, emotional, and verbal abuse, hard labor, starvation, and medical experiments on the children. At least 6,000 Indigenous children are estimated to have died while in the care of the residential school system.[18] Sainte-Marie's song came approximately thirty years before the final school closed and decades before there was any public recognition of the real-life horrors inflicted on thousands of Indigenous children and their families over multiple generations.

"Now that the longhouses 'breed superstition'/You force us to send our toddlers away/To your schools where they're taught to despise their traditions/Forbid them their languages," Sainte-Marie sings. Read as a poem, "My Country 'Tis of Thy People You're Dying" is a scathing indictment of colonization and a lament at its cost.

> For the blessings of civilization you brought us;
> The lessons you've taught us;
> The ruin you've wrought us;
> Oh see what our trust in America got us.
> My country 'tis of thy people you're dying.

In Sainte-Marie's original version, her vibrato resonates most deeply when exploring the in-between moments of rage and sadness, the space occupied by frustration, heartbreak, and hope.

> "Oh what can I do?" say a powerless few.
> With a lump in your throat and a tear in your eye:
> Can't you see how their poverty's profiting you?
> My country 'tis of thy people you're dying.

As in many of Sainte-Marie's songs, she asks the listener to bear witness. Her testimony becomes a light, an awakening, and the listener might at first dwell in the shame of complicity. But Sainte-Marie knows the futility of that guilt. Gentle but firm, her words are an education, not a lecture. "You don't give it to people in an enema," Sainte-Marie says. "If you really want to help make the world better, think like Jesus, think like Mohammed— that [level of] generosity. You don't line white people up against the wall and humiliate them. That does nothing. It's counterproductive." One can't talk just about white people's complicity in colonization, Sainte-Marie says adamantly, without addressing their own victimization by the same forces. "White people have been exploited for far longer than Indians by colonialism, by the Inquisition, by the same people who came up with the Doctrine of Discovery," Sainte-Marie says. "And I don't ever let Native educators forget that: Before they ever came after us, look what they were doing to their own people. Look what they were doing to their own relatives. Do you understand what the Inquisition really was and how long it lasted? You probably think it lasted for three or four years? No, for eight hundred years they ran that thing, including on white people."

Colonization was tantamount to genocide for Indigenous people throughout the world, "not because of race but because of greed," Sainte-Marie says. European settlers wanted more— they felt they deserved it and that the land and people were theirs to exploit because they could. She points to the Doctrine of Discovery and its legacy of entitlement and violence that is still in practice today. Issued by Pope Alexander VI in 1493, the papal bull *Inter Caetera*, which was later known as the Doctrine of Discovery, became the central framework for the Spanish conquest of the New World, for all European claims in the Americas, and later for western expansion in the United

States.[19] It was a framework for explorers that states that all land uninhabited by Christians may be conquered and inhabited by Christians, and it exhorted explorers to overthrow the "barbarous nations." The residual effects of this doctrine, Sainte-Marie says, are at the heart of systemic colonial inequality and inequity.

Sainte-Marie says that "'My Country 'Tis of Thy People You're Dying' is, in a song, 'Indian 101.' I wanted to let audiences know how Indigenous people got to be in the state that they're in today. I knew it wasn't fair fights, majority odds, and superior weaponry. That's bad enough, and that is what most people think. 'Oh, you poor guys, you were outnumbered, and we had guns. I mean, it really wasn't fair for you—poor you.'"

But it was more than that. Sainte-Marie felt compelled to address the legacy of European colonization all over the world—centuries of bullying and sexual violence. "I wasn't hearing about residential schools on television," Sainte-Marie says. "Television didn't talk about it, ever. They didn't teach about it in schools, not even in college. I found out about it through people who were actually there." She quickly realized why there was a collective silence in the Indigenous community. "No one talked about it because they'd all gone to residential school, and if you'd gone to residential school, you'd probably been molested or raped. Everybody had. It was common and it was horrifying. In the 1960s, there was no audible sense of outrage, just shame and helplessness."

According to Sainte-Marie, another taboo subject was how Europeans treated children, particularly the vulnerable children of the poor. "There was no sense of inequity within Indian country or the general public. It was just—this is what life is like. Which is also weird because the horror about residential schools was no secret. It was covered in newspapers as early as

1907, when Dr. Peter Bryce busted the scandalous mistreatment of First Nations kids." The Bryce Report was an investigation by Dr. P. H. Bryce into the high mortality rate in Canadian residential schools. After his first report in 1907, the *Victoria Daily Colonist* ran a story with the headline "Indian Schools Deal Out Death" and quoted Dr. Bryce's report, which declared, "We have created a situation so dangerous to health that I am often surprised that results were not more serious than they have been."[20]

As Sainte-Marie's fame continued to grow and her profile increased, she often heard the same question from members of the press: "Why are you so angry?" Racist stereotypes of the "savage Indian" were (and continue to be) plentiful. In the mid-1960s, a female performer who presented as anything beyond the narrow categories of sweet virgin or sex kitten meant trouble. If she wasn't deemed aggressive or hysterical, she was stereotyped as angry. A 1970 *New York Times* interview literally begins: "Buffy Sainte-Marie, the singer, is an angry woman."[21] In this case, the journalist leads with quotes from Sainte-Marie regarding the fashion industry's appropriation and misrepresentation of Indigenous designs.

"It is most insensitive in the light of Indian poverty to be publicizing those clothes and giving awards to people who design them." She grabbed a copy of a recent issue of Look *magazine, which contained both a cover and several inside color pages of "Indian" fashions. "No Indian would wear those things," she said. "And look—all of the models are white. Usually they have a few Black girls to portray Indians. They never use real Indians. You know, I'm really dismayed by all of the magazines and the fashion industry. They can't be deaf, blind, and dumb."*

"I wasn't 'being an angry woman,'" Sainte-Marie says in retrospect. "I was pointing out an inequity!" But many journalists emphasized outrage over inequity, and in failing to interrogate the systems perpetuating those injustices, the media helped to erase her victories from the public record. "I don't seem like somebody who's going to be throwing rocks and spitting venom and pissing on people's Shakespeare," Sainte-Marie says. "I feel as though it's a misperception, and in the long run, I guess I must not be doing my job properly." Sainte-Marie has only ever wanted to be effective, empowering, and positive. Sure, she's been angry, but she made a conscientious effort to approach her songwriting and her activism from a very different place, and so it can be disillusioning and exhausting to be repeatedly misinterpreted as simply angry. "In those days, there weren't very many people writing [songs] about American Indian issues at all," she says. "Peter Lafarge ['The Ballad of Ira Hayes'] wrote a couple, but they were mostly written in anger. There was no sense of solution or compassion for the listener. I want the listener to get on board. I don't want the listener to just get pissed and leave. I mean, I have had that happen, but it was not my intention."

In the early days of Sainte-Marie's fame, some audience members got riled up when she sang "Now That the Buffalo's Gone" or "My Country 'Tis of Thy People You're Dying." "People asked for their money back," she says. "I really offended some people just by being accurate! They were not ready to see that what I was saying was true. Which is another reason why I make it so crystal clear for short attention spans. If you read 'Now That the Buffalo's Gone' or 'Universal Soldier,' or 'My Country 'Tis of Thy People You're Dying,' it's basically the facts. And every one of those facts can be fact-checked. I was writing the song as if it had footnotes. I thoroughly researched the song so it wasn't coming from a place of hate, but many, many people who had never heard those facts or who'd never paid attention to them or who'd never seen them sewn up in a two-minute-forty-second bundle all at the same time were really—I don't know if offended is the right word, but they questioned it. Because they'd never been exposed to it before, they thought I must be just sour-grapesing."

The "angry Indian" stereotype is part of colonization; when marginalized or oppressed minorities speak up, those who hold power fear the disruption to the status quo that has benefitted them in visible and invisible ways. "Angry" is a way for power holders to dismiss and delegitimize activism and protest. But Sainte-Marie understands why people default to "angry" as a descriptor, even if she feels they're wrong.

"I do think that people from 'le showbiz,' who are usually from the city and very often from second-generation immigrant families from Europe, are themselves angry," Sainte-Marie says. "These journalists assume that I am too; they're projecting their own anger. I think they're saying, 'Holy shit, we got fucked over, but Indians got fucked over even worse, and if I were an Indian, I would really be pissed.' Like, pick up a gun or act in some 'savage' way. But in the history of Native American people, you haven't seen this. And in my associations with Native American historians, scholars, professors, activists, schools, school kids, and community people over the last fifty years, I have not seen a lot of angry people. Determined, dedicated, depressed, disgruntled, disappointed, defeated, demoralized, and in despair—yes. But for Native American people, it was almost like being an abused child or wife: Anger would just make the bully more dangerous, so you were careful not to become a target. To me, this is not cowardice—it's common-sense survival. I'm not saying there haven't been or aren't any angry Indigenous people;

I just tend to spend my time with elders, women, kids, artists and musicians, highly educated Native lawyers, and seasoned activists who know how to survive the work in spite of emotion, and how to redirect adrenaline to a more effective use than just spewing anger. I don't hang out with tough guys. I don't pretend to be a warrior. I don't throw snowballs and insults at people with guns. I tend to be patient. Maybe I lack testosterone, but I seldom feel angry. Some people will argue that I'm not angry enough... and they might have a point."

As Sainte-Marie's fame grew and her profile expanded internationally, she continued to take musical risks. On her 1967 album, *Fire & Fleet & Candlelight*, she recorded a few songs orchestrated by Peter Schickele (a.k.a. P. D. Q. Bach), who had worked with Judy Collins and Joan Baez. But she continued to raise the profile of Indigenous issues every time she got behind a microphone, and eventually Hollywood beckoned. In 1968, she was approached for a guest-starring role on the popular NBC western television series *The Virginian*, which aired from 1962 to 1971. Director Leo Penn, who had been blacklisted for his support of the Hollywood Ten[22]—they refused to name names when called before the House Un-American Activities Committee—wanted Sainte-Marie for the role of an Indigenous woman who goes to school back east and then must decide if she wishes to return to her home. The singer-songwriter had two demands before she'd sign on: Actual Indigenous people had to play all the Indigenous roles, and the writers had to give her character more complexity, elevating her beyond that of the one-note, Hollywood cliché.

"I said, 'No Indians, no Buffy.' The reason I did that was not solely to 'stick up for the Indians.' It was also because any production is going to be better if the people involved are familiar with the cultural experiences in which it's set," Sainte-Marie says. "It was just common sense, you know. Sometimes in my life and in my career, I've had people look at something [I've done] and celebrate it, but for the wrong reasons. Well, not for my intended reason. The smaller point with *The Virginian* was that it was going to be an Indian show with an all-Indian cast. Wow, that's a first! Yay, aren't we terrific? But the bigger picture was that in any production, familiarity with the cultural group it depicts—why would you do it any other way?"

Sainte-Marie says her demands weren't about railing against Hollywood's racism problem; instead, she offered Penn and the producers and casting directors some alternatives to their default resources. And it worked. The show hired Indigenous actors from Jay Silverheels and Lois Red Elk's Indian Actors Workshop to play all the Indigenous roles, thanks to Sainte-Marie's insistence. "They had never thought of expanding their own network until I helped to make that possible," Sainte-Marie explains. "My gripe was never against Hollywood for being racist, 'cause griping wouldn't change that. I think it's better to light a candle than to curse the darkness. I think it's better to turn these people on to where they can find Native American actors than it is to stand there, shaking my fist saying, 'You bastards! You don't let the Indians in!' But that's what a lot of people call protest. If instead you can do something that actually solves the problem, then wow, that's actually being effective! That's empowerment."

The media brought the story to the public's attention. The *Los Angeles Times*' Hal Humphrey covered the historical moment for the paper in 1968, and called it an "unheard-of request" because in Hollywood real Indigenous people were never hired to play Indigenous people in westerns. Humphrey explained that the Screen Actors Guild had a "large assortment of Mexicans, Italians and mixtures who pass." He then quoted

Sainte-Marie: "They always used the excuse that real Indians can't be found, but I have made it so they cannot say that anymore. Do you know there are 20,000 Indians in the Los Angeles area, representing 110 different tribes?"[23]

Sainte-Marie also didn't have anything to lose by making her demands because she didn't actually care if she took the part. "It was much more important to me to pull off that kind of coup than to get my stupid face on a TV show," she says. "As soon as I could provide accredited people, everybody was happy. It was definitely a win-win situation. It shouldn't be looked at as though, 'She won a fight.' It wasn't like that. No, I provided an alternative, which is different from winning a fight."

CHAPTER 7

BETTER TO FIND OUT FOR YOURSELF

CREATING ALTERNATIVES TO established narratives was already something of a Buffy Sainte-Marie trademark when she Indigenized *The Virginian*, but 1968 also marked another major new direction in her life: her visit to country music. On the surface, at least through one lens, the crossover presented an Indigenous woman infiltrating the perceived whiteness of the genre. But the idea of country music as the domain of white artists was just another example of colonization. Country, folk, traditional, roots, and bluegrass all have deep roots in African-American, Indigenous, poor white, and other racialized communities. Sainte-Marie had been experimenting with country music in subtle ways throughout her recording career, including in her 1965 song, "The Piney Wood Hills," which sounded perfectly ready for the Grand Ol' Opry—and was. In fact, country artist Bobby Bare covered the song in 1967, and country great Chet Atkins also covered it as well as Sainte-Marie's "Until It's Time for You to Go." Sainte-Marie had written a number of bluegrass and country songs that she'd yet to record, so the timing seemed right to explore the genre.

Atkins and Sainte-Marie became friendly—both were natural musicians who didn't put any stock in reading music—and when he called Vanguard Records and suggested that she travel to Nashville to make a record with him, she didn't see any reason to say no. "My life is pretty much my own," she explains. "And whether you're thinking about emerging technologies or taking a chance on *The Virginian* or singing whatever I wanted to on my albums or having the guts to go to Nashville—see, I thought that I had already peaked, so why wouldn't I?"

She traveled to Nashville to join the highly-respected guitarist and producer, and together they got to work on her 1968 album, *I'm Gonna Be a Country Girl Again*. Sainte-Marie's new musical direction and her work with Atkins sparked the interest of *Billboard* magazine, which described the arrangement as Sainte-Marie working under the "guidance" of Atkins, and specified that "Atkins did not produce the session. He offered advice and suggestions as 'a personal favor to a great artist.'"[24]

In fact, Atkins did co-produce the record, but would have to remain uncredited because his own recording contract precluded him from doing work with another label. Sainte-Marie liked Atkins's easy-going, friendly personality, and she says she felt at home in Nashville. She rejects "that terribly offensive, New York assumption of the 1960s, that everybody in the South was a redneck. It's just not true," she says emphatically. "And there are plenty of rednecks other places too. With Chet Atkins, you could not have a more wonderful introduction to Nashville. What a gentleman, and he loved songwriters. He loved guitar players. He loved musicians."

The critical reception to *I'm Gonna Be a Country Girl Again* was lukewarm for the most part, but Sainte-Marie was creatively restless and always looking forward. She wanted to physically explore the planet—ride dog sleds in the Yukon, spend time with Aboriginal people in Australia, and she still thought she was going to India—but she had a contract with Vanguard to satisfy, so she channeled elements of that risk-taking trait into her sound.

For her sixth album, she opted to continue to experiment, this time focusing on new technology, and the result was the groundbreaking, if utterly unappreciated (at the time) *Illuminations*. The 1969 electronic music record was about thirty years ahead of its time and severed her connection with the folk world. It was a departure from the more acoustic sounds of her first three albums. Her guitars, vocals, and interactions with a Buchla synthesizer were experimental in ways that wouldn't become de rigueur in the music scene for many years. In 1998, *The Wire* magazine ranked *Illuminations* amongst its "100 Records That Set the World On Fire [When No One Was Listening]," writing, "If Dylan going electric in 1965 turned folk purists into baying hyenas, Buffy Sainte-Marie going electronic would have turned them into kill-hungry wolves, if they weren't already a spent force."[25]

Illuminations opens with the almost five-minute-long lyrical song-poem, "God Is Alive, Magic Is Afoot," written by Leonard Cohen and set to music composed by Sainte-Marie. Her voice circles the listener and closes in, picking up speed and urgency. It feels mystical, and it's also largely acoustic, like a welcome mat that lets the listener know that the terrain will be mostly familiar and safe but maybe not quite the same as it was before. This track lays the foundation for what's to come: a record on which almost every sound was taken from either Sainte-Marie's voice or her acoustic guitar and then synthesized. Arguably, it's Sainte-Marie at her most brilliantly, willfully experimental and impossibly cool.

The second track sounds almost mournful, a loping, religious meditation called "Mary," and then makes a jarring shift as she launches into "Better to Find Out for Yourself," a rollicking middle finger to terrible boyfriends and bad men. Sainte-Marie delivers every burn with a vocal flourish that bounces against the band's psychedelic rock groove. The song fades out into

Star Wars–like laser gun *pew-pew* sounds (although *Star Wars* wouldn't exist for eight more years). It's a lost gem. These three tracks are just the entry point, and they can't quite prepare the listener for the penultimate track, the bewitching and bracing "He's a Keeper of the Fire," which features Sainte-Marie's most daring vocal performance on a record filled with them. She sings in so many different registers, her voice stretching from wilderness to solar system and back again, moving back and forwards in time, and occupying spaces and sounds that are almost otherworldly. The record closes with the hauntingly affecting "Poppies," which finds Sainte-Marie venturing into gothic-opera territory. It's unlike anything else that existed commercially in 1969.

"I was doing things in the sixties and seventies that Annie Lennox did in the eighties, and I was thrilled when she did that, overdubbing with several different voices instead of trying to sound like the same character all the time," Sainte-Marie says. "I used to love it, and it became kind of a signature for me, especially when singing harmonies and [at] powwows. Nobody else much caught onto it. Many years later, I spoke to Annie about that, just the idea of singing in four different voices. [On 'Mongrel Pup' from 1975's *Changing Woman* album], I was singing in two different voices, and in a third I whispered, and in the fourth I shouted, and it just gave an emotional quartet to the song. Love it or hate it."

By the time she began to work on *Illuminations*, Sainte-Marie knew that the sound she'd cultivated on her previous albums wouldn't carry the underlying energy of the songs she intended for this record. She wanted a more radical, ambitious, and artistic record, almost a concept album. She saw each song on *Illuminations* as its own movie for which she needed to provide a compelling score. Folk songs and rock wouldn't cut it. "I heard them differently in my head, and my job was to get it into your head the way I was hearing it, and electronic music seemed to make a lot of sense," Sainte-Marie says. Using the relatively new Buchla 100 series synthesizer, *Illuminations* became the first quadrophonic electronic vocal album, a technological innovation that would eventually lead to 4.0 surround sound.

Matrix synthesizers were a new musical technology in the 1960s. Sainte-Marie had played with one on *Fire & Fleet & Candlelight*, but she decided to embrace synthesizers almost entirely for *Illuminations*, which made the recording process unlike anything she'd ever done before. "Picture yourself sitting down at a desk. There's something like a pegboard full of holes in front of you. You plug a sound cord from one of those holes into another one—that's what we're talking about. You have pins of a certain size that fit into an input [hole] of a certain size, and it's almost like the idea of an old-fashioned telephone switchboard. It wasn't as though there was an electric keyboard, it was too early, and I don't think there was a brand name for it at the time. We just called it a matrix, a bunch of possibilities you could connect in various ways to modify sound waves."

Today, *Illuminations* is referenced as a precursor to gothic rock, and it also sparked Sainte-Marie's friend, punk rock fashion icon Jimmy Webb, to later refer to her as one of the pre-punk punks. Genesis's Steve Hackett frequently cites *Illuminations* as a source of inspiration for the band's sound. He listed *Illuminations* first on his list of ten favorite albums in an interview with *Rock'n'Roll Journalist* in 2013, saying, "The album has an interesting blend of electronic and folk music. Buffy has a beautiful voice. She puts so much heart into her songs."[26]

But at the time, the album was largely ignored. There was some blowback when people found out she was using computers. "Believe me, folk singers at the time had no interest in that," she said in E. K. Caldwell's 1999 book, *Dreaming the Dawn: Conversations with Native Artists and Activists*.[27] Friends and fans alike were not excited about her innovations. "I've been experimenting since the very beginning, since *It's My Way!*, but nobody cared," Sainte-Marie says. She's matter-of-fact, not self-pitying, and perhaps this is because she'd make music no matter what, whether she was doing it professionally or not. "I've had a lot of times when I've been doing something so cool, and I just knew that nobody was ever going to know about it."

Rumors persist that Sainte-Marie disowned *Illuminations* because it did so poorly, in terms of sales and on the charts, but actually she loved it. It represented her first major foray into electronic music before the term really existed, and as someone who embraces technology and has, in many ways, always lived in the future, it's a record that holds a special place in her heart. "Even in 1978, I was writing and using a Synclavier to score the movie *Spirit of the Wind*, but the music business itself still was not interested in electronic music," Sainte-Marie says. "I was real early with electronics, and I just got used to this typical music-biz resistance—it was like spitting in the wind. Most of these boys—whether musicians or record company guys—did not want to seem old-fashioned or out of the loop. They didn't want somebody else—a girl like me—to be ahead of them. It's another form of what I call sideman misogyny."

Although *Illuminations* suffered commercially for its avant-garde futurism, Sainte-Marie wanted to continue her creative evolution, and some of her groundbreaking musician peers were also excited about her changing sound. Phil Spector's right-hand man and Neil Young's producer, Jack Nitzsche, called up Vanguard and begged to produce her next record. He said he'd fallen in love with her picture in *Cashbox*, a music industry magazine. But first, he asked her to help record music for the 1970 rock 'n' roll crime film *Performance*, which was also Mick Jagger's acting debut. Sainte-Marie contributed "Dyed, Dead, Red" with Ry Cooder and "The Hashashin," which is largely instrumental and features her overdubbed mouth bows. These days, she laughingly suggests "smoking one up" before watching the movie, which she says is good. But the music is *really* good.

"It's a really hot album—rocking, but quite different from other Mick Jagger albums. It's a Jack Nitzsche movie score and has me and Randy Newman and Ry Cooder. Mick is on at least one song, of course, but the score itself is gorgeous. Jack knew who to hire and what to do; he did not mess around with also-ran musicians. The people that he worked with were just really tops; all the sidemen and recording people and engineers. Jack was a weird person, [and he] knew it, couldn't help it. Kinda nuts." She laughs. "A lot of people just hated him, but his taste in music was really interesting and impeccable." The soundtrack was also the first time that Randy Newman conducted an orchestra for a record.

Sainte-Marie continued to be involved in film composition on her own, which she says was the only place to further explore electronic music. She contributed songs to 1970's *Strawberry Statement*, a cult film about the counterculture and student protests in the 1960s, but she scored her first big movie hit writing the title song for the 1971 film, *Soldier Blue*.

"*Soldier Blue* was really the first big-time movie that dealt with the North American genocide [of Indigenous people]. I could have written a tough song like 'Bury My Heart at Wounded Knee,' you know, castigating the generations of politicians including some contemporary warmongers. Instead, what I wanted was to give the audience something different. I wanted them to get a picture of the beautiful way that Indigenous people think of Mother Earth, nature, the universe, the cosmos, and the entire natural world—the antithesis of the violence portrayed in the movie."

Inspired by the 1864 Sand Creek massacre of the Cheyenne in the then-Colorado Territory, the film was adapted from Theodore V. Olsen's novel *Arrow in the Sun* (retitled *Soldier Blue* after the movie came out). The film made immediate waves for its shocking and frank depiction of brutality and violence. The massacre scene involved horrific and graphic depictions of Cheyenne women being raped, tortured, and killed, children being slaughtered, and men being tortured and killed—all at the hands of American soldiers.

While it was lauded as a groundbreaking film by some critics and was a success in Europe and Asia, *Soldier Blue* was in and out of American theaters in a flash. In part, this was because of the film's graphic violence and nudity, the likes of which had rarely been shown before on the big screen. But it was also viewed as an allegory for the Vietnam War, particularly the horrific My Lai massacre of 1968, when U.S. soldiers slaughtered more than five hundred unarmed South Vietnamese civilians.[28]

Sainte-Marie says that, at the time she was writing the song, she wasn't even aware of the massacre in Vietnam. Riding buses and airplanes, touring all over North America, Australia, and Europe, it was easy to miss the headlines until after the fact. When the parallels were pointed out after the movie's release, the film disappeared from American theaters, even though it was described by *New York Times* writer Dotson Rader as "among the most significant, the most brutal and liberating, the most honest American films ever made."[29]

"The movie was about violence," Sainte-Marie says. "And it's really an exposé on the difference between love and rape, or in the case of loving one's country, the difference between matriotism [love of the Motherland, Mother Nature] and nationalism." The distinction between love and rape is as crucial now as it was when Sainte-Marie wrote the song. In writing about *Soldier Blue*, many critics conflated sex with rape, describing the film's depiction of "violence and sex," but they were actually talking about violence and rape. The film's poster for the European release sexualized the image of a violated Cheyenne woman, depicting her from behind, naked and on her knees, arms bound at the wrist, a feather in her hair, and two long braids down her back.

Although it vanished in the U.S., the film was a success in Europe, and Sainte-Marie's song became a top-ten hit in several countries. It's rousing and anthemic, but she also deliberately wrote it in opposition to the film's violence. There's one line of protest in the song—"Soldier Blue, can't you see there's a better way to love her"—but the rest is all about the loving relationship Indigenous people have with Turtle Island. "I wanted to give [audiences] the feeling of the Indigenous people the day before that massacre, when we were in love with nature and with the Americas, with the birds and the crickets," Sainte-Marie says.

"Soldier Blue" is included on Sainte-Marie's 1971 album, *She Used to Wanna Be a Ballerina*, but it is the one track that wasn't produced by Nitzsche—she recorded it with Roy Budd in London in 1970. The recording process during *Ballerina* was difficult thanks to Nitzsche. He was a genius but he was also volatile, which hadn't been as obvious when he worked with Sainte-Marie on *Performance* but became a huge problem when they worked together closely on the album as artist and producer.

"I liked Jack just fine," she says, recalling the first meeting arranged by Vanguard. "He was charming and shy. He obviously liked my music. I mean, you can tell from another musician whether they're just doing it for a job or whether they really are a fan of what you do. And I could tell that he really did have a deep appreciation for the various kinds of music that I had been making up to that point, so I kind of trusted him in that way. I didn't think that he was just some business contact. I thought he was a like-minded, talented musician and that there was a mutual respect. I hadn't known much about his music. He had been mostly working and making huge hits with Phil Spector. I would hear Phil's hits, but I wasn't on the West Coast and I wasn't in that part of the music business, so I didn't know any-body. Jack could really be warm, sincere, funny, charming, and genuinely humble—at least it seemed so."

Sainte-Marie remembers, however, that even early on in their working relationship, Nitzsche was a person of extremes. He either loved an artist or he had no time for them at all. He genuinely liked Willy DeVille, Keith Richards, Neil Young, Ry Cooder, and Sainte-Marie. "Jack seemed to like uniqueness. That seemed to be the common denominator. He really, really liked Keith Richards, but he didn't like Mick. He seemed to go for the artistic as opposed to the show business. He distrusted show business, and he hated actors and actresses. He genuinely liked my music for all the right reasons, I thought. I hadn't col-laborated with a lot of people up till then."

What Sainte-Marie did find refreshing was the fact that Nitzsche seemed to see her. Vanguard Records, on the other hand, wanted a bigger commercial success than *Illuminations* had been, and consequently five of the album's eleven tracks were covers of songs by contemporaries such as Leonard Cohen, Carole King, and Neil Young. Nitzsche had actually wanted to take the album in the direction of *Illuminations*, and he could see the rock 'n' roll side to Sainte-Marie. "He could see past what Vanguard was trying to sell—Indian folk singer—he could see beyond that. Jack had an acquaintance quite early in his own life who was a Native American guy, and he had a feel for Indigenous people, and it was always genuine."

But their collaboration was awful. "I wasn't willing to admit to myself how awful it was going," she says. "I was trying so hard to make it work. There have been times in my life where it's been like that, where something was obviously not working, but I would think, 'Oh, it's not working yet because we haven't found the key or the formula. We're not there yet.'"

Nitzsche brought in guitarist Ry Cooder, whom Sainte-Marie adored—"he was a hero to me"—and bassist Russ Titelman. "I didn't really hit it off with Russ on a musical level. Also if you were in the elevator with Jack and the guys that he had hired, the talk in the elevator, despite my being there, was all about getting pussy. Ry wasn't doing that. I guess maybe they thought it was sexy to talk like that in front of a woman, but I found it really kind of childish, boring, and demeaning—to them more than to me."

In the studio, Sainte-Marie says she was happy to experiment and try out songs that Nitzsche wanted her to tackle with musicians whom she didn't know. He had an excellent reputation as a producer, after all, and was often nice to work with. "But then these conflicts would appear in him and there'd be something wrong, and I had absolutely no power to know what it was," Sainte-Marie says. "It was like this boys' club of musicians and the engineer, and it just wasn't right."

Some of that discord is evident on the record, though Sainte-Marie doesn't really think there's anything wrong with the songs, per se. There's the folk tune she learned from Leonard Cohen, "The Song of the French Partisan," and songs by Neil Young and Carole King. "'Smackwater Jack' was a Carole

King song, and I was crazy about Carole King," Sainte-Marie says. But it wasn't the kind of easygoing collaboration Sainte-Marie had enjoyed with Chet Atkins a few years earlier. She and Nitzsche were always trying to find common ground, and now and then they would hit something creatively, but "we weren't two halves of anything. It was kind of me putting the maestro on a pedestal, and Jack putting the star on a pedestal, and neither one of us getting what we wanted musically."

Their contentious relationship only reaffirmed Sainte-Marie's increasing desire to have more autonomy in her music, more respect in the studio, and more control over her career—and all of those feelings dovetailed with the looming end of her seven-year contract with Vanguard. She'd signed this contract in 1964 without a lawyer of her own, and Vanguard was anxious to continue with it, no matter what.

CHAPTER 8

UNTIL IT'S TIME FOR YOU TO GO

N 1971, SAINTE-MARIE lay in a hospital bed feeling like she was going to die, recovering from a recurring digestive problem that had caused convulsive vomiting. "I was in the hospital and really not doing very good," Sainte-Marie remembers. "When I woke up, this guy was standing next to my bed, and he showed me a picture." It was Vanguard's art director, Jules Halfant, who was a well-known painter and printmaker in his own right. "He shows me the cover that they were proposing to use for *The Best of Buffy Sainte-Marie, Vol. 2* [album], and I just hated it. Greasy-looking orange face, green hair—not hip, just gimmicky, bad art. And he said, 'Well, Maynard [Solomon] says this is the one that we're going to use if you don't re-sign with us.'"

The previous year had seen the release of the first Sainte-Marie compilation, *The Best of Buffy Sainte-Marie*, and it gave her the only gap in what was otherwise a demanding annual record-release schedule that had begun in 1964 with *It's My Way!* and didn't end until 1976 with *Sweet America*. These compilations were in addition to her contracted output of new material. The double album compilation in 1970 was rumored to have been a response to the financial loss of 1969's *Illuminations*. Sainte-Marie's relationship with Vanguard was already fraught, and it didn't improve much after the release of the Nitzsche-produced *She Used to Wanna Be a Ballerina*, which also failed to find an audience or much radio play. But, after "Soldier Blue" became a hit in the U.K., Sainte-Marie's 1968 song, "I'm Gonna Be a Country Girl Again," found a brief second life and also charted overseas. To capitalize on the success of these two songs, Vanguard wanted to release a second best-of double album, 1971's *The Best of Buffy Sainte-Marie, Vol. 2*, featuring the album cover that Sainte-Marie despises to this day and calls "the blackmail album."

The threat to use a photo she hated if she didn't do what they wanted made her feel like she'd come full circle. After all, when Vanguard first signed Sainte-Marie and learned that she didn't have a lawyer, they offered to "let her" use theirs. "God, was I green. I signed a seven-year deal." This time was different. She did not want to re-sign with them, having fulfilled her contract with her seventh album, *She Used to Wanna Be a Ballerina*. But she felt like her hands were tied, and so she gave in. They used the photo anyway.

The album cover looks like a literal red-washing of Sainte-Marie's face, her hair is windswept to one side, and her smile doesn't quite reach her eyes. It's the expression of someone who looks reluctant, someone who's being forced. And it wasn't the first time Sainte-Marie's image had been altered in this racist way. "For the U.K. release of *It's My Way!*, the London guys tinted my face red for that—to be sure everybody got the point that it was a 'real red Indian,'" Sainte-Marie recalls. But this new cover was glaringly out of place with most of her North American album art up to that point, which was more artistic, inventive, and creative. It looks like the punishment Sainte-Marie says it was. "They put that one [*Vol. 2*] out, and I just didn't want to work with them anymore," she says. "I didn't want to re-sign with them, and they knew it. I still hate that cover."

In addition to Sainte-Marie's illness (the result of a small deformity in her digestive tract, which she still manages with medicine to this day) and the "blackmail album," 1971 also marked the end of her marriage to Dewain Bugbee. She was on the road all the time, and at first he joined her, but he hated being away from Hawai'i and their farm. After a number of years of long-distance phone calls and not-too-frequent in-person visits, they decided to divorce.

But 1971 also brought her into teenage crush Elvis Presley's orbit when he heard her song, "Until It's Time for You to Go," and fell in love with it himself. The song had appeared on Sainte-Marie's 1965 album *Many a Mile*. "I didn't even tell people I wrote it for the longest time," Sainte-Marie says. "I wasn't ashamed of it, but I didn't tell anybody I wrote it because it's a pop song." That's how intense the anti-pop sentiment of folk and protest musicians was in 1965. Had she wanted to capitalize on its popularity, Sainte-Marie could have had another career as an in-demand pop balladeer. It seemed like everyone making pop and rock music in the sixties and seventies recorded their own version of Sainte-Marie's unusual love song.

"Until It's Time for You to Go" is Sainte-Marie's most covered song and her most conventional pop standard as well, but it's still a little different and subverts many of the trappings of standard love songs. Its melody is not quite as sentimental, its bridge progression is wonderfully unconventional, and its themes are decidedly progressive; the narrator's expectations are realistic and mature but still passionate. It's the exact opposite of "undying devotion" songs in which love is cement-glue and side-by-side coffins, a suffocating blood oath that can't be broken. Those kinds of songs have a certain romantic appeal, but that's not what's happening in this song. This is about a love that is not forever and will not last, and no one is blind to its brevity or lying to themselves or to each other.

Lesley Gore's 1963 performance of "You Don't Own Me" was thought of as an early feminist pop anthem, and it was, but the song was written by two men. Sainte-Marie released "Until It's Time for You to Go" two years before Aretha Franklin's gender-flipping, jaw-dropping performance of "Respect" hit the airwaves, and though Sainte-Marie's song wasn't heralded as a feminist anthem, there's something radically empowering about it. It's sung from the perspective of a woman who has total agency, who is actively resisting gendered stereotypes and the coding of forever-love as a girlish dream. She has a shared vision for what this partnership will—or could—look like. "Don't ask why, don't ask how/Don't ask forever of me/Love me now," she demands.

The song wasn't a hit for the songwriter herself, but it was for Bobby Darin, the Four Pennies, Neil Diamond, Andy Williams, and, most significantly, Elvis Presley. Cher, Barbra Streisand, Roberta Flack, Françoise Hardy, Bette Davis, and many others also put their spin on it, while Nancy Sinatra and Glen Campbell covered it separately and then turned it into a duet, extracting the song's gentle melancholy. Its wildest treatment is the soulful and sexy R&B kiss-off offered up by the New Birth featuring Susaye Greene's spellbinding lead vocals.

At first Sainte-Marie wasn't thrilled about the idea of anyone else covering it, particularly because it was a love song and pretty personal to her, though she declines to specify for whom she wrote it. "It kind of bothered me a little bit because it's a different kind of song," Sainte-Marie remembers. "The first person who covered it was Bobby Darin. His musical director either felt that I had made an unintentional mistake or he totally missed the very cool melody that came to work against what's going on in the chords. He turned it into a very vanilla thing. In my original, changing the chords under that melody, it gives the song a certain delicious, suspended, totally unique feel. Chet Atkins was the first person to suggest that maybe I had written a standard, something that was just plain different from anything anybody else had done. Chet couldn't get over the suspensions and the bridge progression. They [Darin and his musical director] overlooked it; they turned it into an ordinary thing, like a Protestant hymn. To me, that was totally blowing the sexy. He turned it into bus tickets instead of sexual tension."

And as more people covered the song, some would cover it her way, while others built upon Darin's version or the "Vegas version" as she sometimes calls it. "I had to go through this thing where I had to let the song go and have a life. I came to understand that, actually, it's a huge compliment no matter how much some other artist might reinterpret or just plain get it wrong," she laughs. "Gradually I've really come to appreciate other artists taking it into their lives because I know what's involved with that. You fall in love with a song. You take the time to learn it and to learn how to play it and you teach it to other people and other people teach it to the band. It just takes on a life of its own. That artist gives it to his or her own audience, and that's really something. Now I look at it with great gratitude and appreciation because some of my songs that have been done differently from the way I would do them are just lovely. It's like seeing your child grow up."

Sainte-Marie also took ownership of "Until It's Time for You to Go" publicly, though, of course, people continued to attribute the song to others. "I actually had somebody claim that they wrote it," she says. "It was just some bozo trying to exploit something. It took two minutes to straighten it out because he was lying and I had the proof. We didn't spend any time on that." There was even a rumor that Rod McKuen, the American poet and singer-songwriter, had written the song. It seemed like people wanted to attribute "Until It's Time for You to Go" to anyone but Sainte-Marie. It's hard to say exactly why, but it's easy to deduce that racism, sexism, and classism were all factors. What was a young, Indigenous protest singer doing penning a pop standard and breaking through, at least partly, into the mainstream?

The song was shot into another stratosphere of recognition thanks to Elvis Presley. By 1971, Presley had already mounted one comeback and a lengthy Las Vegas residency and was moving into a new phase of his career. Sainte-Marie was in Nashville recording her 1972 album *Moonshot* with musician-producer Norbert Putnam. Putnam was part of the famous Muscle Shoals Rhythm Section, had been in Presley's band, and had also worked with all of the top session players at the time, such as his music partner David Briggs and the Memphis Horns, many of whom had also played with Presley. Sainte-Marie was recording one of Presley's songs, a B-side from one of his earliest albums called "My Baby Left Me," by Arthur Crudup.

"I memorized all of Elvis Presley's first few albums, and I loved that song," she says. "We finished the take and the phone rang and it was one of Elvis's associates, a guy that I had met through Chet [Atkins] many times. When you're in Nashville, and you go out to dinner with Chet, you're going to meet a lot of people," Sainte-Marie remembers. "I got to meet a lot of the business people that ordinarily would not have come into my life. And so this associate of Elvis's called and said, [she puts on a deep southern drawl] 'Buffy? Elvis just recorded your song, "Until It's Time for You to Go."' By this time, I was pretty much over Elvis; he was singing mostly formula stuff," Sainte-Marie says. Still, when Presley's associate called, Sainte-Marie could barely contain her glee. "It was Elvis Presley, come on!" Sainte-Marie laughs at the memory. "Don't think of Tom Parker Elvis; think of Elvis before that horror got hold of him. When I was thirteen, Elvis was fresh. He was young. He was healthy and beautiful, and he was sexy and a natural musician. He was everything. He was just everything."

There's almost no expression of love that's more pure or more intense than first love; that early devotion still stirs up a bit of a giddy, amazed feeling for Sainte-Marie. "It was just a total surprise," she admits. "Elvis had already gone into kind of a different style. He no longer had that young rebel thing going for him. And the army and church—you know, he was a pretty conservative guy. But when he recorded 'Until It's Time for You to Go,' it was just amazing. It was as if Santa Claus had said yes to coming to your birthday party." But then Presley's associate followed up with a demand. "The guy said, 'We're going to have to have some of that publishing money, honey,' and I said no."

Presley might have been on the decline, but he was still one of the biggest artists in the world. Presley's managers could effectively argue that his stardom would elevate the song and he deserved a cut for the increased sales, but Sainte-Marie wasn't interested. "He hadn't written it, period, and I felt that it was [an] unfair [demand]," she says. "I had given away the publishing to 'Universal Soldier' for a dollar about ten years earlier because I didn't know what I was doing, and I certainly was not going to do that again. I had already made up my mind that I was never going to have a big career in show business. It was just me. It's not right for the lawyers to come along and ask for a cut of a song that they had nothing to do with. Elvis hadn't written it. If he had, I would have split the publishing [profits], but he hadn't.

So it was a very easy decision. I said, 'No, I can't do that, too bad.' So I let it go and figured, well, he's not going to record it."

He not only recorded it—he recorded it at least nine times, including live versions, and put it in movies. It quickly became one of his signature songs. Presley first released his cover in 1972, but later that year he and Priscilla Presley would file for divorce (finalized in 1973). It had been, ostensibly, a love song from him to his wife, and it did become their anthem, but it was also more complicated than that. Presley's rendition of Sainte-Marie's song is performative to a certain extent—he'd had an affair and so had Priscilla, and he needed some image rehab. There was incentive to perform his heartbreak publicly so that women would still worship him. But it's also a convincingly rueful treatment—he really does sound regretful, a little lost, and like he let love down.

Consider how differently the song presents in Presley's version with the slight lyrical changes and gender flip compared with Sainte-Marie's version. When Sainte-Marie sings "I'm not a queen/I'm a woman/take my hand," it can be interpreted as a declaration of autonomy and equality. So often when a woman is put on a pedestal by a man, there's an element of misogyny at work: her personhood is erased, she's held to an impossible set of standards or expectations, and he doesn't need to deal with her in any real, messy, day-to-day ways. But a woman telling a man that he's not a "dream" or an "angel" is different than a man telling a woman the same thing. The difference is in the power dynamics of language, the coding of vulnerability and softness, clichés of femininity and masculinity, and gendered romantic ideals. In Sainte-Marie's version, "take my hand" sounds like an invitation; in Presley's, it sounds like a demand.

And did Presley and his team continue to make demands of the songwriter? "Every time Elvis was about to record it again, they would call me: 'Buffy, we're gonna have to have some of that publishing [money].' My lawyer would say, 'They called again,' and I would say, 'No,'" Sainte-Marie remembers. "It was just a business ploy. Elvis still hadn't written the song, and there was a principle involved, which I felt would also benefit other songwriters. I mean, why should I have given him publishing money? It's not as though Elvis was an up-and-coming, struggling artist. Elvis didn't need the push. My song was already a standard. I knew it, and I really didn't care whether or not anybody else ever recorded it. I just didn't care."

Despite Presley's obvious affection for her song, the two artists never met, though she says she would have loved to. "But I'm sure we would not have become friends," she says with a laugh. And even though Sainte-Marie hasn't loved every cover treatment her songs have received, she has gained an important perspective that she offers up to other songwriters and artists. "The way I look at it now is, you can't kill a good song. That's one of the beautiful things about music."

To this day, Sainte-Marie's friend Randy Bachman (of The Guess Who and Bachman–Turner Overdrive) is impressed by her versatility as a songwriter. "When your songs get recorded by Elvis and Bobby Darin, really big heavyweight dudes, that is an absolute testament to how great your songwriting is," Bachman says. "She's very much like the Beatles or the Rolling Stones or like Neil Young, and I try to be like that too, but her next song or record is not at all like any previous ones. There's a changing songwriting format, even though the themes are usually peace, love, and rebellion against the evils in the world."

Buffy Sainte-Marie
on fame

I'm surprised I get any credit. I really do count my blessings. With the way publicity engines work—we know how come the same face is on every magazine at the same time. It's all an inside job. Showbiz is an inside job. There's only so much space and everybody's competing for that two-inch column in *Rolling Stone*. They might like you as an artist, but they really like the fact that the record company you are with has fourteen other artists. You're not going to get much say and it's going to get boiled down to the lowest common denominator that would reach the most people. And there's a certain kind of boneheaded logic to that. Most people are governed by business. Those of us who are not governed by business are very few. And if you're not governed by business, you may be considered unbuyable, suspect, a loose cannon. In Hollywood you certainly are, and certainly in the record business. If you're a certain kind of artist, people like Clive Davis are going to come and get you and they'll just propel you. And if you're not, if you're a different kind of artist, if you are somehow outside the system so that you're not part of the social life of meetings and deals, you're going to get left out.

Buffy Sainte-Marie at the Newport Folk Festival in the mid-1960s.

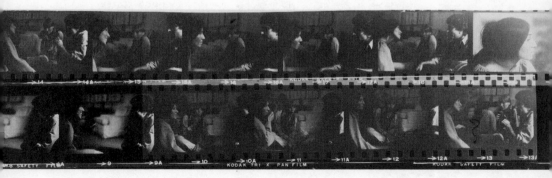

These pictures, taken at the Chelsea Hotel, are from a proof sheet that has survived two hurricanes, and are the only photos that Buffy Sainte-Marie has of her with Joni Mitchell and Leonard Cohen.

Buffy Sainte-Marie with
Leonard Cohen.

PHOTO COURTESY OF BUFFY
SAINTE-MARIE

Buffy Sainte-Marie in vintage
fringe.

PHOTO BY GUY WEBSTER

Buffy Sainte-Marie in her backyard in Hawai'i.

PHOTO BY JIMMY FUJITA

Emile Piapot, Buffy Sainte-Marie, and Clara Starblanket Piapot.

Buffy Sainte-Marie basking in the sun in the 1970s.

PHOTO COURTESY OF BUFFY SAINTE-MARIE

Buffy Sainte-Marie in concert in Nashville.

PHOTO BY MARSHALL FALWELL

Buffy Sainte-Marie in Paris.

PHOTO BY VINCENT ROSSELL

Vintage press photo of Buffy
Sainte-Marie.

Buffy Sainte-Marie performing in
the 1970s.

Buffy Sainte-Marie with her mother, Winnie, holding a baby monkey in Australia, around 1975.

Buffy Sainte-Marie giving baby Cody a bath in a bucket at the Piapot Reserve, around 1976.

Buffy Sainte-Marie with her Piapot family at the reserve.

Cody peeking out of a teepee around 1977.

Cody in a bucket around 1977.

Buffy Sainte-Marie getting ready for baby Cody's luau. *Sesame Street*'s cast and crew also attended the celebratory luau, filmed on location at Sainte-Marie's home in Hawai'i around 1977 (the episodes aired in early 1978).

Floyd Westerman, Buffy Sainte-Marie, and Dennis Banks
in the 1970s.

Buffy Sainte-Marie with Cody, age sixteen.

Buffy Sainte-Marie holding her Oscar in 1983 after winning the Academy Award for Best Original Song for co-writing "Up Where We Belong," the theme song from *An Officer and a Gentleman*.

Buffy Sainte-Marie happily painting.

PHOTO BY DENISE GRANT

Buffy Sainte-Marie standing in front of her painting *Elder Brothers*.

PHOTO BY JESSE GREEN

Buffy Sainte-Marie performing in Ottawa at the National Arts Centre.

PHOTO BY BRIAN CAMPBELL

Buffy Sainte-Marie cuddling with a kangaroo.

PHOTO COURTESY OF BUFFY SAINTE-MARIE

Buffy Sainte-Marie with her band: Jesse Green, Leroy Constant, and Michel Bruyere.

PHOTO BY CHRISTIE GOODWIN

Buffy Sainte-Marie supporting Idle No More.

PHOTO BY KEVIN NORTON

Buffy Sainte-Marie performing in Central Park for Summerfest.

Buffy Sainte-Marie and the author at Catfe in Vancouver, 2018.

PHOTO BY ANDREA WARNER

CHAPTER 9

NOT THE LOVIN' KIND

SAINTE-MARIE'S 1972 ALBUM *Moonshot* was another departure for the young artist, thanks to her new collaboration with Norbert Putnam. Coincidentally, Presley and his team had first called Sainte-Marie while she was in the studio with Putnam, who'd recorded with Presley in 1965. Putnam had just produced Joan Baez's last Vanguard album, 1971's *Blessed Are...* and had played bass for the psychedelic pop band the Neon Philharmonic in 1967. In 1970, he and piano player David Briggs started Nashville's Quadrafonic Sound Studio, where Neil Young's *Harvest* was recorded, as well as Jimmy Buffet's "Margaritaville" and countless other hit rock records.

Working with Putnam was something of a revelation for Sainte-Marie. They even fell in love for a little while, living together in Nashville, and their creative partnership made for some of her most exhilarating forays into funk, soul, and rock. The first track on *Moonshot*, "Not the Lovin' Kind" is one of those songs, a lost gem that, in an alternative history, would have become a much-covered classic by the likes of Heart and Jefferson Airplane and Led Zeppelin. It's a bracing, bruising rock song that embraces soul, country, and psychedelic flourishes. Sainte-Marie spits out every line with a snarl and some snark, and you can practically hear her eyes rolling at the excuses of the male subject on the receiving end of these lyrics, but also at her song's narrator for succumbing to his nonsense one too many times. "I think I've learned your secret/to keep from getting burned," she sings. "Love for you is a matter of no deposit and no return."

Putnam and Sainte-Marie were well matched in many ways, not the least of which was a shared love of soul-baring vocal performances. "I read an interview where Norbert said that, for him, it's always all about the emotion of the song and the singer in the song, and I always loved him for that. If [the emotions] are not there, then the record's no good," she says. "I can appreciate non-emotional music—you know, some music is real mathematical—but the emotion that comes through songs is always what's most important to me. And Norbert had pointed out, in whatever article that was, that most producers don't even think about that. And I guess maybe he's right. It's just not talked about in music production schools or camps, the emotion of a song."

Sainte-Marie made four albums with Putnam—1972's *Moonshot* and 1973's *Quiet Places*, both on Vanguard, and 1974's *Buffy* and 1975's *Changing Woman*, both on MCA. She left Vanguard once and for all after *Quiet Places*, thanks to her lawyer, Abe Somer, who worked to get her released from her contract—something she'd wanted since the *The Best of Buffy Sainte-Marie, Vol. 2* fiasco. In 1974, Vanguard released yet another compilation, *Native North American Child*, which Sainte-Marie says was done without her agreement. "If I had wanted to make an all-Indian album, it sure wouldn't have been this one and it sure wouldn't have had [Vanguard] in charge," she says.

Working with Putnam, however, made a world of difference. It made her a better singer, she says, as did working with musicians who genuinely loved the music. It was the first time she'd worked with a band of like-minded individuals, and it was as if she'd unlocked a door to a secret garden. The players were largely from Putnam's own band, Area Code 615, or Putnam's friends, and included the likes of his studio partner David Briggs as well as Billy Sanford, Kenny Buttrey, Charlie McCoy, and Eddie Hinton. She felt comfortable talking about music with them because they too were natural players, often self-taught just like her.

"Working with Norbert and his band was easy," Sainte-Marie says. "It was friendly; it was no struggle at all. I didn't have a record label breathing down my neck, and I didn't have snobby musicians trying to make me feel like less because I couldn't read music. The musicians in Nashville approached music conversations the same way I did in that they didn't talk the way that music-school musicians usually talk, which is kind of like lawyer-ese. But in Nashville, we thought of how the chords related to each other. It's a much more natural way of relating to music. So I felt comfortable there; it was a lot of fun, and I think it shows in the music. The passion that I had for those songs—I couldn't have done that in New York with Maynard Solomon in the room. It wouldn't have happened. It had to be loose and fun. It was beautiful."

Sainte-Marie was thrilled to finally work collaboratively with other musicians. "I didn't have a band not because I didn't want a band, but who the fuck's going to play with me?" She laughs. "I mean, in 1960 or something, who's going to play along with 'Cod'ine?' Who's going to play along with 'Universal Soldier?' I didn't know anybody, and boys in bands being the way they were then—you can see how that wouldn't have happened."

The musicians in Nashville proved the exception. Sainte-Marie acknowledges that Greenwich Village had terrific musicians, but they were working for other people, and she wasn't about to steal somebody else's band. ("It has happened to me," she says, "but I've never done that.") Vanguard co-owner and Sainte-Marie's "somewhat distant producer" Maynard Solomon paired her with a handful of musicians, but she felt like they were just working another job. And no one tried to position her as the front person of a band.

"I would have loved it, though!" Sainte-Marie says. "When Bob Dylan went to play with The Band, I was thrilled. Some of my favorite songs were [those they did] together." She holds up The Band's "The Weight," written by Robbie Robertson, as one of the best rock songs ever written, and the admiration between the two songwriters is mutual.

"I found out about Buffy after I joined up with Bob Dylan and was first introduced to the folk music world," Robbie Robertson says. "When I heard her, I thought she had such a unique voice and delivery, and I liked that she was singing songs with strong meaning. On top of her talent and great voice, she was also a First Nations artist, and that made me want to discover more and more about her music and story. Years later, when we did get to work together, I was even more impressed with her artistic durability, powerful advocacy, and downright coolness."

The experience of finally finding musicians, collaborative and creative soul mates to help execute Sainte-Marie's vision proved liberating in ways she never anticipated. "Working with Norbert's band freed me somehow to let 'er rip like I did from the very beginning, but their tonality was so superb, it was real easy to play with them," she says. "Just playing with the six strings of a guitar—which can go out of tune in the middle of a song—is not nearly as secure as playing with a band who are all zoned in on A440 [tuning standard for musical pitch]. But I don't want to portray that as restrictive in any way. It was expansive, not restrictive. I lost none of that original emotion or passion, and I didn't learn how to sing vanilla. It was just so much fun working with them because I sang all the time and more and more of my musical wishes came true. Norbert had written one of the most beautiful melodies I ever heard and I added words. It's called 'Nobody Will Ever Know It's Real but You' and it's my favorite vocal of my whole career."

Sainte-Marie's first real, full-band touring experiences happened with Putnam and his band. She remembers one show around 1972 or 1973 in Boulder, Colorado, in a large club. "I loved it! It was rockin', it was hot. It was so good. I was doing things like 'Sweet Little Vera,' 'Not the Lovin' Kind,' 'Sweet Fast Hooker Blues,' 'Generation,' and 'Moonshot.' It cost me a fortune because not only were there string players and backup singers, there were horns, too. I had a seventeen-piece band on the road. It was only for about a week. I was wearing fancy short skirts and these stupidly high, five-inch glorious rhinestone platforms."

She remembers playing a concert on that tour at either Carnegie Hall or Philharmonic Hall, she can't remember which, with Norbert's band and sax legend David Sanborn. "The first few songs I did solo, and Norbert told me afterwards that they were all nervous, they were just shaking in the wings as I did my solos. Somebody said, 'Oh my god, how are we going to follow this? She's carrying it.' They were worried that the audience was going to hate them when they came out onstage because the solos were so strong, but, actually, everybody loved it. I just couldn't afford to keep it up financially."

Musically, Sainte-Marie was flying high, but that success didn't come without some problems. Long before email, Sainte-Marie received a lot of fan mail, sometimes hundreds of pieces a day. Most of the time they were nice letters, and occasionally she would answer them. For the most part, she liked to hear from people who were inspired by her music. She got phone calls or met people who wanted to get backstage to meet her in person. Fans liked to send her presents, and she didn't think too much about it—at first. But on one of her tours with the Nashville band she experienced the first of two significant experiences she had with stalkers.

She and the band were in Atlanta, Georgia, and after their show, they returned to their motel, a two-storey building where every room opens onto a common walkway. Someone started to talk to her from outside her door, so she telephoned her drummer down the hall and asked him to look outside. He saw a man and called security. The man went away, and Sainte-Marie didn't think too much about it—until they got to Boulder and one of the roadies found a note on the rental car from the man who'd been trying to see her. The front of the car had been smashed in with a baseball bat. They called the police, but continued on with the tour.

When they got back to Nashville, they resumed recording in Putnam's Quadrafonic Studio. Guitarist Eddie Hinton noticed something weird. "He came in and said, 'Norbert, do you know anything about that truck that's parked across the street? It's been there for a couple of days while you guys have been recording.'" Putnam didn't know, so they called the police who arrived and scoped out the situation. They came into the studio and asked Sainte-Marie if she knew the man who owned the truck.

"I knew his name because he had been sending things to the studio, like two big boxes of vintage clothes he thought I would like," Sainte-Marie explains. "This guy was really trying to get my attention. I had been nice, sending him thank-you notes." She laughs at her own innocence.

Sainte-Marie recalls the police explaining the situation to her. "'Okay, here's what's going to happen. You're going to have to go out and confront this guy. And the idea is to turn him off completely and make him think that you are just the worst person in the world, so think something up. Be cold as ice, a real bitchy person who wants nothing to do with him. No sympathy, no turn on, no nothing.'"

She remembers thinking, "Oh, my god," but she went out to his truck to confront him. "The place was fitted up like a wedding caravan," she says. "It was all fancy with lace and pictures. He thought that I was his wife in his last life and all this stuff. It was really sick." She had spoken to him once before on the phone. He'd found out her phone number and called her, and she didn't know who he was but he had a big, deep voice. She'd imagined him as a massive guy, an intimidating figure who the police would need to be careful around. He wasn't.

"He was this little skinny hippie with dirty hair, really kind of strange," Sainte-Marie says. "He asked me if I was still an Indian or was I just a hippie now. It was just weird. So I was very cold [to him] and then went back into the studio. When the police came in later they said, 'Well, we don't think you're going to hear from him anymore.' They told him to stay out of the state." It was dramatic, but she wasn't traumatized. "I was a little concerned," she recalls. But a few years later, another "super fan" with a criminal history prompted Sainte-Marie to call in the FBI.

"I used to get love letters from this guy. I did *not* answer them, and I told the post office that if I got any packages from this guy not to accept them, because he had been involved in mail bombings." Sainte-Marie is pretty sure that the person who told her that her stalker was also a mail bomber was Doug Weston, owner of the Troubadour, the famous Los Angeles club that helped establish many of the major musicians and bands of the sixties and seventies. Weston knew the man and gave Sainte-Marie the heads-up.

One day in Hawai'i, after returning from touring, she inadvertently signed for packages that included one of his. "When I saw who it was from, I was still at the post office. I said, 'No, no, no, I'm not going to take that.' The postmaster came out and, what a shithead, he refused to let me give it back because I had mistakenly signed off on a package from this nutcase." Sainte-Marie's lawyer called in the FBI and they handled the matter.

In the early- to mid-1970s, she had less dramatic, if equally memorable, tours. One of Sainte-Marie's favorite adventures was a handful of gala concerts in support of UNICEF. While on tour, she appeared in both Europe and Asia with other celebrities such as Dinah Shore, Dusty Springfield, Danny Kaye, Harry Belafonte, and Marlon Brando. Everyone was paid thirty-five dollars a day, whether they were a celebrity or a driver. One of the highlights was a stop in Amsterdam featuring one of Sainte-Marie's favorite flamenco guitarists, known as Manitas de Plata (Little Hands of Silver). He was born Ricardo Baliardo in a caravan in southern France. Although he played Spanish guitar, he didn't speak the language; he and his family were Basque.

"I kind of identified with them in a funny way," she remembers. "They were between cultures like I was. I was an Indian with too much education. I was a folk singer from neither a WASP nor Jewish background. I was something else. Manitas was an unusual fit, and so was I."

Sainte-Marie had been a fan of flamenco music since she'd idolized Carmen Amaya in college. She had seen Manitas de Plata perform in New York, but this was the first time they'd shared a bill. As they waited in the big theater for the rehearsal to get underway, they grew restless. "It just takes forever, so we all decided, 'Aw, heck with this. Let's go down in the basement where the catering was,'" Sainte-Marie remembers. "They [de Plata and the band, consisting of de Plata's nephews] were playing flamenco and I was dancing and singing fake flamenco in French, and somehow it fit. I have this flamenco vein that goes through me to this day. I take a dance class on Wednesdays. I practice secret flamenco. I'm a closet flamenco singer, and I take dance lessons because it's so much fun, and it's just so beautiful. Manitas de Plata's nephews went on to become the Gipsy Kings."

But Manitas de Plata wasn't the only hero she met while touring. Sainte-Marie was also a huge fan of sixties- and seventies-era Chinese cinema. She loved the language, the costumes, the makeup—everything. "I had a crush on a couple of Chinese movie stars," she says with a laugh. "Where I live in Hawai'i, my local theater used to show Chinese movies and I would go all the time." When she was invited to perform in Hong Kong in the early 1970s, she was paired with Bruce Lee, who acted as her celebrity ambassador. "He was very nice to me, and he invited me over to where they were filming the nunchaku scenes in *Enter the Dragon*," she recalls. "His arms were all bruised, and he was laughing about it. He said, 'We've been working on this for days!' just trying to get it right in one take. He was all bruised up. He was very nice and a brilliant person. I think he was just so wonderful, and it's too bad he died so young."

And Sainte-Marie wasn't just meeting other celebrities and artists. She was also working as an activist to support the increasingly powerful young Indigenous leaders rising up against their oppressors—namely, Sainte-Marie says, "the money and power behind local, state, and the U.S. governments' mining and ranching interests in Indian country."

CHAPTER 10

BURY MY HEART AT WOUNDED KNEE

N THE EARLY 1970s, Sainte-Marie was working with well-known collaborators and enjoying a spike in popularity overseas thanks to the success of her song, "Soldier Blue." She was also on the road constantly—but no matter where she was, she never stopped advocating for the rights of Indigenous people. She believed that if only everyone else understood the inequity they faced, they would want to help. Hope is integral to her resistance, and her resistance is equally paramount to her hope. Everything she'd instinctively cultivated in childhood and youth—her sense of humor, imagination, music, and love of nature—was part of a survival strategy that allowed her to thrive. In the early 1960s, she'd gained a deeper understanding of that innate resistance after spending time with her family on the Piapot Reserve, meeting and connecting with young Indigenous activists in the National Indian Youth Council, and traveling as often as she could to other reservations in North America. She made some life-changing friendships and forged relationships within the activist community.

In the late sixties, Sainte-Marie met Annie Mae Pictou Aquash, a fellow activist whom she liked right away. Sainte-Marie can't remember exactly where they met—"Cities start to look alike when you're traveling around with a guitar," she says—and even though Aquash was a few years younger than her, they bonded quickly. Like Sainte-Marie, Aquash was originally from Canada (she hailed from Nova Scotia). When they met, she was living in Boston, 130 miles from where Sainte-Marie had gone to school. Aquash was also Mi'kmaq, like Sainte-Marie's adoptive mother, Winnie. Sainte-Marie was encouraged by Aquash's work with the Boston Indian Council. "Twenty years before, most people in Boston didn't know that there were any Indians," she says. "They just plain had never come across it; it had never crossed their screen. But Annie Mae knew, and she was involved with some other 'invisible Indians' in Canada and Boston."

Through their activism with various groups, including the National Indian Youth Council and the Boston Indian Council, Sainte-Marie and Aquash also knew the activists leading the American Indian Movement (AIM), an Indigenous civil rights group founded in 1968 by several young activists, including Dennis Banks and Clyde and Vernon Bellecourt. Russell Means, who had a strong leadership role, became AIM's national director in 1970. They were resisting racist U.S. government policies and policing, protesting broken treaties, and advocating for Indigenous sovereignty as well as land claims and resource rights. Both strip mining and uranium extraction were behind treaty violations and had severe consequences—pollution, exploitation, displacement, environmental and financial ruin, cancer, and even death—for Indigenous people.

Sainte-Marie saw something truly empowering about these early days. "In my heart, and in the hearts of others, there was a real resistance," she says. "There was a genuine grassroots movement, and I was fortunate to be a part of it and learn from it and sometimes help it along by spotlighting an issue."

From the *New York Times* to the *Washington Post* to the *Chicago Tribune*, the young Indigenous activists were continuously

framed in the media as "radicals" and "militants" who chal-
lenged the status quo, which, in turn, was fiercely enforced
and upheld by rich settlers, who often identified themselves
as "patriots," but whose notions of morality and propriety were
shaped by capitalism and exploitation. Government and big
business had vested interests in silencing Indigenous activists,
and even when it wasn't done overtly, they had other, more subtle methods of oppression.

"They owned it all," Sainte-Marie says. "They didn't hire us
outspoken artists at their universities and theaters or support
entrepreneurs who may have needed their support, their ads,
their permits to put on a concert or a speaking event. I may have
been famous, but I wasn't playing in the heart of Indian country,
and that was a great shame. If we'd understood at the time, we
might have had a stronger impact where it was most needed.
If there's one thing that I could have done differently, I would
have had a real business shark in my corner who also understood the stakes and potentials in Indian country, but there was
no such a person in my corner. And even had there been, who
knows? It was probably just impossible at the time. We were
obviously marginalized citizens out-powered by huge energy
companies, and our voices were not to be heard by the public.
So they weren't."

Early on in her career, Sainte-Marie could book shows in
major cities like Toronto, Miami, New York, and Los Angeles, but she was never invited to Oklahoma City, Phoenix, or
Wyoming, or other places that make up what she calls "Indian
country." Sainte-Marie and the Santee Sioux activist-poet John
Trudell later discussed their suspicions that big energy companies like Standard Oil, Peabody Coal, and their ilk not only
quietly blocked activist shows in "Indian country," but they also
ensured that major newspaper stories about Sainte-Marie and
other positive Indigenous activists weren't picked up by editors

of the local papers. Sainte-Marie traveled both coasts via coffee houses, colleges, and Indigenous friendship centers, but was conspicuously absent (in hindsight) in places like North and South Dakota, Oklahoma, or Nebraska. It wasn't a confrontational persecution of her, Sainte-Marie says, but rather a negation of anything that corporate entrepreneurs—motivated by profit, competition, and bullying—saw as bad for their bottom line.

But they persevered. "John Trudell was getting out of the army at the time, but he was becoming an activist, and we wrote letters back and forth. Dennis Banks, Russell Means, Clyde and Vernon Bellecourt, and Eddie Benton Banai, the people who founded AIM, had recently gotten out of jail and were beginning to advise local people about their rights. All of us were emerging from having had our hands tied, sometimes totally unfairly, unjustly, by a system that we all wanted to change."

Some of the people on the National Indian Youth Council had earned law degrees that they used to confront the executives, the system, and local issues. Others organized, as AIM did in Minneapolis-St. Paul and the Native American Committee did in Chicago and Annie Mae Aquash had done with the Boston Indian Council. Sainte-Marie was doing it nationally and then internationally through music and education and eventually through philanthropy. "I had traveled enough in Indian country to know what one fixable problem was," Sainte-Marie says. "Maybe somebody else would have diagnosed a different problem. But I saw that there were a lot of Native American people who, after they finished high school, were about to work for some energy company, and carry uranium in and out of the mine."

With her own money, Sainte-Marie started the Nihewan Foundation for American Indian Education in 1969, which for the next fifty years awarded financial scholarships to Indigenous people who wanted to continue their education beyond high school. "Students just didn't know how to negotiate the path between high school and getting to college," Sainte-Marie says. "Meanwhile, many scholarships from big foundations were available but went unused. The Nihewan Foundation was different because it required and helped students to apply for other support as well." Sainte-Marie's hope was that it would empower future Indigenous leaders and scholars who otherwise might not have considered college or post-graduate education possible, particularly those who saw no life for themselves other than working for the energy companies that had swooped in to extract resources and exploit their land with assistance from the U.S. government.

The same year Sainte-Marie launched her foundation, a group calling themselves Indians of All Tribes began their occupation of Alcatraz Island, the site of the infamous prison near San Francisco that had been closed in 1963. Her friend John Trudell was right out in front. The 1868 Treaty of Fort Laramie between the U.S. and several Indigenous nations had guaranteed that any abandoned or out-of-use federal land would be returned to the Indigenous people who had once occupied it. Alcatraz fit the bill, but the government refused to negotiate. As the occupation began to receive media attention, thanks in part to high-profile visits from celebrity allies like Jane Fonda and Marlon Brando, the government attempted to control the situation, frequently cutting off electricity to the island as well as telephone service. Access to clean, fresh water was almost impossible, so Sainte-Marie offered financial support to provide clean water to the Indigenous occupiers, including Trudell, who was on-site with his family. According to one interview in 1970, Sainte-Marie donated $300 a month to get clean water to Alcatraz, but it still wasn't enough.[30] The government also made deliveries difficult, so food and other necessities remained scarce.

Sainte-Marie performed at a benefit for the Alcatraz occupation on December 12, 1969, in Stanford University's Memorial Chapel. It was broadcast on KPFA public radio's open hour the same night. Tapes from the evening are archived with Pacifica Radio Archives, which also holds thirty-nine tapes from Radio Free Alcatraz, a show hosted by Trudell and designed to "give a voice to the voiceless minority of Native Americans."[31] On December 22, 1969, KPFA began its first live broadcast from Alcatraz, under Trudell's direction. Each episode began with a recording of Buffy Sainte-Marie singing "Now That the Buffalo's Gone." Trudell's final broadcast was in September 1970, but the occupation continued until June 1971 when the U.S. government forcibly removed all of the remaining activists from the island.

In the early 1970s, Sainte-Marie signed with a booking agency in Los Angeles, and around the same time, Aquash arrived in L.A. from Boston. She reached out to Sainte-Marie and also let her know that she was looking for work. Sainte-Marie introduced her to her publicist, Karen Shearer, who needed an assistant. Aquash helped Shearer facilitate some of Sainte-Marie's personal appearances, including a project with the award-winning actor and then activist (now conservative Republican) Jon Voight. Having Aquash as a part of the team during that time made Sainte-Marie feel less alone and less othered on the road. "If I had a personal appearance, I would usually be working for white people in exclusively white show business," she says. "And this would bother me. I would say, 'Where are the Indians?' Night after night, singing to only white faces—ask Jimi Hendrix how that felt," she laughs. "You're not rejecting the fact that there are white people there, but you're wondering, where's everyone else?"

Aquash also helped Sainte-Marie expand the agency's perspective to recognize the value of reaching out and targeting a broader audience and in making sure that Indigenous people were included rather than forgotten or excluded. "Annie Mae and I knew this [Indigenous] world, but almost nobody in L.A. show business did. I was glad to have her injecting some perspective into how to bring Native American people together to support the initiatives we championed, and how to bring national and local efforts together. You have to understand the bonehead mentality of otherwise brilliant publicity folks when it comes to Indians. They know the alcoholic stereotype and they know the romanticized savage Tarzan stereotype, but they have little real-world experience to draw upon regarding Indian realities, so they come up empty."

Aquash eventually began to work more closely with AIM. Sainte-Marie remembers that Aquash worked with fellow AIM activist Leonard Peltier but neither was particularly prominent compared with the two men whose names constantly appeared in the paper, Dennis Banks and Russell Means. "Dennis and Russell were very colorful, very powerful speakers, although very different from one another," Sainte-Marie says. "They really made sense, especially to 'the boys' in media and 'the boys' in politics. Marlon Brando didn't spend a whole lot of time talking to me or Annie Mae or to Mary Crow Dog. Marlon Brando spent time talking to the boys about guy things on a guy's level in that rough and tumble way of camaraderie, that locker-room kind of talk. Marlon and the guys from AIM were all on the same page. I'd just leave at a certain point."

In the earliest days of AIM, sexism and misogyny were rampant, despite the burgeoning feminist movement. Sainte-Marie can name it, as she could then, but she contextualizes it within the time period. "Those guys were just getting out of jail, and although they were doing great work in informing urban Indians of their civil rights, they also loved having teenage girls just in from the reservation looking up into their big brown eyes," she says. "I felt they were exploitative from the start."

Grassroots or city, Sainte-Marie was tired of being surrounded by groups of men, so she was particularly grateful for the women who occupied her various worlds, among them Aquash, Crow Dog, and Joni Mitchell. Most men at the time, whether they were bands, record executives, or activists, were obsessed with two things: having control of the microphone and what she calls "GP."

"What's 'GP'? Getting pussy. I got so tired of the conversation always coming back to getting pussy—same like it was back in the elevator with Jack [Nitzsche] and the recording boys—and especially in showbiz biographies I've been reading lately. I find it boring, even though I like women a lot," Sainte-Marie laughs, but there's an edge in her voice. "No, I do. However, the only times I ever said anything to my 1970s men friends was in a kind of hesitant, little, ridiculing tone, but it was also full of hurt, resentment, and 'How dare you?' And 'Boy, are you AIM guys ever missing it,' I thought. At the time, they were not smart or experienced enough to listen to women, including me. And they were surrounded by wonderful women. The women who were supporting them—their mothers, wives, girlfriends, sisters, and aunties—they were just wonderful. But you didn't hear about them... Nobody ever gave us the microphone. Later, grassroots women finally—without hurting any of the men—just stepped forward and blew through the rudeness and the misogyny that we had all experienced, and did whatever we could."

By 1973, Sainte-Marie and Aquash's lives had diverged. Sainte-Marie was on the road, and Aquash was more deeply involved in AIM's on-the-ground activism. "She became quite crucial to the American Indian Movement," Sainte-Marie says. "She was part of the inner circle who were doing things that I would hear about only after they were either set up or had happened. At this point, I was [traveling] all over the world—Hong Kong, Nashville, Europe, Australia."

While Sainte-Marie was on the road in 1973, tensions began to escalate on the Pine Ridge Reservation in South Dakota. Approximately two hundred AIM members and Oglala Lakota occupied the infamous site of the 1890 Wounded Knee massacre, a location chosen deliberately for occupation.[32] Less than a century before, American soldiers killed an estimated three hundred Lakota, including women and children, near Wounded Knee Creek. For the activists, reclaiming the site wouldn't just be symbolic, it would be historic. Their occupation was meant to protest the failed impeachment of Oglala Sioux tribal chairman Richard "Dick" Wilson, who was accused of widespread corruption and politically motivated violence. Protesters were also critical of the U.S. government for failing to uphold its treaties with Indigenous people.

On the same day that the occupation began, U.S. law enforcement, including marshals and FBI agents, surrounded the town, set up roadblocks, and began to arrest people who attempted to leave. It turned into an armed standoff that lasted seventy-one days. In what became known as the Wounded Knee Incident, gunfire was exchanged at different times throughout the occupation, two Indigenous activists were killed, and one U.S. marshal was shot and paralyzed.

Sainte-Marie personally experienced a frightening act of protester violence in 1974, when she and Aquash were briefly reunited in Gresham, Wisconsin, to support the Menominee occupation of an abandoned Catholic abbey at the invitation of activist Ada Deer. The day after the two women arrived in Gresham, the conflict escalated. "The National Guard saved our butts," Sainte-Marie remembers. "Annie Mae and I were ducking bullets, and the National Guard helped us to not get killed when those vigilantes began attacking Indian people. So I'm not unwilling to admit that people who sometimes seem like the opposition also sometimes seem like friends."

By 1975, Sainte-Marie was still closely involved with Indigenous rights issues and she showed up to do the work, but she didn't work with AIM on a day-to-day basis. She spent much of her time on the road and in support of a variety of different Indigenous activist groups. It wasn't the gunfire that made her hold AIM at arm's length, but rather her awareness of her role in the eyes of some AIM leaders. Occasionally it was her celebrity that proved most attractive to those in leadership positions, rather than her input, intellect, or power as a leader in her own right. "I might show up and bring the press with me to some big deal, but those boys were not about to hand over the microphone to me."

She remembers one incident when she was in Santa Fe with her friend, Navajo artist and anthropologist Rain Parrish. They were alone in the nearby Tesuque Hills doing a fabric and jewels ceremony, and when they came down, Parrish received a call from a friend who was attending an AIM event. When she heard that Parrish was with Sainte-Marie, she asked, "How can you be with Buffy? Buffy's here. She's going to be at the AIM thing tomorrow." The friend had seen posters that announced Sainte-Marie's presence at the event, and hundreds of people expected her to be there.

"Some of the activist guys would use my name, get a thousand people in the room, and then say I was a no-show, which I never was, ever, not even one time," Sainte-Marie says. "I never said that I would show up to something and didn't. This time, I actually got on a plane and went to confront Russell Means in the parking lot. He didn't do it again."

In 1975, Sainte-Marie was also falling for a fellow activist. At an AIM rally in L.A., she met Sheldon Peters, the brother of her friend Ernie Peters. "Ernie was Dakota from Minnesota, and he was part of the American Indian Movement," she says. "Very soft spoken, quiet, a thinker, a traditional kind of guy. He wasn't like a headline grabber or anything like that. I met his brother, Sheldon Peters, and we became a couple. That's what was going on before I wrote 'Starwalker.' I was spending time with not only the Piapots and other [Indigenous] people in Canada but also in different movement situations in the U.S."

Sainte-Marie began to write "Starwalker" in 1975 as a way to acknowledge Indigenous leadership in and out of the spotlight. To this day, it's still her favorite song, in part because of how personal it is. "I was thinking of all the people in the movement that I really admired and I wrote the song for them, not for any one person," she says. "There are some real names in [the song], but Starwalker is not one person. Starwalker is my own personal Indigenous hero or heroine, like a Jay Silverheels or, today, a Sylvia McAdam kind of person. Sober—not somebody who goes out and gets drunk and ruins things. A real hero or heroine. A 'star walker don't drink no wine.' That's a very deliberate line, and I think it's one of the reasons why the song continues to be a favorite of mine because I have always feared the destructive part of alcohol. I know people can have fun on it and all that, but the downside of it is so terribly destructive. I've always felt it's a huge blessing in my life that I never went down that road. So many loved ones I've seen go through horrifying lives because of alcohol."

Sainte-Marie says that the "Wolf Rider" character in the second verse is more specific: female, strong, someone who creates connections and opens doors. It might be a certain part of herself, she says, or someone like Annie Mae Aquash or activist and scholar Winona LaDuke or the women who founded and continue Idle No More. "'You've seen her opening doors,'" Sainte-Marie says, quoting one of the lines in "Starwalker." "There were a lot of people in the American Indian Movement days who opened doors too."

The character of "Holy Light" was a real person—Ernie and Sheldon Peters's grandfather—and this verse also marked the song's musically groundbreaking moment: a sample of traditional singing. "Nobody was using samples at the time, and certainly not Native American samples," Sainte-Marie says. "Indigenous music was not being heard at all. You could go to the Smithsonian and borrow a 78 or listen to Indigenous music on Ampex tape... but it was very, very hard to find Indigenous music at all in the seventies unless you were home on the rez. The music business hadn't discovered sampling yet, and they sure didn't care about Native American music. I used a little bit of sampling, but I also used some live singers when I recorded 'Starwalker' for the first time. When I re-recorded it on *Coincidence and Likely Stories* [in 1992], I overdubbed my own powwow vocals six times in different voices and added new sampling."

"Starwalker" also contained a warning or, at the very least, some pointed advice from Sainte-Marie to her fellow resisters. "When it says, 'Sisters, Brothers all together aim straight/stand tall,' I'm not talking about pick up a gun and aim it at a camera to get your picture in the paper," Sainte-Marie says. "'Aim straight,' really means, 'American Indian Movement, stay clean, don't get caught up in the rackets or any of the pitfalls that are out there when you're attracting attention.' It's so easy to go right when you should go left."

Unfortunately, there was more violence and tragedy ahead for the American Indian Movement. In June of 1975, Joseph Stuntz, a twenty-four-year-old Coeur d'Alene Indigenous man from the Lapwai Reservation in Idaho, and two FBI agents were killed in a shootout at Pine Ridge, South Dakota.[33] Special Agents Jack R. Coler and Ronald A. Williams were allegedly investigating an altercation and burglary (of a pair of boots). The suspect was a man named Jimmy Eagle, who was also wanted for questioning in connection to the assault and robbery of two ranch hands. The agents followed a vehicle that matched the description of the truck Eagle was driving when someone, or multiple people, opened fire on the agents. The agents radioed for backup but were killed. A few hours later, a Bureau of Indian Affairs agent shot and killed Stuntz, an AIM member who'd allegedly been part of the shootout.

But Leonard Peltier was also a suspect in the shootout, and after fleeing Pine Ridge, he ended up on the FBI's Ten Most Wanted Fugitives list.[34] He fled to Canada and was eventually apprehended in Hinton, Alberta, and extradited back to the U.S. Peltier is still in prison to this day, the sole AIM member to be convicted in the deaths of the two agents, despite the fact that the casings from the bullets that killed the agents allegedly did not match Peltier's gun. Two other AIM members were charged and tried separately but were found not guilty. But the violence wasn't over. In December 1975, Annie Mae Pictou Aquash disappeared. Like many other activists, Sainte-Marie feared the worst.

On February 24, 1976, an unidentified female body was found on the side of the road on the Pine Ridge Reservation.[35] Initially, it was reported that she'd died of exposure, as the coroner somehow failed to notice the bullet hole at the back of her head at the base of her skull. Her hands were cut off by the coroner and sent for fingerprinting to the FBI headquarters in Washington. Rather than wait for confirmation of her identity, the body was quickly buried and marked as "Jane Doe."

Eventually the body was identified as Annie Mae Pictou Aquash. She was just thirty years old when she died, leaving behind two little girls, Deborah and Denise. On March 10, 1976, her body was exhumed at the request of her family and members of AIM. A second autopsy was performed, and the real cause of death—that she was shot in the back of her head—was confirmed. Rumors began to circulate, allegedly instigated by the FBI, that Aquash had been an FBI informant killed by AIM members because of information she'd provided about Peltier's involvement in the shooting of the two FBI agents.

For decades, Aquash's murder remained unsolved. Over those same decades, Leonard Peltier's conviction and sentencing was held up as proof of the systemic injustice against Native Americans. This is the background to Sainte-Marie's song, "Bury My Heart at Wounded Knee," which took fourteen years for her to complete. The song is something of a time capsule, filled with the information Sainte-Marie had at the time.

"There were a lot of things going on," Sainte-Marie says. "There were tragedies. Leonard Peltier's trial was a grotesque travesty and a mockery of American justice, and he's been in prison ever since, even though the bullets didn't match the gun. Three people were killed at Pine Ridge. Later, Annie Mae Aquash was murdered. We didn't hear all this information in a three-minute song one day. The incidents at Wounded Knee continued to unspool and come to light over many years."

The fourteen years it took her to get "Bury My Heart at Wounded Knee" right was the longest Sainte-Marie has ever

worked on a song. "When I was putting it together, I was trying to do a lot of things," she recalls. "Obviously, I was trying
to quell some kind of emotional turmoil in myself to come to
grips with what had happened, to resolve it in a way that I could
share with other people and have it all hang on irrefutable facts.
It's kind of like making a movie. And I do care that it hangs on
irrefutable facts because I know that people can challenge it.
Sometimes they do—usually they don't, though, because I did a
pretty good job and even people who check find out, 'Holy shit.
She was right.'"

There were numerous twists and turns to Peltier's impris-
onment, and mysteries about Aquash's tragic murder, and after
Sainte-Marie released her song, events continued to unfold.
In 2004, AIM member Arlo Looking Cloud was convicted of
Aquash's murder.[36] In 2009, AIM member John Graham was
charged, along with Thelma Conroy-Rios, for the kidnapping,
rape, and murder of Aquash.[37] Graham was convicted in 2010,
and Conroy-Rios pled guilty in exchange for a reduced sentence.[38] All three were held accountable for Aquash's murder,
and speculation remains that Peltier was involved too. Aquash's
daughters, Debbie and Denise, believe that high-ranking AIM
members ordered her execution due to fears that she was an
informant.

"I'm very hesitant to talk about Annie Mae for some very
strong reasons," Sainte-Marie says. "Barack Obama lost the last
chance to pardon Leonard Peltier, and some of Annie Mae's
family believe that Leonard's story impacts Annie Mae's in terrible ways. And I cannot shed any light since I wasn't there. I
have to admit that although I knew both Leonard and Annie
Mae years ago, I really can't speak to what happened in those
days. However, all these years later, I know Annie Mae's daughters and sister, and I do believe their research, even though it

implicates some old friends in terrible ways. I loved Annie Mae, and I just have to kind of step aside and not comment about what I don't know."

CHAPTER 11

GENERATION

I N 1975, *SESAME STREET* had only been on the air six years, but already it had revolutionized children's television and was considered a cultural institution. From the beginning, it was a hit. "*Sesame Street* Dazzles in Television Premiere" read a headline in *Variety*.[39] The show was aimed at preschoolers and had specific goals about reflecting accurate and nonjudgmental depictions of the lives of inner-city kids; it was set in a brownstone tenement and the cast included strong African-American characters Gordon and Susan (who were the cornerstone of the street), and Hispanic characters Maria and Luis (added in 1972). White characters were deliberately in the minority. They also cast everyday kids, not child actors, to play the children of *Sesame Street*. According to author Michael Davis's 2008 book, *Street Gang: The Complete History of Sesame Street*, at the end of its first year, *Sesame Street* was in the homes of 1.9 million Americans, and a decade later, more than nine million American kids under the age of six watched it daily.[40]

Sainte-Marie didn't expect the phone call from *Sesame Street*'s producers asking her to be a typical one-shot guest on the show, and in fact, she almost said no. She was busy with other ventures and she didn't really want to go all the way to New York just to count to ten like everyone else who made a guest appearance. But before she hung up she asked a question. "I said, have you ever done any Native American programming?" she recalls. They hadn't, but they called her back with a new offer to include her as a writer and contributor and appear as a semi-regular cast member. She knew it would be a good opportunity to reach millions of young children and their parents with the same message she had been bringing to her concert audiences for years: "Indians exist."

Among Sainte-Marie's first *Sesame Street* appearances was a location shoot in Taos, New Mexico, for a full week of shows. Producers even temporarily changed the theme song to begin with, "Sunny day, coming to Santa Fe," and end with, "We're a long, long, long, long, long, long way from Sesame Street." Sainte-Marie takes Big Bird and his human friend Maria to visit Taos Pueblo, an Indigenous community in New Mexico. Sainte-Marie's performance is quite natural, and her rapport with future lifelong friend Sonia Manzano, who played Maria, was immediate. Through a handful of scenes, Sainte-Marie manages to convey some vital information about Indigenous people, including that while she's Cree from Canada, there are hundreds of different tribes and nations with their own languages and customs and culture, and that she's a guest there, too. She also sings a few songs and plays the mouth bow, and they find out about the children's way of life in the pueblo.

Accurate representations of Indigenous life in pop culture were painfully rare in 1975. "It's very hard to create a presence when all of the seats are already filled by the same old people who've been doing it the same way forever," Sainte-Marie says. So it was additionally important to her to make the most of this opportunity. "The fact that Indians exist—that was really important to get through to little kids and their caregivers. It's important to get that message through before any kind of stereotyping makes a presence in their lives. So that when somebody says, 'Indians are no good,' little kids can say, 'Oh, no, Big Bird says Indians are okay.'"

When she was growing up, Sainte-Marie had very few visible touchstones or pop-culture role models of people who looked like her. The landscape presented a largely white, homogenous North America, but she hoped to change that through *Sesame Street* and through songs like "Generation," a thundering, bluesy track recorded for her 1974 album, *Buffy*, which addressed inequality and was also anchored in real life happy memories.

In the chorus, Sainte-Marie sings, "Me, I don't want to go to the moon/I want to leave that moon alone," a line she took from a conversation with her Cree father, Emile Piapot, while they were walking around in Regina one day. In another line, Sainte-Marie sings, "The media is saturated but the sweetgrass still grows tall." This references a conversation she had with her friend, the broadcaster, activist, and artist John Trudell. "He was talking about the fact that the media is saturated, which means column space is already prescribed, and they have a reserved sign on almost every seat," Sainte-Marie says. "If you're seen as an American Indian or First Nations Canadian or an Aboriginal Australian or an Indigenous Sami person from Sweden, Norway, Russia, or Finland, even if you have a brilliant idea, nobody's going to notice because they're still thinking about you in terms of the 1800s and some costume from a movie. Yet that doesn't mean that our traditions don't still exist. We do have things going for us that nobody points out or that people have tried very hard and systematically to strip away. All of these songs are written with that in mind. I feel that I've had great advantages in knowing two cultures. I do understand that the media is saturated and that the sweetgrass still grows tall."

Her first *Sesame Street* appearances were so successful, Sainte-Marie became a recurring cast member. She balanced her ongoing commitment to the show with her activism, her new relationship, and a tour to Australia. In 1975, she was looking for a new road manager when she met her future best friend, Kayle Higinbotham.

"I was in the recording studio at A&M records with [engineer] Henry Lewy and Joni Mitchell," Higinbotham remembers. "Joni was doing an album. Henry gets a call at the studio, and it's from Buffy. She says, 'I'm going on tour to Australia, and I need a road manager. Do you know of a road manager you could recommend?' Henry said, 'Hold on a minute,' and he turned to me and said, 'Hey, do you want to be a road manager?' I had never been one before, and I said, 'Sure.' We met very shortly thereafter and had a lot in common, so we went off to Australia. It was my first gig as a road manager—on-the-job training—and she was incredibly patient with me. We've been friends ever since."

Sainte-Marie recalls that, on tour, "Kayle thought maybe I had a sweetheart or that she was just being left out, because she'd come by my hotel room and there'd be two dinner trays. Only, that was all me! I was real hungry, and I'd call room service and say, 'Yeah, I'll have the roast chicken, and what'll you have?' I'd cover the receiver and then say, 'Oh, the spaghetti, too, right?' to an imaginary roommate. Well, anyway, when I got back from that tour, I found out I was pregnant! That's why I was eating so much!"

"We didn't know each other that well. But in front of her [hotel] rooms, there'd be all of this room-service food!" Higinbotham laughs. "'Oh, she's got a boyfriend or they had parties and didn't invite me,' I'd think. We found out when she got home that she was pregnant with Cody. We can always know how long we've known each other by how old Cody is."

Sainte-Marie hadn't harbored any long-held dreams of being a parent and was surprised when she found out she was pregnant. "Very much surprised! And very happy." She and Sheldon Peters married and welcomed Dakota Starblanket Wolfchild, or Cody, to the world in 1976.

"Sheldon didn't yet have an Indian name," she says, explaining how the name Wolfchild came to be. "We were about to visit the Rocky Boy Reservation, a Chippewa/Cree reservation in Montana. My Cree dad, Emile Piapot, had relatives there and he suggested we go see his cousin, Henry Wolfchild. It was Henry who gave our family, Sheldon and Cody and me, the family name Wolfchild. As usual with Cree name givings, it was a beautiful little ceremony."

The name-giving ceremony also provided Sainte-Marie with a powerful coda to some of the feelings and issues the pregnancy had raised about being adopted, her complex childhood, and being reunited with her Cree family. "It wasn't until I was pregnant with my son that I talked to a psychiatrist about various things, including this kind of parentage issue and who's your family and who's not, and how much does that matter in the world, and all that kind of deep thinking that comes later in life. Especially when you're going to have a child, you have to get things straight. So you're coming to grips with knowing that there are some things that you'll never know about yourself. And I don't know certain statistical things [about myself], and it used to bother me a lot, but finally I just said, 'You know what? I'm not going to let this bother me anymore. I have two families, so fuck it. If somebody else wants to get into it, more power to you,'" she laughs.

Sainte-Marie loved reading to baby Cody, making up songs to narrate their time together, communicating with him constantly. When *Sweet America*, her 1976 album, failed to garner much attention, she matter-of-factly assumed that the day she'd always known was coming had arrived: her guest appearance in show business was over—though, by then, it had lasted twelve albums longer than she thought it would—and it was time to move on. She'd concentrate on raising Cody, do a few concerts a year, and keep writing songs, just not explicitly for the purpose of putting out a record. She'd also keep working part-time on *Sesame Street*, folding her little family into the mix as well.

"When I became pregnant during my first year on *Sesame Street*, I thought they'd probably let me go," Sainte-Marie recalls. "But they didn't. They really got into it." Producers invited Wolfchild to join Sainte-Marie on the show sometimes, and after Cody was born, he was also a frequent guest. A baby introduced a lot of new, exciting dynamics into *Sesame Street*, as did the family's Indigeneity and Sainte-Marie's adoptive cultural practices related to her home in Hawai'i. "When Cody was either one or two, we had a baby luau for him, and that's a traditional thing in Hawai'i," Sainte-Marie says. "I married into a Hawai'ian family in my first marriage, so I was real comfortable with Hawai'ian people anyway, even after Dewain and I parted. *Sesame Street* wrote up the scenario for Big Bird as, 'You're going to Hawai'i for Cody's baby luau, and you're going to visit Buffy and Sheldon.'"

Sainte-Marie had long had a teepee set up in the backyard of her Hawai'i home in what later became her goat pasture. Hundreds of people showed up for the luau, including locals and the *Sesame Street* cast and crew who'd come over for a few weeks of taping. Oscar the Grouch found a temporary new home inside an old truck that she hadn't had towed yet from her yard. "With our local people and the *Sesame Street* scouts, they found a mountain that kind of looked like Snuffleupagus, who was Big Bird's imaginary friend," Sainte-Marie recalls. Sainte-Marie's character was, initially, the only adult who could see Snuffleup-agus, which was part of her bond with Big Bird, who was for a while hugely jealous of baby Cody.

"Their thing on sibling rivalry was just brilliant," Sainte-Marie says. "Unfortunately, most grown-ups fail to prepare kids for what having a new baby will be like for them. You know, the grown-ups are all saying to the kids, 'Oh, you're going to have a little brother or sister! Won't that be wonderful?' And it's not wonderful [for kids]; it's awful. *Sesame Street* set it all up so that Big Bird turned out to be quite disappointed. And that had nothing to do with ethnic things either, so I've got to hand it to them, they never tried to stereotype me. They just had it right every time. We did specifically Indian things, but we also did everybody things."

Sainte-Marie would sometimes sing the little songs she wrote for Cody on the show, like his bath-time song that went, "Wash your little feet now, yep, yep, scrub your little feet now." And, in 1977, Sainte-Marie became the first woman to nurse a baby on mainstream national television. She'd suggested this to producers, in hopes of helping to normalize nursing, and they loved the idea. The brief scene, which lasts less than a minute, is incredibly simple and effective. Big Bird asks Sainte-Marie what she's doing, and she says, "I'm feeding the baby, see? He's drinking milk from my breast." Big Bird replies, "That's a funny way to feed a baby," and Sainte-Marie calmly, sweetly explains, "Lots of mothers feed their babies this way. Not all mothers, but lots of mothers do."

"I didn't know it would ever become a big deal," she says. "And I really didn't care. But I did know how hard it was for mothers like me to get information and encouragement about breastfeeding even from their doctors, and I just wanted to be a part of fixing that. Now people will get a chip on their shoulder on one side or the other, but then it was no big deal." It's also not a big deal to Big Bird. He's curious and asks a question, and Sainte-Marie respects his curiosity and answers his question, and then he goes back to playing, just like real little kids.

When she was shooting the show, Sainte-Marie, Wolfchild, and Cody would spend a few weeks or a month in New York, usually in a hotel close to Lincoln Center and Central Park. A typical day started when she arrived early at the Reeves Studio at 81st and Broadway and headed upstairs to her tiny dressing room. The wardrobe woman would show up with the day's outfit, or Sainte-Marie brought her own clothes. They often shot two shows a day, which for Sainte-Marie meant memorizing two scripts with a baby on her hip. It was exhausting. And, rightfully so, the adults really came third in the list of *Sesame Street*'s priorities, right behind the Muppets and the children.

Sonia Manzano, who played Maria, offered her some very specific advice when Sainte-Marie joined the show. "She told me to be prepared to look ugly because the lighting was all for the Muppets," she says. "She said, 'Actually, we have a pretty good-looking cast, but we all look ugly because of the lights,' and boy, was she ever right. You had to kind of leave your ego in the dressing room. If the Muppets messed up, you had to do it over again. But if you messed up, you might not get a second chance, because filming Big Bird and the other Muppets was so crucial. The live cast, we were all second bananas. But very happy bananas," Sainte-Marie laughs.

While the adults rehearsed the scenes, the kids who appeared on *Sesame Street* would play in a different part of the theater, a big, decked-out playroom packed with things to do and people to watch them. When the cameras and actors and puppeteers were ready, the kids would step into the scene.

Sainte-Marie also remembers being impressed with the sheer

size of Big Bird. Caroll Spinney, who has played Big Bird since 1969 (and who is still officially credited with the role, though Matt Vogel is usually the one in the costume now; Spinney pre-records Big Bird's dialogue), is tall anyway, but Big Bird's costume stands eight foot two. Sainte-Marie sighs. "Most parents are so stupid, they just don't even think of what that's like for a little child. Parents used to stop me in airports with a toddler in their arms, 'Look who it is! It's Buffy from *Sesame Street!*' and they're pushing this poor little kid into my face, and the kid is not putting two and two together because for a child watching on television, I'm eight inches tall and Big Bird is twelve inches tall."

Sainte-Marie has a soft spot for both of Spinney's characters, Big Bird and Oscar the Grouch. "He said they were two sides of his personality," she laughs. She also had a special affection for Frank Oz's blue monster character, Grover. "I always liked Grover; he's shy, retiring, doesn't have any confidence. I did one scene I'll never forget with him about self-esteem. The *Sesame Street* photographer took a beautiful picture, and I turned it into a poster that we used to use for the Cradleboard Teaching Project about self-esteem," she remembers. "I had to say, 'Everybody needs self-esteem. You too, Grover.' Like, it's okay to feel good about yourself and to be happy. A lot of people don't learn that it's okay to be happy. As in, 'If you're happy, you're being selfish!' We need to break that old-fashioned cycle of negativity. It's obsolete and destructive."

Sainte-Marie also taught the Count how to count in Cree, and Wolfchild taught him how to count in Dakota. "Most Americans don't realize that American Indians have language and have numbers. 'Pre-Columbian'—they think cavemen," she says. "They don't think about astronomy and cranial surgery and mathematics and families and agriculture and things like that. I tried to give them what they could not have found on their own. I was trying to fill in that blank that they could not themselves bring into the lives of children; simple stuff like our existence. We're considered the vanishing Americans, like we're a myth, a Halloween costume, instead of a reality. *Sesame Street* provided just the loveliest way to do the same thing that I had been doing through songwriting: bring things to light that people might not be able to find on their own."

Sainte-Marie only met the now-deceased Muppets creator Jim Henson once. "He was really nice, but I never got to spend any real time with him," Sainte-Marie remembers. "[I met him] at the Golden Globes [a few years after she appeared on *Sesame Street*] when I was nominated for 'Up Where We Belong,' and Jim was wearing a green suit (of course). I wish I could have known him. I think he was a very important artist. Also Kermit Love [his real name, but not Kermit the Frog's namesake, it was just a wild coincidence], who actually created the Big Bird costume, helped develop the character and took care of the costume and all that. It's hard to tell who Big Bird is: Is it Kermit or is it Caroll? One person's inside it, and the other is taking care of the outer Big Bird. Kermit was very close with Jim, and they did a lot together, building the Muppets."

Sainte-Marie's stint on the show came to an end in 1981 when the Reagan administration made budget cuts that hit PBS and put an end to travel and rural filming, but the impact of the experience continued to help shape the direction of her life. "*Sesame Street* really was on the side of children," she says. "No B.S. about it; they really meant it. I can't think of any group in show business for whom I have more respect."

CHAPTER 12

UP WHERE
WE BELONG

N 1978, THE American Indian Movement made news again when they led a spiritual journey across the country that became known as the Longest Walk.[41] The walk aimed to support Indigenous sovereignty and to bring awareness to proposed legislation that would have, among other things, nullified land treaties and limited water rights. It began with a ceremony on Alcatraz Island on February 11, 1978. Thousands of people participated, representing many nations and tribes, including Indigenous people from Canada and throughout the world and non-Indigenous allies. Led by elders, the group reached Washington, D.C., on July 15, 1979.

Sainte-Marie thinks a lot about the Indigenous individuals who worked out of the spotlight on that event. "The bigger movement itself was glorious," Sainte-Marie says. "It brings tears to my eyes when I think of the unappreciated work that so many people did in those days. A lot of the real power and common sense and drive came from the women, who were kept tangential or who were—it was just their way—to remain in the background."

Sainte-Marie was one of the few women in the spotlight as one of the headliners at the Longest Walk benefit concert, and her connection to this event was personal: Sheldon Wolfchild and his brother Ernie Peters (also known as Ernie Longwalker) were instrumental in creating the Longest Walk with AIM. And among the participants were her two teenage nieces from Saskatchewan, Marlyn Obey (who is now deceased) and Debra Piapot. The walk was a revelation for Piapot. "We didn't really know at that time what was going on in terms of Indian issues," she says. "We weren't paying attention; we were young teenagers in Regina with a very closed view of the world. I remember thinking and believing some of the negative messages that I got bombarded with at school and by other kids, teachers, and neighbors."

There's a great photo from the benefit of Sainte-Marie seated at a piano next to Muhammad Ali, and surrounded by Floyd Red Crow Westerman, Harold Smith, Stevie Wonder, Marlon Brando, actor Max Gail, Dick Gregory, Richie Havens, and David Amram. Piapot remembers the massive event in Washington, D.C., and the huge support from the African-American community as well as from white supporters and even several Buddhist nuns and monks. More importantly, the Longest Walk resulted in real change when in 1979, the U.S. agreed to honor the treaties and vote against the proposed legislation.

"Just to be sixteen and in the thick of it—my whole world expanded," Piapot says. "It was the first time I understood that there were Indigenous peoples across the world. There were Sami people from Scandinavia, Aboriginal people from Australia, the Maori people from New Zealand. It was a really informative, exciting time, and it was all because of Buffy. Everything was around her voice and her vision and her songs, and that unique ability to bring everyone together."

But in the following year, Sainte-Marie's personal life began to fall apart. Her relationship with Sheldon Wolfchild was strained, and like any breakup, there were a few factors that contributed to the dissolution of their marriage. Where to live was one disagreement. Sainte-Marie's heart has belonged to Hawai'i since the 1960s, but Wolfchild had been in the Vietnam War and the similarities to Hawai'i were overwhelming. "It reminded him a lot of Vietnam, and he never was comfortable here. That's a lot to overcome. He had a love for Minnesota, where he came from, but I didn't want to live on the mainland," Sainte-Marie says. Having a child also occupied a lot of their time, and like many new parents, they found it challenging. There was no chance to nap or have a bath or do any of the things that non-parents took for granted. Prioritizing Cody was easy for her, but multitasking work, travel, motherhood, and marriage wasn't just hard—it became impossible. By the time Cody was about four, Sainte-Marie was a single parent.

"When I was traveling, that was very hard on everybody, but I wasn't about to give it up completely," Sainte-Marie says. "In part it had to do with being the one with an obviously greater income. But I have to admit that it was also who I am and what I did and how I contributed to trying to make good change in the world, and I wasn't about to turn into a regular stay-at-home wife and mother instead of being who I am. I've always been clear about being a breadwinner in my life. Nobody has ever supported me. If the marriage is not going to work, there comes a point where a parent has to say, 'You know what? I think this is going to be easier unmarried than it is married.'"

The pair officially divorced in 1981. "It's not always for the kinds of dramatic things you see on soap operas—somebody cheated or they hate each other now. No, if it's not working, you have to figure out how to distribute your attention between your marriage and your parenthood. And I don't know if anybody gets it right. Anybody in show business, anyway."

Sainte-Marie says the balancing act between motherhood and her artistic life was also tricky. She remembers how just twelve weeks after giving birth, she was already back on the road, Cody in tow. In Rapid City, South Dakota, she performed a solo concert at the local prison with Cody asleep in her open, velvet-lined guitar case, and Wolfchild by his side. After a series of interviews, Sainte-Marie eventually found a nanny to accompany Cody on the road with her. Sometimes, she'd go out on tour alone for a week and leave Cody at home with the nanny, whom he called Nana.

"It always felt like skating on thin ice to be away from Cody," Sainte-Marie says. "But he loved Nana and she loved him, too, and was very good to him, and he had playmates among Nana's grandchildren. Although both Nana and Cody seemed fine with my travels, I didn't like being away, but concerts were my only real income. Hawai'i's a great place to hide from show business, but there's really not much of a music scene where musicians can work steadily, mostly just hotels and bars playing for tourists. Solo concerts, without added airfares, was how I supported us."

The same year her divorce from Wolfchild was finalized, Jack Nitzsche came back into Sainte-Marie's life. They hadn't seen each other since he'd finished producing her 1971 album, *She Used to Wanna Be a Ballerina*, an experience that she called "awful." His moods were mercurial and unpredictable, and in hindsight, it's easy to see that there was also something predatory about his focused pursuit of Sainte-Marie and how that hinted at darker elements of his personality. "I hadn't realized at the beginning of recording *Ballerina* how crazy Jack was," Sainte-Marie says. "And I don't mean fun crazy."

After Sainte-Marie and Wolfchild had split up, Nitzsche called her to say he was coming to Hawai'i. Could he see her? "He said he needed a melody for a movie that he was working on, *An Officer and a Gentleman*," Sainte-Marie recalls. "He couldn't come up with a melody, and he thought maybe if he came and saw me, we could come up with the melody together, or maybe I had something or seeing me after all these years would spark an idea. Jack used to say that I saved his career because I had that melody for *An Officer and a Gentleman*. It certainly didn't save my career, but he thought it saved his."

Nitzsche painted himself as a reformed drug user. He told Sainte-Marie that he'd fallen into addiction since they'd last seen each other ten years before, but that he had pulled himself out of it. He was clean, and he felt healthy now. "He claimed that he had failed [raising] his own son, and he was so happy for me and Cody that he wanted a second chance to be a father and to give his own son a brother," she says. "During that [first] visit, he carried Cody around on his shoulders and played silly with him, and made lots of fun. He was always in a good mood. I didn't question why he was in a good mood; he just seemed like a normal person in a good mood to me."

Despite personal hardship, he'd flourished professionally since the last time they'd seen each other, moving away from producing rock giants like the Rolling Stones and Neil Young and into film scoring and composing. He earned his first Oscar nomination in 1975 for the music from *One Flew Over the Cuckoo's Nest*, and now he wanted Sainte-Marie to help him with *An Officer and a Gentleman*. But he wasn't just looking to work together. A few months after their re-acquaintance, the two were on the phone and Nitzsche declared that he still had feelings for her. He wanted a chance to get it right and be a father to both his own son and Cody. She responded somewhat neutrally, and he was devastated.

"He said something like, 'Oh, my heart. I was just walking up and down Beverly Hills looking at engagement rings.' And I said, 'Oh, my god.' I mean, what can you say to somebody when they say that? It wasn't like a proposal, but he was coming on like, 'Now I'm wounded.' I decided to give him a chance because I didn't want to wound him. Typical woman, eh?" There's a shade of incredulity in her laughter as if she still can't believe she said yes. "But this was not just a con man, and this wasn't just an act. He really did want a good life. I believe he genuinely did think that if he could be a father to Cody—I mean, he and I had been friends and gotten along, and we do have some things in common. We're both real smart in an artistic way and quite naïve in business ways. We both liked to talk about spiritual things. He really did want a good life, but he just couldn't maintain it."

Nitzsche and Sainte-Marie married in 1982, but she has scant recollections of the wedding itself. Electronic music pioneer and composer Jill Fraser, with whom she had recorded the music for the film *Spirit of the Wind*, stood up for her at the ceremony as a witness, and writer and director John Byrum stood up for the groom. Nitzsche knew the minister, and she's pretty sure the ceremony took place at his house. "I wore a white Mexican gauze dress with ruffles that my girlfriend Alicia had given me years before, kind of a soft flamenco thing," she says. "Cody was there with his nanny, and Jack was mad at me forever because I looked at Cody [during the ceremony]; I was trying to include him. Anyway, I don't even remember doing that, but Jack never really forgave me. Said I'd married Cody instead of him."

It didn't get much better after the wedding day. It turned out that Nitzsche wasn't clean—he was still using drugs and drinking, too. He went on a methadone program right after they were married, but that meant that he couldn't travel. And because Hawai'i didn't have a methadone clinic at the time, Sainte-Marie felt like she had no choice but to live in L.A. "I didn't realize when I married him that I was going to give up my home in

Hawai'i," Sainte-Marie says. "That I would no longer have a car or my clothes and all my personal girl junk, all my makeup and stuff, all my Indian stuff. I didn't have anything of my own life."

Nitzsche's mood swings worsened, and he could be controlling and cruel even when he was clean. "He didn't believe in other people's happiness if he was in those black moods," she says. Nitzsche told her that he had "mental issues" that dated back to his childhood. He'd grown up in the 1940s as the child of German immigrants and had been made to feel like an outcast during and even after World War II. Nitzsche was easily influenced by men he admired or perceived to be powerful. "Jack's personality reflected an awful lot of Phil Spector's behavior," Sainte-Marie says. "All of that kind of nasty, smarmy, misogynistic stuff." Nitzsche became obsessive and possessive of Sainte-Marie, demanding all of her time and energy. "My career, once we had married, was over for that time period. It wasn't like I could accept offers of work unless it came through Jack. He would just freak at the mention. I'd do a concert now and then, but big offers for myself were out of the question."

Sainte-Marie and Nitzsche's creative collaboration did have one major payoff. Together (along with Will Jennings, who penned the lyrics) they wrote "Up Where We Belong," the theme song for *An Officer and a Gentleman*, which won an Academy Award in 1983. Sainte-Marie became the only Indigenous person and the first folk singer to win an Academy Award, and although it should have been a catalyst for publicity and high-profile songwriting gigs and collaborations, there was little opportunity to leverage the honor.

Nitzsche began to push Sainte-Marie into the background. She became his copyist, supporting his career rather than advancing her own. Sainte-Marie says that he would wait until the last minute to write something for a movie score, and when suddenly he knew what it was going to be, he had to act fast and write it down immediately. Sainte-Marie would sit there with her pen and her ruler—this was before computers—and set up music charts for him, numbering all the bars and putting in the cue numbers. "My mom asked me one time, she said, 'How did that happen? Jack used to be an employee of yours.' He was never an employee of mine; he was an independent contractor and very talented. But my mom thought that he was kind of an employee of mine, and suddenly he was 'The Boss' and pushing me around. How did that happen? How come he got to abuse me?"

Nitzsche did what many abusive, controlling men do to women and isolated Sainte-Marie from her friends. Kayle Higinbotham, Sainte-Marie's best friend, remembers that when she was around Nitzsche, her skin would crawl. "I didn't know what it was or what it was from, but I had a very physical reaction to him and fear of him," Higinbotham says.

"None of the people who were around Jack at that time would see me privately," Sainte-Marie says. "It's not as though I ever got to have a real conversation with, like, Leslie Morris, [who] was one of our mutual friends... It's not as though Leslie and I could ever be left alone in the room to talk together. None of Jack's other friends knew what was going on in our marriage. I had no confidants at all. I was really isolated. It was hard."

When Nitzsche loved an artist, it was hero worship, Sainte-Marie says, but if he hated them, he truly loathed them. "He was either putting you up on a pedestal or he was pulling you down," she laughs. "Jack used to say, 'Jesus Christ, they ought to have closed the border after Neil Young came in.' He hated Joni Mitchell. 'Oh please, don't ever bring up Joni Mitchell because I just can't stand to hear it,' he'd say. He didn't like Leonard [Cohen] either. I've never met another person in the world or [even] in fiction who could tear someone apart the way Jack could. It's as though he was proud of it. It was really something."

Sainte-Marie describes Nitzsche as a "cyclical alcoholic." If you imagine a clock, this was his pattern: At noon he was fine, but by ten after the hour, he would get uncomfortable and start giving her the side eye, finding fault with little things and complaining. By 12:30, he'd be boiling. "If he was driving, you started to worry that you were going to have an accident. And by the time he pulled up to the restaurant, well, the poor valet would just get an earful. Jack could be so cruel to strangers, to waiters and waitresses, anybody who happened to be in his way when that nightmare was coming on. Dinner out almost became impossible; it was so embarrassing. And it wasn't as if he was making a scene to be seen and heard; it was coming from inside him, in an awful rage. [At the restaurant], it wasn't directed at me, at first, but an hour later, he tried to push me out of a moving car."

The threatening behavior continued to escalate, but Sainte-Marie believed that Nitzsche was suffering too. "Jack had no control over his mood disorders. During the time I was married to him, three different psychiatrists talked about it in terms of being bipolar, borderline personality, narcissism, and possibly schizophrenia. Even without alcohol for a month, he'd suddenly get a squirt of brain chemicals and turn mean."

Sainte-Marie says that he also manipulated her to get what he wanted. "He was not beyond playing me—as many men do with family members they perceive as weaker. It's probably what they got away with, with their moms, only their moms saw through them and thought, 'He'll grow out of it.' Guess what, moms? They don't grow out of it. They just put it on their partners!"

"I thought I was strong enough to be his support person," she continues. "One of the hardest things for me was that he changed psychiatrists three times during our marriage, and each time, in order for Jack to be accepted as a patient, I was required to agree to enlist as a support person for at least eighteen months... I 're-enlisted' twice, totally against my better judgment. In those circumstances, I thought that I probably could do it. I am strong and I've been strong with other people too, when they were in dire straits. But Jack took the cake."

What Sainte-Marie liked about Nitzsche was his introspection and his intelligence. He could be very funny, and he made her laugh a lot. Even in the middle of being absolutely awful, he'd think of something funny and he'd laugh, too. His sense of humor was self-deprecating, like that of the best comedians, she says. And when he wasn't suffering, their conversations were wonderful. He was also a brilliantly talented musician, though one of the key differences in their musicality intrigued Sainte-Marie.

"Jack was incredibly gifted, but he couldn't improvise," Sainte-Marie says. "I can sit down at any piano in the world and start playing anything, stuff nobody's ever heard before, including me. Jack couldn't do that. On the other hand, he could sit down at a piano with a blank piece of music paper in front of him and start writing things down and then play them! He could write these beautiful melodies and incredible orchestrations. There were other wonderful movie composers, but Jack's music was nothing like theirs—it's unique. Since Jack came on the scene, a lot of people tried to copy him and learn what they could about his orchestration. He was a true movie composer; he never used a ghost[writer], which is what most busy composers do."

He was self-aware enough to know that he was "difficult," but usually it was after-the-fact, once the outburst had passed.

Nitzsche suffered some consequences for his outbursts—in a drunken 1974 interview, after he and Sainte-Marie had lost track of each other, he complained at length about Neil Young, and their friendship never recovered—but mostly he got away with a lot of bad behavior. People still wanted to work with him, and even though he was considered among the best in the business at the time, he was sick with self-loathing. "His inferiority complex was probably the most outstanding part of his personality, I think, to anyone who knew him. He was not the cutest pup in the litter, and he hated how he looked. The best that he could do was to try to copy Phil Spector, who he kind of resembled in certain ways. You would think they were cousins. He also looked a little bit like Roman Polanski, only Roman had kind of a Hollywood polish to him and that European accent."

When Sainte-Marie married Nitzsche, she didn't know that just a few years earlier, he'd violently assaulted his ex-girlfriend, actress Carrie Snodgress. The two became involved in 1974 after she and Neil Young broke up. Snodgress and Nitzsche eventually split up too, and in 1979, Nitzsche broke into her home and badly beat her, threatened to kill her, and allegedly raped her with his gun. The rape by instrumentation charge was later dropped, and he pled guilty to threatening her and was sentenced to three years' probation.[42]

"Poor Carrie Snodgress. I've never spoken to her, but Jesus," Sainte-Marie says. "He hated actresses so much, 'They lie for a living,' Jack would say. He insisted they were no good. He would turn his own inferiority complex and self-deprecation against other people. He also felt marginalized, I believe, and told me at length about his abusive mother." But none of it excused Nitzsche's threatening behavior and the escalating violence, which he backed up with props. "A couple of times he threw a big ring of keys into a sock and started pounding it into his fist to threaten me. He narrowed his eyes and said, 'Now what're you gonna do, ya pig?'"

Sainte-Marie slipped into old patterns of deference, making herself small in order to survive. "Any woman who has lived with a bully or an alcoholic probably knows what it's like," she says. "I 'crawled under' his dominance again and again, hoping to raise his self-esteem as self-defense. By not arguing and trying to avoid making it worse, I would make myself a smaller target by diminishing myself. 'I know I'm nothing, and of course you're God,' that kind of thing."

She didn't know that this was a common survival reaction that abused women used until years later, when she read Louann Brizendine's book, *The Female Brain*.[43] In response to intimidation, Sainte-Marie adopted typical female survival techniques that Brizendine describes in her book: stay small, hide, monitor his aggression, make mental notes of the exits, avoid escalation, communicate, and do not confront his confrontation because you cannot win in a fist fight. "I should be very clear that Jack never hit me," Sainte-Marie says. "But Jack, in his threatening ways and intimidation, in his belittling and verbal assaults, could really reduce you to something that you weren't. And you'd better convince him that you believe you are nothing, or it continues. It continued until he was convinced that I was broken. I was conquered. I was dead. Just make it stop."

Dr. Brizendine claims that when a woman finds herself in the position of being in a losing fight with a man, especially a man who weighs fifty pounds more than she does and is in the "gorilla stance" men take when they're angry, the female brain can be on the edge of seizure. "Until I read her book, I didn't realize that was that feeling that I was having," Sainte-Marie says. "I would go into the same mental state that I did when I was a child and my brother would beat me up. There's a feeling where you give up, and you know they're going to do their worst. With Jack, I would stay calm in my behavior, although I was terrified. I'd be subconsciously checking for the exits and strategizing how to protect my son. And in spite of all that tension, I continued to feel compassion for him. I could empathize. I knew that he was in trouble, even more than me. I continued to feel sorry for him and to respect his talents and skills while hiding my own, but it was hard on me.

"I remember being relieved every time [that he didn't hit me], and making mental notes that next time could be worse," she says. "He also liked guns. But most of all, he liked to threaten. Looking back on it now, I can see that he liked to threaten."

Sainte-Marie managed to work on a couple of film projects of her own, which Nitzsche approved, during their seven-year relationship. She composed the score for a 1986 docudrama titled *Stripper* about a group of professional strippers on their way to Las Vegas for a contest. Sainte-Marie got to know some of the dancers during the filming and found them fascinating. She also scored *Harold of Orange*, a short film starring her friend, comedian Charlie Hill, and wrote its theme song, "Trickster." But she was operating in Nitzsche's shadow. He not only minimized her contributions to his work, sometimes he even took the credit.

"There's a lot of music in movies that nobody realizes I wrote during the time that I was married to Jack because Jack sometimes would forget to tell people," Sainte-Marie says with a laugh. "For the longest time, he couldn't tell Taylor Hackford [the director of *An Officer and a Gentleman*] that I had written the melody for 'Up Where We Belong.' He didn't know how to tell him. Jack was supposed to write it himself... Taylor wasn't very happy about finding out that I had actually written it because he thought Jack had. Taylor was always very nice and polite to me, but I think he was just concerned that Jack hadn't told him. There wasn't any kind of kerfuffle about me writing it, but about the way it went down."

Sainte-Marie sang or played or wrote for a number of films that Nitzsche worked on. Sometimes she'd be credited, sometimes not, and she wasn't usually paid. "One time, I think it was for *The Razor's Edge*, a Bill Murray movie, Jack wrote a beautiful, beautiful melody for it, just a fantastic melody, which he always thought was a bit too grand for the movie itself. Jack was a very harsh self critic. He didn't hold back. He would criticize himself, and if he thought he'd made a mistake, he was very honest about it. Anyway, I had gone with Jack to London when he was recording the music. I sang on some of the movie cues, but instead of having a contract and earning a thousand bucks for having sung something, when I was on the way out, the guy in charge handed me fifty quid [pounds] like I was a hooker. It was so ugly."

Sainte-Marie was still writing her own songs in secret and recording her private thoughts in her diaries—but then Nitzsche read her diaries. Once he found something she'd written about an old boyfriend who'd died years before, and he went into a rage. But even all of his erratic, threatening behavior couldn't prepare her for what Nitzsche would do one night towards the end of their marriage. "I think I probably slept with one eye open all the time I was married to Jack," Sainte-Marie says. "One time, when I was asleep, he did assault me but not by hitting me: he shot me up. He skin-popped me with heroin while I was asleep."

That violation finally pushed Sainte-Marie over the edge. "I had never chosen to be involved with opiates—I mean, I had been addicted [to prescription opiates] in the 1960s—you know the 'Cod'ine' story—so my body recognized it. That was the only time I had been involved with opiates, having been given codeine against my will by a doctor. I hated opiates after that experience, but Jack just thought they were so wonderful that, when I was asleep, he skin-popped me and woke me up. I hated it. It gave me the creeps. The whole world looked like horror. He was dangerous, there was no doubt about it."

Sainte-Marie started to formulate a plan. She was afraid for herself, but she also became afraid that Nitzsche would hurt her son. "Jack would say terrible things about my little boy. If Cody would make a noise down the hall in his room or cry Jack would go into one of his horrible black moods and say, 'Go. Go to your baby Jesus, your goddamned baby Jesus in there.' It became really frightening."

She set up her escape with the help of Kayle Higinbotham. "I had packed carry-ons and hid them in Cody's little closet. At four in the morning, I got up, picked up the suitcases, put them by the door, lifted up my son, walked out the door, got in [Kayle's] car [and] went to the airport. Cody said, 'Where we going, Mom?' I said, 'We're going home, Cody.'"

After returning to Hawai'i, Sainte-Marie never went back to Nitzsche's, not even to pick up her belongings. Nitzsche came to Hawai'i once after she fled, but she never allowed it again. "I never wanted to be in the same room [with him] again, 'cause it was over. It was just done. I wanted nothing to do with Jack." She didn't care whether he paid back the $25,000 she'd given him in the first week of their marriage so he wouldn't lose his house in Studio City, California, and she had no interest in alimony. "I just wanted my life back, and I wanted to be Buffy again. I didn't even bother getting a lawyer. I didn't want to talk to him on the phone. He'd say, 'Come on, c'mon, you don't mean it.' He used every trick in the book. He'd say, 'Well, are you going to divorce me?' and I'd say, 'I want nothing to do with you. I don't even want to see you for a divorce.' That's how much I didn't want to see him. So I said, 'If you want a divorce, you divorce me.' He was so worried I was going take his money. I had no interest in his precious money; all I wanted was never to have to look at him again. Eventually I got some papers in the mail, and I signed 'em and sent them back."

Even with the divorce papers signed, Nitzsche tried to get Sainte-Marie back, to control the situation and her. "Jack didn't give up. Until the year before he died [in 2000], he was still trying to get in touch with me. He would call me and try to convince me that I didn't know what I was doing. There was no arguing with Jack because he understood clearly that he hurt people, for which he would apologize sincerely. He really did. He did know that he'd often treated me very cruelly. I felt sorry for the neighbors who had to hear me cry all the time. He was a terrible, terrible bully and liked me to be frightened. He loved to threaten, but he knew how wrong that was. He was terribly apologetic every time that it happened. But he had no control over it, so he said. And I believe that he didn't, but it doesn't make any difference. I couldn't live with him." The situation was intolerable and no amount of apologies or explanations could make it worthwhile.

Sainte-Marie is glad she left when she did, but knows that some people won't understand why she stayed for seven years. In some ways, she's not even sure. Nitzsche's relentless bullying was part of it—the isolation and the threats and the violence of his language and his intimidation all factored in—but so was her generous heart and compassion for his suffering. She thought she was doing something important and valuable in staying with him, not abandoning him, and she believed in his creative genius.

"But was it worth it? No," Sainte-Marie says. "Sisters, it was not worth it. Please, don't go through it; it's not worth it. Your sacrifice or martyrdom to Bluebeard means nothing. God is not giving out points for women's service to bad men. You have a brain: use it. Find a safe way out, find support, make a plan, and escape. Survive. Don't put your beautiful heart under the thumb of some monster who thinks that your love can heal him. It can't. It's sad, but it can't."

Buffy Sainte-Marie on happiness

I'm not a recluse just to hide from the spotlight. I mean, there's some of that. I get tired of airplanes, working, lights, camera, action, concerts, long drives. But for the most part, it's the opposite. I live in the country very privately because it's so wonderful; not because the alternative is so horrible. I like living with animals. That's where my happiness is. Yesterday I had my nose to my kitty, we were lying down, having a nap together. And she was looking at me and I was looking at her and we were cuddling. I was thinking, *this is heaven, this really is where I live*. One of my goats died last month, she was old, and I was there with her day after day as she was getting ready to die. I didn't know if we were going to be able to save her or not. But just being with an animal throughout their lives, you love them. They become your friends. It's a different kind of beauty.

CHAPTER 13

THE PRIESTS OF THE GOLDEN BULL

SAINTE-MARIE'S "REAL" LIFE was essentially on pause while she was married to Nitzsche. When she returned to Hawai'i in 1989, she wasn't so much starting over as reclaiming and reunifying what was hers. "I had my son, and I could still draw and paint," Sainte-Marie says. "I still had music and words in my head. I didn't realize that I would be giving up so much of my identity when I married Jack, and I was really, really glad to get [it] back."

She may not have written or recorded much music in the eighties, but throughout the decade she continued to experiment with cutting-edge technology. In 1984, for example, she was one of the first people to purchase a Macintosh computer, and she used it to create digital art. "I still have my original 128k machine. MacPaint and MacWrite saved my sanity while I was married to Jack," Sainte-Marie remembers. "To have had that kind of fun toy, maximizing and recording the stuff I already loved to do, was a real joy."

In Hawai'i, she continued to explore various techniques and disciplines and computer programs, utilizing emerging tech for photography, painting, pointillism, and more. "I always say I have both a digital studio and a wet studio," Sainte-Marie says. "I wasn't the kid in class who could draw things. I was never very good at drawing—many painters aren't. I've always loved to splash around with colors and paints and paste and put things together like songs, I have that kind of mind." The art Sainte-Marie began to create in those years has since appeared in a variety of exhibits around the world, including the Glenbow Museum and the McKenzie Gallery in Canada, and several pieces are permanently housed in the Institute of American Indian Arts Museum, the Tucson Museum of Art, and other galleries throughout North America.

"If I look at a blank piece of paper, I'll see stuff," she says. "Or if I look out the window of an airplane, I'll start to rearrange and color things. I think it's just some kind of mental masturbation," she jokes. It's not that she has a low tolerance for boredom; rather, in the space of absence, Sainte-Marie comes alive. "When there's nothing to do, that bothers some people. But I start doing artsy things. I'll play with words or I'll play with music or I'll start rearranging things in my mind. Re-coloring things, turning things upside down and inside out. Instead of getting bored, I have fun."

It's also, in essence, the way she's approached music throughout her life, and new innovations in computer technology have signaled creative possibilities. It wasn't a stretch to make and record music using a computer since she'd already experimented with electronic music instruments like the Synclavier and Fairlight, which are combination synthesizer/digital sampler/music workstation units. To Sainte-Marie, it looked like IBM and Microsoft were designed for keeping secrets, making war, and doing taxes, but that with Apple, it was different. She liked its origin story—invented by two hippies in a garage—and felt that finally there was a computer for the rest of us. "I wasn't thinking of war and taxes at all, not even business," she says. "I saw incredible potential. Musicians, artists, grandparents,

Indigenous people, everybody—we weren't trying to keep any secrets. No! We were trying to record our artistry and get the news out. Early on, it involved some programming and it was hard, but the results were thrilling. Once the Macintosh came along, I was just shoutin' it from the rooftops! Anybody can use this!"

When Sainte-Marie returned home to Hawai'i after leaving Nitzsche, she resumed making demos of songs in her home studio, not sure if she actually wanted to make another record. By the time her son was a teenager, she had some freedom to get back into the studio. But she had also been out of the recording business since 1976. She'd thought that this was mainly by choice, but—unbeknownst to her—it had also been influenced by the actions of two different presidential administrations.

Sainte-Marie knew that her activism may have cost her career in some ways, but she believed it was a consequence of seeking justice. Many other Indigenous activists and friends, after all, had paid a price far worse. But in the late 1980s, a bombshell of a story dropped into Sainte-Marie's lap. She was being interviewed on radio when the interviewer apologized for having participated in a campaign to suppress her music in the sixties and seventies, when Presidents Lyndon Johnson and Richard Nixon were in power. Sainte-Marie was floored.

"[The interviewer] had a letter on White House stationery commending him for suppressing this music which 'deserved to be suppressed,'" Sainte-Marie said.[44] Not only was she blacklisted, meaning her music wasn't played on the radio and often shipments of her records would just vanish, she was also monitored by both the FBI and the CIA. Her work with the American Indian Movement and her pacifist condemnation of Vietnam were also factors in the blacklist. "I got so lucky so young, I guess that I was not being self-protective," she says. "I didn't know enough. I'm just not defensive. I think that's why I was so surprised when my lawyer suggested I might have FBI files." Sainte-Marie laughs. "What? Me?!" Sainte-Marie says the FBI had a thirty-one-page file on her, and in 1999, ex-CIA agent Charles Schlund confirmed the governmental blacklists of rock music.[45, 46]

She acknowledges the damage being "put out of business" did to her career but she brings another perspective to it now. "People say, 'Oh, poor Buffy, she got blacklisted, not so lucky.'" She laughs. "Many, many people that I know look at show business as the pinnacle of life on Earth. They really do believe that. For me, it's kind of the frosting on the cake of something else entirely. And, I should qualify this: I don't think I'm above money. It's not that. I just never really had that big shot at making a corporate-level fortune so I haven't had to worry about it as much either. It's a lot to take care of."

Although she'd been blacklisted by her own government, Sainte-Marie had also unknowingly ensured that the bastards wouldn't keep her down. She'd survived the blacklisting and an abusive marriage and still managed to cultivate exactly the kind of life she'd always wanted: she had a little farm in the middle of nowhere in Hawai'i, surrounded by animals that she coaxed into the world and whose lives she made more peaceful when it was time for them to go. "Fame and fortune are great," she jokes, "but have you delivered a baby goat?"

Discovering the truth about the blacklist did raise one big question about making another record: Was it even worth it to try again? But as an activist, how could she not? She'd never shied away from the truth, and the world had welcomed her perspective before. Being silenced by the government was just further proof of the real power of protest music. She'd poured more than a decade into slowly writing "Bury My Heart at

Wounded Knee," and the blacklisting only strengthened her resolve that the song needed to be out in the world. This was also the head space in which Sainte-Marie wrote one of her most damning protest songs yet.

"The Priests of the Golden Bull" is viciously astute, a bold evisceration of profiteering and racketeering in the energy sector. It's almost a spoken-word song, and every sentence weighs heavily in the listener's mind. It demands and rewards repeat plays as she offers up Colonization & Racketeering 101 in less than four minutes. "It's delicate confronting these priests of the golden bull/They preach from the pulpit of the bottom line," she sing-speaks. "Third worlders see it first/The dynamite, the dozers, the cancer and the acid rain/The corporate caterpillars come into our backyards/And turn the world to pocket change." A record was taking shape, but it was 1990, fourteen years since her last album, *Sweet America*, and it wasn't just the music business that had changed; music itself had changed, as had the culture. Her last few records had, for the most part, flopped and, perhaps because of the blacklist, never even been heard by her fan base. Would there even be an audience excited about her return?

Sainte-Marie's lawyer, Abe Somer, was. He was the same man who'd helped her free herself from the Vanguard contract, and he was also a long-time fan of her music. He shared her new songs with his friends Nigel Grainge and Chris Hill at Ensign Records in England, and they asked if she'd be willing to make a record. Sainte-Marie eventually said yes, but she had a stipulation: she wanted to make the record mostly digitally—remotely, from Hawai'i. She didn't want to live in London since she was still raising her son, and besides, she had recording equipment at her house. She expected pushback, but she was used to making people—artists, producers, activists—comfortable with computers. "By the 1990s, I already had twenty years' experience with my own hands-on electronic music, and they didn't even know what it was. Even then, I still had Windows people tell me that Apple would be out of business in six months. Being a woman in electronic music when other people were stuck in the old genres was—well, you get a lot of misogyny and you get a lot of just plain cockblocking and attitude."

But to Sainte-Marie's surprise, Ensign Records thought it was a great idea and connected her with producer Chris Birkett. Birkett had just co-produced for Ensign one of the biggest records of 1990, Sinéad O'Connor's *I Do Not Want What I Haven't Got*, featuring her chart-topping cover of Prince's "Nothing Compares 2 U."

"Nigel phoned me one day and said, 'Guess what? I just signed a legend—Buffy Sainte-Marie!'" Chris Birkett remembers. "And I said, 'Who's that?'" The English musician and producer grew up on Led Zeppelin, Deep Purple, Yes, and Genesis. "I was not familiar with a legendary folk singer from Canada," he admits. Grainge named tunes like "Up Where We Belong" and "Until It's Time for You to Go," and Birkett realized that he, like many people, knew the songs, but not the woman behind them. Grainge positioned the project as Sainte-Marie's comeback album, and Birkett was intrigued. "I thought she was a very smart, compassionate, intelligent woman, and very aware," he says. "We got on really well, so we decided to give it a go."

Ultimately it was technology that bonded Sainte-Marie and Birkett. "What closed the deal for me and Chris [working together] was that Chris, too, was using CompuServe, one of the very early platforms for sending files," Sainte-Marie remembers. "The word 'internet' was not in common use—nobody knew what it was. Nobody knew what 'online' meant. It was 1990."

"Buffy's friend Roger Jacobs was kind of a tech genius and he organized a thing through CompuServe," Birkett says. "In those days, it was really low bandwidth; you could send about a mega-byte at a time, so he fixed Buffy up with a system that would enable her to transfer her finished MIDI [musical instrument digital interface] files." The MIDI files were low bandwidth because they weren't audio—they were digital information about everything from pitch and tone to notation and velocity, and they could link multiple devices.

"Between Buffy and Roger, they sent me the keyboard parts for all the new songs," Birkett says. "I had a tech engineer working with me, and he was really much smarter than me as far as tech stuff goes. But all I had to do was mirror Buffy's keyboard setup and then dump the information into those modules. And the sound that she was playing in Hawai'i arrived in my studio in London instantaneously. It was really cool."

Coincidence and Likely Stories was released in 1992, and it claimed the honor of being the first record to be made over the internet. It was also the first record in her career on which Sainte-Marie took a co-producer credit. She'd planned to produce it herself, but Ensign wanted Birkett involved, so they acted as co-producers. "And that's the way it's been ever since," Sainte-Marie says. "I know what I do. I know what I bring to the table. Same with Chris." Wikipedia indicates co-producer credits on some of the records she made with Norbert Putnam in the early 1970s, but Sainte-Marie says that he deserves sole credit. He set up the sessions and contributed musical ideas, both towards the records and through the musician friends whom he'd hired to play.

"With Chris it was different," she says. "In the first place, I don't have all those great musicians around like Norbert provided. All I got is me. I'm at home coming up with all of the musical ideas myself. When I was working with Norbert, I was writing the songs and a lot of the licks, I was writing the hook and all that, but the players Norbert hired were super musicians, much better than I was. But in working with Chris, I was doing most of the actual musicianship as well."

The songs on *Coincidence and Likely Stories* positioned Sainte-Marie on the other side of some of the massive, life-changing moments where she'd left off, at least publicly, in 1976. There was the joyous before and after of having a child; the activism at the heart of the American Indian Movement followed by the disturbing and tragic fall-out of Pine Ridge and the murder of her friend Annie Mae Aquash; and the discovery of the questionable roles of the FBI and the government in her career. As well, she'd shut the door behind her on two marriages, one of which had left her almost broken.

You can hear her contending with all of these things in some capacity, directly or indirectly, throughout *Coincidence and Likely Stories*. The tracklist includes "Bury My Heart at Wounded Knee," which she had begun writing in 1976, and the bluesy "Bad End," which teems with danger. Her vocal performance is languid and dark, and the tension is rooted in a defeated kind of exhaustion that stems from surviving an abusive relationship. Whether the words reflect her experiences or not—"Now there's bruises in the bed at night/Needles in the drawer/There's blood all in the mirror/And there's strangers at the door/And I believe I'm coming to a bad end"—we feel the singer's fatalistic, heartbreaking ruin.

On "Emma Lee," the saxophone deepens the slinky, moonlit vibe, and as Sainte-Marie sings "Emma Lee she take the power in her own hands/She just take her time," there's something quietly defiant in her voice, and it's sexy but slightly menacing. That edge of darkness threads through most of the record, particularly "Disinformation." Musically, it's uncomfortable and disquieting—which is perfect, because we're supposed to be off-kilter, we're supposed to be on edge and suspicious, because we've just been informed and reminded that everything is a lie and we need to do better in sourcing our information, in challenging our biases.

"Starwalker," from Sainte-Marie's 1976 album *Sweet America*, is considered the first powwow-style rock song, and Sainte-Marie included a re-recorded version of the song on *Coincidence and Likely Stories*, amping up the production even further. Her digitized powwow and powwow-inspired songs and chants effectively smashed boundaries between traditional Indigenous music and pop and rock. "As I'd done in my early albums, and Annie Lennox did much later, I used many 'different voices,' although they all were my own," Sainte-Marie says. "It gave a richness to the powwow choruses that nobody else has matched." She even named the different "vocal characters" in order to keep them straight during the recording and editing processes. There were times, however, when even those closest to Sainte-Marie and her music didn't, couldn't, or wouldn't appreciate what she was doing. At the very least, they got out of her way.

"Nigel Grainge just couldn't figure out why I would want to put 'Starwalker' and 'Bury My Heart at Wounded Knee,' on the album," she remembers. "Chris Birkett and I talked him into it, but he just didn't get it. [She sings some of the powwow-style melody.] He didn't even hear it as a hip ethnic sound; he just didn't get 'Starwalker' at all."

In 1996, Sainte-Marie released a compilation album, *Up Where We Belong*, which opened with an all-out powwow pop song titled "Darling Don't Cry." The melody for the powwow part of the song was written by Edmund Bull from the well-known grassroots powwow group, the Red Bull Singers. Sainte-Marie thought she could turn the melody into a great pop song, so she approached Bull and asked his permission to include his melody in her new song.

Like so many of her creative decisions, Sainte-Marie put a lot of thought into the judicious presentation and use of both technology and powwow-style music. "How much powwow you use and how you use it makes a difference to how listeners of the time are going to perceive it," she says. "And if you're doing powwow with a chip on your shoulder, it's not going to sound the same. 'Darling Don't Cry' is a love song. I knew that if I just started singing pure powwow in the early 1990s, most listeners were going to think that they tuned into the Smithsonian folklore channel. They didn't recognize it as legitimate music; it was just that 'screaming thing that Indians do.' I had a producer actually tell me that! 'Yeah, it all sounds like screaming to me.' And he should have known better, too, somebody I loved and adored."

"Darling Don't Cry" provided the perfect entry point to powwow music for the average listener. The melody is a traditional song that Edmund Bull and his mother sang, and Sainte-Marie first introduces it in a soft, loving, romantic, seductive way. "I'm singing it the way I'd sing a pop love song," she explains. "I'm not singing it the way that we're singing at the end when Red Bull are singing with me. The odd elements—the elements that vanilla listeners have never heard before—I kind of get them ready for it in the beginning [of the song], and that's almost a metaphor for how my career has been. Music, whether it's pop music or movie scores or whatever, is destined for the ears of an audience much bigger than me and my friends. I know that it's going to reach new people. Some people may be miseducated, some may not be knowledgeable, some have not been exposed to Indigenous music before, but I thought that I could give it to them in a way that they would really like. It's as simple as that, but I was a little strategic about it, too."

Sainte-Marie's powwow songs pushed boundaries both sonically and technologically, but few at the time noticed her pioneering digital leap. "*Coincidence and Likely Stories* became the first album done over the internet," Sainte-Marie says. "Why didn't everybody stand up and say, 'Yay, Buffy did something new!'? Because nobody was in a position to even understand what the internet was. You couldn't hire a publicist to put out a story about how cool I was to be the first person to use the internet to deliver an album because nobody had a clue what that was. There are other things, too, but the timing is part of it."

Sainte-Marie's technical innovations had planted a seed in her mind that bloomed in the conversations she had in the internet's earliest "chat rooms." Online chats are entirely common today but were incredibly rare in the early nineties. "It was great fun to sit around and talk [online] with people who were just envisioning what we see today and what we've seen in the last twenty years. 'What's going to happen when artists get hold of it? What's going to happen when families can use it? What's going to happen when people can speak their minds to one another?'"

Inspired by this bold new world, Sainte-Marie began to imagine something extraordinary, something that would marry her passion for technology, her background in education, and her Indigenous activism.

CHAPTER 14

WE'RE ONLY GETTING STARTED

BEFORE THE INTERNET was big and the world got a little smaller—in a good way—children learned about the world primarily from the communities in which they were raised, from whatever they saw on television, and, at least in North America, from school curricula that were prescriptive, standardized, and entirely Eurocentric. History books presented a collection of pro-settler fairy tales as Indigenous people were killed and thousands of years of language, culture, customs, methodologies, practice, knowledge, and wisdom were suppressed, appropriated, and eradicated. And for many kids, school was boring and monotonous, no matter the subject, and the approach, for the most part, was formulaic and uninspired. The discrepancy between the education offered to privileged kids and disadvantaged ones was—and continues to be—criminal, particularly when it comes to the technology available.

That was the environment in 1996 in which Sainte-Marie would formally launch a radically new, Indigenous-focused education curriculum for children, built on a foundation of emerging technology, multimedia, and digital communication initiatives such as chat rooms and video conferencing. It would be a bridge between Indigenous and non-Indigenous children thousands of miles apart. It would be the future.

It's easy to see the Cradleboard Teaching Project as a gift to Sainte-Marie's childhood self and to countless generations of colonized Indigenous children who may have grown up without their culture, who were made to feel ashamed of it or were torn away from their families, traditions, and customs. It's also easy to see how the material could teach non-Indigenous students about Indigeneity and help de-stigmatize Indigenous people, raise awareness of Indigenous realities and cultural practices and customs, and hopefully eradicate systemic racism towards Indigenous people.

Sainte-Marie founded Cradleboard officially in 1996 as an initiative of her Nihewan Foundation, but she had begun developing the curriculum in the eighties after one of Cody's teachers, Adria Siebring, approached her. "She told me she was required by law to teach an Indian unit but that the material was all baloney." Sainte-Marie says Siebring was embarrassed by the curriculum. "And she wanted to know—could I help?" In many ways, Sainte-Marie's entire life had been moving towards this moment, or at the very least, it was certainly a relevant part of her circle. With her songs and television appearances, she'd already spent decades mapping historical and contemporary Indigenous experiences and contextualizing them for modern, mainstream audiences, Indigenous and non-Indigenous alike. "It really started in the 1960s when I was just a young singer with too much money, and I had all these aeroplane tickets," she told an interviewer for *The Guardian* in a 2009 interview. "They're the link to my whole existence because they've enabled me to travel. And if I have a concert in Stockholm, it means I can visit the Aboriginal people in the Arctic. Or if I'm playing in Melbourne or Sydney, I'll go out and visit the Aboriginal people in the bush. The Cradleboard Project is a result of my experiences living in two worlds—the fancy show business world of hotels and aeroplanes—and spending time with interesting people who have a lot to say. I'm a bridge—Cradleboard helps connect people in Indigenous communities with the rest of the world."[47]

Her background in teaching and philosophy, as well as philanthropy and Indigenous cultural practices, helped Sainte-Marie craft a hands-on, interactive, multimedia learning curriculum for public grade schools that was embedded in core studies and still happened to reflect Indigenous people. It wasn't an after school "extra" about beads and feathers, circular rubrics about north-south-east-west, or Boy Scout–type legends. It was core science, geography, math, music, and government studies as found in actual Indigenous communities both ancient and modern. She felt no need to argue with the ways schools taught or tear anything down. Instead, she felt that there were ways to incorporate Indigenous realities into what was already in place. These would enhance the way most core subjects were taught without subtracting from valuable teacher time. It would obviously improve the self-esteem of Indigenous kids, but it would also add value to what non-Indigenous kids had to study anyway, by the inclusion of culture. More than that, because it was multimedia and interactive, it would be more engaging for all students.

The curriculum she developed for Cody's school was an extension of what Saint-Marie had started in 1969 when she founded the Nihewan Foundation to help Indigenous youth get to college. Nihewan didn't just give Indigenous youth scholarships; it also helped them navigate the process of applying to school, finding other financial aid sources, and breaking down barriers to entry in academia. She's incredibly proud of the fact that two Nihewan scholarship recipients became Tribal College presidents, and it validated Sainte-Marie's belief in this type of giving.

Sainte-Marie found a place in which she could not only channel her teaching degree, but also put into practice what she had done for five years as a regular, part-time member of *Sesame Street*. If she could Indigenize the standard curriculum— both through providing factually correct information about contemporary Indigenous people as well as exploring science, technology, and other core subjects through Indigenous lenses— she could reach new kids all the time and open their eyes to other options. She folded the work into the scope of the Nihe- wan Foundation and began to build towards the Cradleboard Teaching Project. Sainte-Marie kept refining the material over the years, adding units to the existing public school curriculum.

Technology was essential to Sainte-Marie's emerging vision for Cradleboard. Thanks to her early adoption of Mac comput- ers and her lifelong fascination with useful cutting-edge tech, she helped pioneer interactive testing, twinning long-distance classes, and computer-based multi-sensory learning. Because of the relationship building that Sainte-Marie had done in online communities and early chat rooms, in 1991 she suggested con- necting her son's class in Hawai'i with a classroom on a reserve in Canada.

"We connected a class at Island School in Hawai'i with a class in Saskatchewan at the Star Blanket Reserve where my cousin was teaching, first through pen pals and faxes, and then online. Both classes had been studying our new lessons," Sainte-Marie recalls proudly. "But when the kids connected, it all came alive. The early online remote connectivity required tech help and patience, but it was worth it to see the kids interacting live with their far-away partners." Sainte-Marie wrote on Cradleboard's website: "The kids also exchanged letters and boxes of local goodies and information about their communities, their schools, and most of all themselves. They also had their first experience with email and Live Chat on a computer, which was very new at the time."

But what added unique value to the classroom partnering, she says, is that all the children in both communities were suddenly studying their old school subjects in a new way, "through Native American eyes. It was the combination of live partnering and new culture-based curriculum content that stunned the education community."

A 1998 feature in *Wired* magazine talked about the importance of Cradleboard's online space in creating connection between youth who might otherwise never meet. Sainte-Marie referred to that connection metaphorically as "the fire." "They ask anything they want: 'Do you live in tepees? Do you hunt buffalo? Do you still smoke pot in those peace pipes?'" Sainte-Marie told *Wired*. "By looking at the questions the kids are asking, we learn the scope of what needs to be done."[48] For core subjects, she developed the Cradleboard lessons for three distinct levels—elementary, middle, and high school. Building the lessons to be delivered on interactive CD-ROMs, she and her team provided teacher lesson plans, tests and quizzes, automatic grading, progress reports, interactive maps, videos, audiotapes, charts, and numerous other features. "Many of them were actually fun," Sainte-Marie says. "The teaching tools and books used in North American schools never provided any idea that Indigenous cultures had their own intellectual collateral and ways of teaching regarding science, geography, social studies, and government. Everybody thinks the Greeks invented everything like science and democracy. Actually, everybody who has survived has done so because of their own successful ways of doing science. And the Haudenosaunee Confederacy, which kept the peace for 1,100 years, actually practiced democracy, which the Greeks only talked about."

As an educator, Sainte-Marie wanted students of all backgrounds to have the option to learn about the fascinating collateral of Indigenous innovation and invention and for educators using the program to have access to alternative methods and thought processes. There was so much to be learned from traditional Indigenous models of life and learning, she says, so many friendships possible despite the fact that much had been eradicated through colonization, assimilation, and extermination. This was an opportunity to emphasize alternative models that could benefit everybody.

Cradleboard emphasized the concept of living in a circle, seeing one's self as part of the continuum, and therefore affected by everything that came before—beginning, middle, and end. In studying government through Indigenous eyes, fourth-grade Cradleboard kids learned about the Haudenosaunee Confederacy, the Plains Tribes' and the Pueblo forms of government, and discovered that—surprise, surprise—there are multiple ways to govern, not just one based in parliamentary hierarchy. Without tearing anything else down, Cradleboard taught that there are alternative ways of governing not rooted in colonialism.

"At Cradleboard we didn't even bother to include history," Sainte-Marie says. "It's what many people expected we were doing, maybe because that's what they would have done. 'Oh yeah, the Indians must be mad. Now they want to educate us by shoving it up the white man who has told so many lies!' No. Cradleboard has nothing to do with 'getting even' or building a business or any of that. Cradleboard is this additional option to learn core subjects through Indigenous perspectives without shaming anybody. It's about information. Besides delivering core science—which has no ethnicity—Cradleboard methods allow people to see the beauty, fun, laughter, joy, and power of

Indigenous cultures while doing their science lesson. It's sharing the principles of science through culture in a way that most students would never come across, and it's a lot of fun."

The program's multimedia features were new at the time, but according to Sainte-Marie, they also simplified the learning process, making it more natural and instinctual. More than twenty years after its inception, she still gets excited about the way in which aspects of the curriculum worked to inform a whole. "Here's an example of how it works at grade six when students are required to study the principles of sound. Frequency and amplitude—which have no ethnicity—have usually been taught by reading about them in a book, which is hard to understand. We presented the lessons as interactive multimedia, via video and computers, so that the kids are learning from hands-on experience themselves instead of just reading about them. To see the difference between frequency (pitch) and amplitude (loudness), the students can operate the same kind of sliders we use in recording studios. They can actually see and hear the sound waves get louder and quieter as they raise and lower the amplitude slider with their own fingers. That's called multisensory learning. And cultural experts, kids, and teachers from the [Indigenous] communities did the video presentations, so children could see some actual Indigenous faces on camera."

Sainte-Marie had endured a lifetime of Indigenous people being viewed as decoration, of having cultural traditions appropriated by "unknowledgeable movie vultures" or artists who would champion their "love" for Indigenous people, but really didn't do anything to help. Most North Americans "saw us in the way that a child sees someone in a parade" she says.

Sainte-Marie recalls one example of this in her own life. It was during one of two Pete Seeger shows in which she performed. At the finale, everyone gathered onstage together to sing Woody Guthrie's famous song, "This Land Is Your Land." "I just couldn't do it," she says. "Pete was wonderful but like everyone else onstage, completely oblivious to how that song impacts Indigenous listeners. As Charlie Hill used to sing, 'This land is your land. It used to be my land.' I told Pete's producer I didn't want to do it. He nicely insisted. I stood onstage but didn't actually sing. It was a real conflict at the moment for me and it became one more of many lessons in patience, doing what we can whenever we get a chance to make positive change without making things worse. Part of the success in surviving this kind of thing is to understand that. In this case, Pete and Woody and company were not my enemies: they just didn't know. There was no reason to create an escalation of negativity. Much later in life, I mentioned it to Pete, and he saw my point. But most people do not listen between the lines, and we need to understand that. That's why I don't restrict myself to show business, and it's partly the same reason I created the Cradleboard Teaching Project: because people who should know don't know—and they deserve to know."

In 1994, Sainte-Marie addressed a conference of Native American women in Montana, in which attendees were encouraged to take a new look at the potential role of Indigenous people and content in education. "I have a passion for content about Indigenous people in the Americas," Sainte-Marie says. Dr. Valorie Johnson, an educator and Seneca program officer at the W. K. Kellogg Foundation, one of the largest philanthropic foundations in the U.S., heard her speak. A few weeks later, Buffy got a call from Norbert Hill, Johnson's colleague and the brother of her friend, comedian Charlie Hill. They wondered whether Buffy would like to present a proposal to Kellogg to support her educational mission. Up until then, Buffy had been funding the work of her Nihewan Foundation, including

Cradleboard, on her own dime—"my leftover singing money," she called it—and had never considered approaching a big foundation. She contacted her friend, former Mohawk chief Harold Tarbell, and together they created the Cradleboard proposal. It was approved by the Kellogg Foundation with a budget of $1.5 million over two years, which Sainte-Marie leveraged thanks to further support from the other philanthropies to model the project. Although Kellogg dollars were mandated to serve American children first and foremost, Sainte-Marie found ways to include Canadian content throughout the new curriculum.

For the curriculum itself, Sainte-Marie secured input from a variety of educators, including scholars from thirty-three tribal colleges. According to Cradleboard's website, within its first two years, Sainte-Marie modeled the project in Mohawk, Cree, Ojibwe, Menominee, Coeur d'Alene, Navajo, Quinnault, Hawai'ian, and Apache communities in eleven states. By 1998, Cradleboard was being used in thirty-three classrooms across the United States.

Sainte-Marie had seen the ways in which non-Indigenous people ignored or put forward a bastardized representation of Indigeneity throughout her life. "The fact is that students in North America have usually studied Indians in the fall, after the volcanoes and dinosaurs, and before Columbus," she says. "Then we show up at Halloween as Halloween costumes. But once Thanksgiving myths and Halloween are over, the important subjects go back to being only, only, only, in italics and underlined and in quotes, only Eurocentric. What kind of message does that give to non-Indian kids and teachers and families about us? That we've vanished or are not part of the serious world of science and government, etcetera. And what kind of message does it give to Indigenous kids and teachers and families? That we're obsolete like the dinosaurs, like a costume;

we're not even real. What a waste of exciting potential, when it's so easy to do it right by including us in the actual core subjects."

The old-fashioned educational system hadn't been enough for Sainte-Marie when she was growing up, trying to fill in the blanks in her life, and she hoped Cradleboard, like her appearances on *Sesame Street* and her songs, would help counter the tokenization of Indigenous people. "Somebody might write a song and be real pissed off at 'how tokenized we are.' But the point is why we're tokenized, and can we fix it. And yes, we can. Little by little, person by person, song by song, incident by incident, rally by rally. It's how it happens in real life. It was never our primary goal to build a big business, to settle old scores, or compete with anybody else. Our goal was to model a way to help children and teachers—both Indigenous and non-Indigenous—to learn core subjects like science, government, and geography, through Native American cultural perspectives."

Most public schools in the early 1990s did not have computers in classrooms and neither did tribal schools. Part of the initial W. K. Kellogg grant was used to provide not only computers to remote communities but, in some cases, the actual data lines. Educators like Pamela Livingston, who is quoted on the Cradleboard website, had never seen anything like it before. "This is the only thing of its type being done. It is the best example I've come across of excellence in education technology. It is such a superb answer to the question: 'What are you doing with all that hardware?' and to the type of anti-computer backlash happening right now. Instead of having kids do Math Blasters, our kids are interacting in chats, live video conferences, e-mail, and via regular mail with children they would never encounter otherwise, while learning authentic Native American history past and present."

In addition to the financial contribution of the Kellogg Foundation, Sainte-Marie had to seek out other partnerships as well.

"Key to our initial success was Harold Tarbell who was the former chief at the St. Regis Mohawk Reservation," she explains. "Their neighboring reservation had built Akwesasne Freedom School, one of the earliest and best Indigenous full-service schools based in their own Indigenous language." Harold Tarbell was familiar with working in organizations large and small, government, tribal, and private on both sides of the border. He became Cradleboard's project director and he and Sainte-Marie brought educators together for regional conferences over the next several years as they continued to expand the curriculum. They included teachers and students from Indigenous communities in the U.S., Canada, Australia, Sweden, and New Zealand. For the U.S. national conference in Hawai'i, teachers learned the new curriculum, software, and Cradleboard methods, while the students played Hawai'ian games, interacted with local multicultural kids, and in the case of Little Black Bear School from Fond du Lac, Wisconsin, sang powwow music with the big drum they'd brought from home while their classmates 4,000 miles away watched on classroom computers.

The group of educators who led the American Indian Tribal College movement were also key partners and supporters of the project. Several of the presidents and founders of the colleges, including the two aforementioned Nihewan scholarship recipients, served on Cradleboard's advisory board. Many of the tribal colleges were already associated with grade schools in their local communities and welcomed the new project with excitement. They helped Cradleboard create classroom partnerships between distantly remote but same-grade classes. The class that delivered the curriculum was the Indigenous partner, and the recipient was a non-Indigenous partner in another part of the U.S.

Despite these partnerships, some teachers expressed discomfort with their own qualifications to teach the material.

"Some non-Indian teachers would say, 'I just don't feel qualified to deliver this material to students. I feel so guilty about the things that have happened in history, and there's just so much I don't know,'" Sainte-Marie recalls. "And Aboriginal teachers would say the same thing but in a different way: 'I just don't feel qualified to teach this. Nobody taught me. I don't really know much, and I certainly can't teach about different tribal communities.'"

One school located on the U.S.–Canadian border, the Akwesasne Freedom School, worried at first that they couldn't teach about other nations like the Navajos and the Apaches. But they didn't have to: all they had to do was provide information about whatever they wanted their partner schools to know about their own group. Expert teachers taught about their own people, and each school called its own shots. Navajos taught about Navajos. Apaches taught about Apaches. "But at first, everybody felt either some lack of knowledge, or some guilt or some bitterness," Sainte-Marie says.

Sainte-Marie has a story that she shares with people when they express guilt or bitterness about the impacts and devastation of colonization. Some teachers advised the children to suppress those feelings, but Sainte-Marie has a different approach. "Imagine some people out on the plains, a long time ago, bending over and picking things up and putting them in a bag. I ask the kids, 'What are they gathering?' And they say, 'rocks,' or 'food.' But it's none of those things. It's dried buffalo chips, which is manure, of course, and the kids all laugh when I tell them. 'No, don't throw it away; you can use it,' I say. What can you do with dried, discarded doo-doo? You don't just throw it away, you take it home and do the thing that only human beings can do: you use it to make fire! If you can make fire, you can make light and heat, and you can make community around the fire—you can read a book around a fire, you can write a book around a fire. You can fall in love around the fire. Or you can take that dried manure and put it on the garden like fertilizer and grow something brand-new!

"Guilt and bitterness and a lot of things in life are like that. Don't just hate it because it's stinky: let it dry out and then use it. But not like makeup or your badge of identity—'Oh, I'm so-o guilty, oh I'm the bitterest person in the world.' That'll get you nowhere. See, you gotta let it dry out. Then you can use it like fuel, turn it into light, use it to grow something else, like a song, or a lesson, or a new attitude about going to college and finding out for yourself what you can do in this world." That there are gifts in everything, even in the shit, is a good philosophy, but this anecdote also speaks to natural cycles and our relationship to the earth, the value of time and distance, and separating ourselves from the mess until the time is right to deal with it. The values in Sainte-Marie's story share space with Cradleboard's values, which are also reflected in her songs, paintings, writing, and thinking.

In 1997, the Cradleboard Teaching Project was commended by President Bill Clinton's One America Initiative on Race as one of more than three hundred "promising practices." Sainte-Marie had major goals to expand Cradleboard into different states as well as to increase the scope of its subject matter. She had begun a partnership with NASA to develop a high school curriculum on astronomy, engineering, and careers in science, when the government experienced a massive political shift with the election of George W. Bush. None of the people at NASA with whom she'd become friendly returned her calls any longer—if they were even there. "People don't realize that sometimes in the U.S., when there's a change of administration, NASA is one of the things that changes," Sainte-Marie says.

"Some of the people who used to have a job? They don't have that job anymore. Bush put his own people in."

Sainte-Marie lost confidence that Cradleboard would be able to continue to secure adequate funding, so she decided to go back out on the road and tour the U.S. and wherever else she could in order to make enough money to sustain the program. "When the Bush administration came in and talked about privatizing charities, I could see the funding drying up," Sainte-Marie says. "I really wanted Cradleboard to work without money, to be delivered free on the internet, but that was too early for most schools, which didn't even have computers. I have a funny relationship to money. I wish that there were an alternative to it, but I don't see it yet. But hopefully someday we'll figure it out."

Sainte-Marie never took a salary from the Nihewan Foundation. "I don't mean just for grants for Cradleboard, but never, since I founded it in the 1960s, have I taken a salary," she says. "It didn't make any sense for me to get paid. For many organizations, it's about providing jobs and building a big infrastructure. But for us, it really was about helping children and teachers and their communities through better education." The project did, however, need to compensate regional and tribal teachers. When Cradleboard had money through grants, they'd hire people locally and regionally to run the program in their own areas. "They were the real foot soldiers who would interact with their principals and school boards," Sainte-Marie says. "They were the first line of contact between us and the school." When the funding crisis loomed, those positions were eliminated, and the program took the hit. Sainte-Marie started to use her spare time while on the road to go to colleges and universities to teach them what she could.

"I would host either a meeting or a Cradleboard presentation on my day off, and I'd let local college educators pick my brain," she explains. "I was trying to teach them how to do what I was doing because it's not that hard to do; it's just a shift in consciousness mostly. I would work with their teacher education programs. I didn't try to 'addict' them to our business, which I was advised to do—I mean, we had a business manager at one point, and I can see how building a brand and growing a business is done, but I don't want to be that person. A lot of businesses are about capturing the public dollar, but, beyond survival, that wasn't our Nihewan Foundation/Cradleboard Teaching Project goal."

Sainte-Marie appreciates the philosophy of Tim Berners-Lee (the inventor of the World Wide Web), who declared that "information wants be free." She shares that belief, which is why Cradleboard was never about building a business. "We were trying to help children," she says. "On the one hand, I was trying to help children and parents of Indigenous backgrounds to have some impact, to be in the driver's seat of knowing who they are and what they had to offer other people. And for the non-Indian children and their teachers and families, I was trying to provide them additional options in studying science, government, geography, and other core subjects through Indigenous perspectives. Most people have still never considered doing things in that way."

In 2000, Sainte-Marie's team created CD-ROMs titled *Science Through Native American Eyes*, which focused on the science of sound, friction, and lodge construction via interactive media, audio, text, animation, and video. It was to be the first of fifteen planned core curriculum CD-ROMs, and Sainte-Marie gave away thousands of discs to interested teachers and instructors. "I still hear from teachers who say that it's just the best thing there ever was," Sainte-Marie laughs. "And they ask, 'Why isn't more education done this way?' But we know why. Because education itself is a very big business."

Cradleboard has been on indefinite hiatus for more than a decade, but the website is still online, a reminder of a workable alternative or addition to colonizer-centered curricula. "I always felt good about the Cradleboard Teaching Project, my foundation, the participants, and everything," Sainte-Marie says. "Our attitude is real, real positive. And we modeled something that really works, even if we were a little bit too early. But we are one of very few foundations whose attitudes are that positive because we're not concentrating on coins. We're about effectiveness and doing things, making things better for real. Helping people to decolonize can be a pleasure, because sometimes you can move people to a better understanding of how those remnants of colonial days still affect us all, and how we can replace the problem parts with solutions without tearing anything down. It's mostly a shift in consciousness, and it doesn't hurt."

While she was working towards launching Cradleboard, Sainte-Marie was also quietly helping broadcaster Elaine Bomberry, who is Ojibwe and Cayuga from Six Nations, and Ojibwe singer-songwriter Shingoose (Curtis Jonnie) establish the Aboriginal category for the 1994 Juno Awards, the annual prizes given out by CARAS, the Canadian Academy of Recording Arts and Sciences (essentially the Canadian version of the Grammy Awards and arguably one of the biggest honors given to professional musicians in Canada). Bomberry had been invited to join the advisory committee for a category that she remembers as a euphemistic umbrella term like "world beat" or "global."

"This was my first meeting with them, and everyone was talking about the criteria, how wide it was," Bomberry says. "I think reggae was in there, soca, and then Native Canadian was listed, but it was, like, written in at the last minute. I just kind of went off. I said, 'Our music doesn't fit here, and it doesn't fit in any of the categories!' The president of CARAS at the time, Daisy Falle, was sitting beside me, and she leaned over and said, 'Well, why don't you start a category?' and I just laughed."

But Falle was serious and asked Bomberry to document fifteen Indigenous recordings from the previous year and fifteen in the coming one. The fax machine in her small office worked overtime as bands sent in their documentation. She ended up collecting information about twenty-five recordings in the previous year and forty in the coming one. Bomberry began to prepare her presentation with Shingoose when she got a surprise phone call. "It was Buffy, and I'm like, 'Are you kidding me?' I let out a little bit of a scream!" Bomberry laughs. "Buffy goes, 'I hear you're doing a presentation to the CARAS board, and I'm just wondering if I can be of any help?'" Buffy's advice was instrumental to Bomberry, though Sainte-Marie now downplays her role. "Elaine was the real brains behind it. I was just window-dressing and confirmation." The presentation went off without a hitch, and the Best Music of Aboriginal Canada Recording category was born, though the name has changed a few times since its 1994 inception.

That also fortified a long friendship between the two women, a bond that was further strengthened the following year when Bomberry was hired to help produce the tribute to Sainte-Marie for her induction into the Canadian Music Hall of Fame during the 1995 Juno Awards broadcast. Bomberry remembers getting a call from Sainte-Marie who was upset at the direction the producers wanted to go in because there were so few Indigenous artists involved. "She was getting kind of discouraged," Bomberry recalls. "She goes, 'You know what they want? They want to bring out Joe Cocker and Jennifer Warnes to sing "Up Where We Belong," and they want all these non-Native singers to sing my songs.'"

Sainte-Marie's words inspired Bomberry, and she organized a tribute that was unlike anything most Canadians had ever seen before. Sainte-Marie was totally blown away. "Without my knowledge, Elaine recruited, booked, and organized a huge group of [102 Indigenous] dancers to enter the arena and dance into the Copps Coliseum in full powwow clothes, while Stoney Park, my favorite drum group from Morley, Alberta, sang an honor song, and Tom Jackson read a tribute."

Decolonizing the Junos was the perfect way to honor Sainte-Marie, but it wouldn't have happened if she hadn't spoken out, and chances are that if Bomberry hadn't been so closely acquainted with the Junos, she would not have been able to pull off what she'd organized that night. The Junos' producers knew enough to hire Bomberry to help produce the tribute, but they didn't understand that it would be essential to Sainte-Marie that her induction ceremony include and prioritize Indigenous artists. Yet again, Sainte-Marie was in the position of being able to open another door for power-holders to walk through.

Throughout the 1990s, she opened more and more doors through which Indigenous people could see themselves and their culture reflected back in education, the arts, and pop culture, and doors through which non-Indigenous people could consider the world from a different vantage point. As the millennium began, Sainte-Marie wasn't just decolonizing the world; she was Indigenizing it, laying the foundation for her most revolutionary record yet.

CHAPTER 15

NO NO KESHAGESH

SAINTE-MARIE WAS SINGING about environmental justice long before most musicians. Indigenous people have been at the forefront of environmental protest—and have suffered from environmental racism—for hundreds of years. And yet, throughout Sainte-Marie's life, she observed a sort of colonization of the movement as environmentalism moved into the mainstream; "green" energy took off amidst anti-oil and anti-pipeline sentiment, food security evolved, and climate change became central to discussions about environmental disasters. In Canada and in the U.S., protests in the 1990s and 2000s—including demonstrations in British Columbia in 1993 against logging old-growth forests at Clayoquot ("the War of the Woods"), the WTO violence in Seattle in 1999, and opposition by various Indigenous groups to nuclear waste disposal on or near their lands—drew international attention. In 2006, former U.S. Vice President Al Gore became the unlikely face of global warming with his award-winning film, *An Inconvenient Truth*, for which he won a 2007 Nobel Peace Prize. But the truth is, Indigenous people were (and are) doing the day-to-day hard work, the actual blood, sweat, and, tears on the ground, the grassroots resistance work, and with little or no recognition.

Sainte-Marie's next comeback album, 2008's *Running for the Drum*, centered Indigeneity in environmental justice and skewed heavily towards protest, activism, and decolonization anthems. She wrote the songs at a time when "people started to really notice climate change and corporate greed and the destruction of the earth that benefited only a few short-sighted people." Show business is not just about money and competition, she says, or besting people you knew in high school, and she rejects the "me, me, me" thinking that's so prevalent in sports, music, and business. The music was bold and visceral, thumping rock tunes that incorporated traditional and powwow elements, like "No No Keshagesh," a powerful rocker about environmental destruction. "Keshagesh" is a Cree word that roughly translates as "greedy guts," and was the name of a puppy at the Piapot home on the reserve who, she says, "used to eat all his own [food] and then want everybody else's." It's a scathing tune, sly and clever and funny, and unrelentingly propulsive with a chorus of pounding powwow-style backing chants and hand claps as Sainte-Marie sings, "No, no, Keshagesh, you can't do that no more."

Sainte-Marie's lyrics are incisive and couched in satire: "Ol' Columbus he was lookin' good/When he got lost in our neighborhood" or "Got Mother Nature on a luncheon plate/They carve her up and call her real estate." The references are often to all-too-real devastations. "These things are so obvious and so horrifying," she says. "God bless Naomi Klein and Winona LaDuke. Some of us have to say something, and this is my way of saying it." In the song, she also talks about how the burden of protecting the planet and advocating for it often falls to Indigenous people with the least resources. "The reservation out on Poverty Row/There's something cookin' and the lights are low," she sings. "People are trying save our Mother Earth," she says, "even though they're broke."

And the inverse of poverty-stricken, exploited Indigenous people attempting to protect the environment are the short-sighted businessmen whom Sainte-Marie calls out, over and over throughout the song. She's particularly pleased with the line, "Oh brother Midas, looking hungry today." "That says a lot, just that one line. Midas is the guy who had the ability to turn anything he touched into gold, and what did he do? He touched his beloved daughter and she turned into gold. That's kind of the Midas thinking behind a lot of short-sighted corporations and greed heads." The lyrics continue, pointed and sharp: "What he can't buy he'll get some other way/Send in the troopers if the Natives resist."

Sainte-Marie laughs knowingly and a little bitterly as she recalls the ways in which non-Indigenous people have repeatedly minimized and dismissed her warnings. "And here comes Standing Rock and all of the in-between things that nobody ever heard about between the 1970s and Standing Rock. It's been going on all along."

"It" is colonial greed and the willingness to sacrifice everything, even one's own capacity for survival, in order to make a quick buck. What she doesn't understand is how, with the full evidence of current corruption and environmental destruction and exploitation, more songwriters aren't saying it with her. "It's kind of obvious right now, and I sincerely don't know what to make of it. People think that they have to join either the Us team or the Them team—things are so polarized right now, everybody feels like they have to be on the right side so that when the shit comes down, they won't get covered in it." She laughs. "But that's not how it is. Somewhere along the line you become a grown-up and start thinking with your own brain and seeing a bigger picture that includes everybody. At least hopefully."

"No No Keshagesh" addresses the past, present, and future, and expresses Sainte-Marie's belief in life in a circle, or how to make it work in such a way that nobody loses. Because so many of her ideas seem to be ten or twenty years in advance of anyone being ready to hear them, she finds that people constantly turn to her for solutions, be they environmental or social. "Every time people ask me, 'How do we solve this problem or that problem in your opinion?' it's always the same answer: Stay calm and decolonize."

Sainte-Marie laughs after she says this, but anyone who's paid attention to her songs knows that this is the mantra she's been living since her earliest days on the folk scene. Well before "decolonize," a term meaning to remove the toxic effects of colonization, entered the vernacular, there were countless Indigenous people—leaders, activists, scholars, defenders, artists, and educators—who advocated for the existence, protection, and rights of their people, including cultural, environmental, and land claims. Among them was Sainte-Marie, whose music communicated a vital personal reality and living history, and who used a microphone and a spotlight to make sure her message made it into as many hearts and minds as possible.

"Helping people to decolonize can be a pleasure, because sometimes decolonizing can help people to understand how that old baloney negatively affects them," Sainte-Marie says. "A lot of people are frightened, especially whenever you mention Indian issues or Black issues. If people are exclusively white, if they've grown up and haven't gone to school with people from other countries or other races, and they're really quite insular— or they might be privileged but still be inexperienced and lack empathy—they may have grown up in a business family where their bottoms are stuck on the bottom line and what matters is the coins. [They fear that] 'those other people are going to try to take something, so you'd better exploit them first!' The old zero-sum colonial illusion."

Sainte-Marie knows that when some white people hear the word "decolonize," this is their assumption. "That's not what it's about. You can have your money. But if you happen to be into charity, please think beyond the usual tax loopholes or what your family has always given to: the opera, the ballet, the diseases. Although these are important, and I support them too, please trust yourself with getting more information, including about innovative start-ups who are not doing it the same old way that has been failing for years. Please understand that many of the most important issues of today are not set up in a way that your accountant would be able to understand at first glance. In other words, life in the hierarchy is the only life that many business people have known, where it's all about 'the Get.' They have never known life in a circle, where it's all about sustaining Life itself for the next seven generations."

Sainte-Marie is heartened when she sees activists' years of work translate into real societal change. For her, one of the most important was the Truth and Reconciliation Commission of Canada (TRC), established in 2008 to address more than 120 years of systemic and institutionalized abuse inflicted on Indigenous people in Canada. "For me, Truth and Reconciliation was really, really important. Years ago, I had written 'My Country 'Tis of Thy People You're Dying,' with my own heart, and [I felt] so alone," she explains. "The stories that my own relatives in Saskatchewan told me about their experiences in residential schools—I was witnessing for fifty years before Truth and Reconciliation came along. I highly supported it. The information just needs to be out there. It's fucking awful, but it needs to be out there and it needs to be addressed."

The TRC attempted to tackle the damage caused by the residential school system, which was funded by the Canadian government and administered by Christian churches for more than a hundred years. The Commission, which concluded its seven-year investigation in December 2015, made ninety-four "Calls to Action" concerning a wide range of issues, from a demand for official apologies to improvements in the justice system and Indigenous health and wellness.

Sainte-Marie sees a connection between the sexual abuse in residential schools and her own sexual abuse as a child in that both are a function of the good-old-boy colonial blueprint that hasn't changed much since Biblical times. "The priests, the ministers, the nuns, and the Indian agents were all sexually repressed people, and like soldiers, they were raised, trained, and expected to be servants of a feudal hierarchy familiar with torture, humiliation, misogyny, and coercion," Sainte-Marie says. "Today, a lot of the descendants of this system are okay with it; they're trying to normalize the abnormal, and they believe that rape is universal human nature—but it's not. Like war, it's just greedy men's dreams. Rape is a choice, a cultural aberration of certain societies, including historical Europe, where rape was a reward for the king's sexually repressed soldiers, and misogyny and child abuse were no big deal and nobody's business."

In Sainte-Marie's view, it leads all the way back through Europe's sick history of bad leadership, mandated by the Doctrine of Discovery. "The big racket as it pertains to children is much bigger than racism," Sainte-Marie says. "Ever read Charles Dickens? Europeans exploited their own children and oppressed their own neighbors before they ever got to us. The slave trade and the king's military were both implicated in the template for how Indigenous children all over the world were treated by Europeans. Little children who were kidnapped from a natural life and sent to live in residential schools without family or community were certainly not a match for such a system. Beyond the established European market for Indigenous child slaves, European literature is full of evidence that suggests bullying and abuse of little kids in their own homes were common, obvious, and no big deal. And, of course, I was one more of the little kids that that kind of men did it to, even without a residential school. And nobody even noticed."

She remembers the trauma only too well. "It's incredibly disempowering to be the slave of an adult and to have to do things that are described as being shameful," Sainte-Marie says. "You're threatened throughout your whole childhood by people who outweigh you, so you're always under stress, always being bullied, having to do even more. [The threat of] being exposed—'I'll tell all your friends'—is just awful. Awful."

Talking about the abuse she experienced as a child is still a work in progress for Sainte-Marie. In the late 1980s, she participated in a support group for adult survivors of child abuse. "This kind of thing never leaves you. It's always in the back of your mind. I mean your lack of identity; not knowing who you are or what the rules are or whether it's fair for people to mistreat you in this big, bad world where men rule everything and older rules younger and more powerful rules less powerful and white rules Indigenous, when you're just trying to find a safe place to fit in unnoticed."

The support group consisted of five women who met once a week to talk about their lives and what had happened to them. After a few weeks, the person running the group asked the women to take part in a healing exercise. "She wanted each of us to envision ourselves as that poor abused kid from way back when—which was very easy for me to do—and she wanted us to go over to that poor kid and tell her, 'I'm going to take care of you now.' Maybe that comes from twelve-step programs or AA, or maybe it's a well-known thing that I just never came across, but I thought it was wonderful."

In doing that, Sainte-Marie recalled an indelible picture of herself at around six or seven years old, standing by the pond where they used to camp in the woods. "I had this continual sense that 'someone' was looking after me," Sainte-Marie remembers. "And I didn't give 'her' a name, a shape, or form; I didn't say she was an angel, I didn't say it was anything. If I thought of her as anything, it was like thinking of my buddy, Mother Nature, who I would eventually grow into. It sounds silly when I say it. But what it connected within me was to envision that little girl I used to be, to go over and comfort her, and to become that little girl's feminine savior person in 'our' own life, who had been there all along; to actually materialize to that little kid who believed in Someday, and let her know that she's safe now, I'm here to protect her. And I guess that was what was supposed to happen, but it still floors me that it did work because I don't usually go along with self-help books, but this was very good."

She believes in sharing her story when it's appropriate and relevant. She also wants to make it clear that sexual abuse isn't just about a physical act; it's also about the psychological ramifications. "Sexual abuse is about bullying," Sainte-Marie says. "Sexual abuse is about an adult or older person having complete control of a powerless person. And the things that follow most sexual abuse—there's the 'act' itself, whatever it is, but then there's the rest of it—the keeping it quiet, the humiliation, the threats, and the bullying. You're frightened all the time that it's going to happen again, he might get me again, he might make me do that again. Or, as you get older, [the threat of] 'If you ever tell, I'll tell your friends what you like to do.' A big person can turn it on a smaller person. Well, that kind of man will always turn it on a woman. I don't care how old you are, he comes back, and pretty soon *you* are the one in the doghouse, right?"

Many of the residential school survivors had never confronted their own abuse until the TRC. "It was just what had
'happened,' and it wasn't the only thing that had happened,"
Sainte-Marie says. The abuse was almost normalized because
of how widespread it was in the residential school system and
how intergenerational the trauma was. And yet it was still a
secret shame that was almost impossible for survivors to put
into words, particularly when they'd spent a lifetime trying so
hard to forget.

"I'm a songwriter; I package my passions and my emotions
into a form that's discussable, and that's what art and philosophy can do," Sainte-Marie says. "But the survivors of war and
domestic violence and residential schools, in order to survive,
don't package it into an episode that they can deal with and get
rid of it. Most of the survivors of residential schools don't have
any money. They don't ever go to a psychiatrist who can help
them to deal with what happened to them. They're told that it's
shameful, bury it."

But when shared trauma has infected most of a community or
an entire family, solidarity can collapse into something harder,
more brittle. "Many sexual abuse survivors are told, 'That happened to all of us. You're not special. Get over it,'" Sainte-Marie
says. "And that's not adequate. We need a lot more help than
that. They were raised without mothering, without hugs, without laughter and childhood fun and parental guidance. They
didn't learn how to make family or be parents. And for us, the
'boogeyman' was real."

Sainte-Marie says that for some adopted people, there's a
real shame in not knowing where they come from. The questions are endless. "'What, did your mother fool around? Were
you a foundling? Did somebody not want you and you were
given away?'" she recalls. "There are all these possible painful

scenarios that you never know. You don't even get to have a damn horoscope 'cause you don't know when or where you were born! You not only don't know who the white soldiers were who raped your great-grandmother, or the name of their sons who raped your mother, or the other guys who raped your sisters, but you don't even know, in most cases, who your Native American ancestors were because the colonials changed people's names. It leaves a big hole where your self-esteem ought to be, and it's heartbreaking, over and over again."

In sharing her personal experiences and framing them in relation to colonialism, Sainte-Marie illustrates not just the ongoing horror of childhood sexual abuse, but also the consequences of colonialism, historical and contemporary. "The problem of decolonizing neither starts nor ends in Indian country," she says. "The family style of contemporary North America needs to change. We need to break the cycle here and now. The pecking order, where dad and his dick and his wallet run everything? Not happening anymore—obsolete, old fashioned, lame. Did pedophilia only happen in residential schools? I think not. Entitlement and abuses of power start in the home, and it is truly time to break the cycles: bullying, abuse, alcohol, and drugs. You might have to get out of town to get away from old family habits successfully. However you do it, just break the cycle. It's not disloyal: it's survival."

Life in a circle speaks to survival, and when Sainte-Marie headed out on the road again in 2008, she knew she wanted to be surrounded by musicians who didn't just understand life in a circle but also lived it. Her identity is the heart of her music, and *Running for the Drum* was her first recording of new material since 1992's *Coincidence and Likely Stories*. It was bursting with empowerment anthems and a challenging, complex sonic landscape of jazz, rock, powwow, and folk. She needed the right artists beside her who not only understood her message but could also amplify it accordingly. She also wanted a band that could rock hard.

Paquin Entertainment, which serves as her manager and agent, set up live auditions in Winnipeg, Manitoba. Over the course of two days, Sainte-Marie auditioned twenty-seven musicians while searching for her new touring band. She chose Winnipeg-based rock band A Gathering of Flies, which included Michel Bruyere (Ojibwe, drums), Jesse Green (Lakota/ Ojibwe, guitar), and Darryl Menow (Cree, bass). She'd never truly had the opportunity to have her own band, her own team, behind her on the road. *Running for the Drum* was the first record Sainte-Marie ever toured with an all-Indigenous band. Sainte-Marie uses the word *waskochepayis* to describe what it was like when they played together. It's a Cree term for the electricity created when thunder meets lightning.

"They all played great, and it helped that what I sang about and where my songs originated is a world they knew too: the passions of Native American realities," she says. "It's powwow rock, like little rez snapshots, it's big love songs, and it's all hot. Feels real comfortable, and it's about more than just the music."

Both Green and Bruyere remember Sainte-Marie from their childhoods. Her music was around, of course, but it was actually *Sesame Street* that made the biggest impression on them. "I was about five years old, I think, and she was with Cody on *Sesame Street*," Bruyere remembers. "That was the first time I saw her. And it blew my mind because I looked at my grandmother, my *kokom*, and I remember I was so excited, and I said, 'Is that us?'"

"Growing up, there weren't many brown faces on TV. She was one of the few that I could see and relate to," Green recalls. "It just made me feel proud to see an Aboriginal person on TV.

It made me think we're in the mainstream, we're not forgotten. We are living in the contemporary world despite what's going on."

The band was crucial in leveling up the live concert intensity on some of the album's biggest rock anthems, like the raucous "Working for the Government," and "Cho Cho Fire," an epic wake-up call to rediscover the power of fun, which included a powwow sample from the famed Black Lodge Singers they heard when they were kids.

Audiences and critics loved the record. *American Songwriter* called it a "triumphant return" and concert reviews lavished praise upon Sainte-Marie, such as the one in the *Telegraph*, which marveled at her "unfeasibly vivacious and passionate set" and described her performances as "dazzling" and "magnificent."[49] *Running for the Drum* won the 2009 Juno for Aboriginal Recording of the Year. When she'd auditioned her band, she advised them to get their passports ready as they would probably be touring the album for two years. Instead, Sainte-Marie and the band stayed on the road for almost six years. It was unlike any tour she'd had before, and it gave her the opportunity to bring the songs and her messages to cities and reservations all over the world.

"It reminded me of when I suspected that Greenwich Village audiences were coming to 'hear the little Indian girl cry,' and my reaction was to concentrate on bringing great, positive shows to the reservations," Sainte-Marie says. "Bring them 'Indian Cowboy' and a rock 'n' roll band—they already had enough tears. I wanted my big love for our people and what's left of our cultures to serve as a mirror in grassroots communities, especially in western Canada, but also in Australia, Norway, Japan. Shine a light on the beauties and realities of who Indigenous people really are, were, can be."

It might not have been obvious at the time, but Sainte-Marie was at the forefront of a major renaissance in Indigenous music, particularly in Canada. However, even she couldn't predict that her biggest comeback of all was still to come.

Buffy Sainte-Marie on decolonization

Racketeers will use misogyny, race, youth, age, anything that they can get their hands on, any of the great "isms." Racketeers will exploit all of those things on their way to the bank because that is their goal, that's their way, that's their dogma. Exploit. Take as much as you can get and give the least you can. We can scream back at them and mention things like racism and sexism, but what's wrong is the basic colonial mentality—the pecking order. The pecking order comes from the barnyard. It is important in the pack, in the flock, and in the herd, but it's not human nature; it's a choice. There are many, many other ways for human beings to live that most people have never observed. That's where inter-community comes in. A lot of us already have decolonized without hatred, without enmity, but with empathy and compassion. Colonialism is obsolete. It should have gone away a long time ago. It doesn't hurt anybody to decolonize. And it doesn't cost nearly as much as maintaining it.

CHAPTER 16

POWER IN THE BLOOD

I N 2012, INDIGENOUS grassroots activists made headlines with Idle No More, a protest against the Canadian government's ongoing abuse of Indigenous people, their land rights, and wide-scale exploitations of the environment for profit. Indigenous and non-Indigenous people alike participated in blockades and flash mobs, while video clips, a Twitter hashtag, and social media helped amplify the message of resisters and activists around the world. Support spread throughout the U.S. as more than thirty reported protests were held across the country, and solidarity protests were held in Sweden, the U.K., Germany, Australia, New Zealand, and Egypt.[50]

Simultaneously, a new generation of Indigenous artists, particularly in Canada, had dug deep into their ancestral and traditional music and fused that with contemporary styles to create bold, vivid, exciting sounds. A Tribe Called Red, the Ottawa-based crew, were crafting electronic powwow tracks that thumped, bumped, and signal-boosted cultural pride–meets-club bangers, songs that were as great on the dance floor as they were at a house party or a protest rally. Tanya Tagaq, an Inuk throat singer and songwriter, had been fusing the avant-garde and guttural for years, but she reached thrilling new levels of genius on her Polaris Music Prize–winning 2014 record, *Animism*.

Sainte-Marie herself was feeling inspired. She had just come off of a seemingly endless tour cycle with *Running for the Drum* and she should have been burnt out, but there was still so much more to say and do. She worked on songs with the band while they toured and revisited material that she'd written and recorded during the blacklist years. It sparked a fire that just wouldn't go out, and when Geoff Kulawick of True North Records asked Sainte-Marie if she wanted to make another album, she said yes. "I flew around North America to interview seven producers to whom I gave a playlist of my homemade demos," Sainte-Marie told *Ottawa Life* in 2015. She chose three: Chris Birkett, with whom she'd recorded before and who had relocated from the U.K. to Toronto; acclaimed pop producer Jon Levine (Drake, Serena Ryder, Nelly Furtado); and Juno Award–winning producer Michael Phillip Wojewoda (Barenaked Ladies' *Gordon* and the Rheostatics' *Whale Music*).

The result, 2015's *Power in the Blood*, was Sainte-Marie's most surprising and incendiary record since 1964's *It's My Way!* It's a powerhouse album from start to finish, containing some of the best material she's ever recorded. Her classic songwriting style—all guts and heart—is intact. Musically it takes huge risks, and thematically it's a cohesive blast of Indigenous identity and authority, autonomy, and power. Galvanized by Idle No More and other grassroots activism, *Power in the Blood* signaled a bold new era in protest music and resistance.

"Indigeneity is such an interesting topic," Sainte-Marie says, "and it's the kind of conversation you couldn't have had fifty years ago, because so many of us were either taken away to residential schools or some other school, or we were adopted out or we got lost in the system, or we were otherwise 'bleached.'" Generations of Indigenous people were legislatively denied access to their mother tongue, ancestral cultures, and philosophies, and were taken from their family homes as children. Numerous systems (both secular and religious) attempted to assimilate and exterminate Indigenous people and their cultural practices. It was something Sainte-Marie had called out back in 1966, in "My Country 'Tis of Thy People You're Dying," with the line, "Now that we're harmless and 'safe' behind laws."

The word "power" in *Power in the Blood* has a double meaning that speaks to both indictment and resistance within her work. The word encompasses negative, colonial aspects, as well as the strength and survival implicit in Indigenous resistance. "One [interpretation] is the power of the feudal system and the patriarchy that's been messing us all around since probably before the Old Testament," Sainte-Marie says. "The other is the power of our own DNA to overcome and thrive in spite of challenges." By anchoring her interpretation of "power" in a binary, Sainte-Marie shows us that these two things do not exist in isolated parallel streams, but rather inform each other while being rooted in the colonizer/colonized paradigm.

The album borrows its name from its first single, and like so many of Sainte-Marie's best songs, "Power in the Blood" is deliberately thought provoking and multi-layered. It's also the rare song that did not originate from her pen. It's a cover, though she also rewrote parts of the song, by the British band Alabama 3, the same artists who wrote and performed the track used by *The Sopranos* (one of Sainte-Marie's favorite shows) as its theme song. "Regardless of [the show's] violence, all the *Sopranos* participants knew and understood the culture in which it was based, so it's especially rich and believable," Sainte-Marie says. "Besides, I was raised in an East Coast home where Dad was from an Italian, working-class family, where some of the boxes of candy hidden in the kitchen closet had 'fallen off a truck' or were 'won in a race.'"

Thanks to the *Sopranos* theme song, she was already a fan of Alabama 3, and when she heard their 2002 song, "Power in the Blood," she loved it. They were fans of hers too, so when she played a show in England in 2014, she invited them. "They came to my concert, and we stayed up all night with them afterwards at their studio. I said, '"Power in the Blood" would make a great peace song,' and, of course, they all thought I was joking." But Sainte-Marie was serious, and she rewrote and rearranged the song into an anthem of resistance. Alabama 3's version talked about being ready for war, but Sainte-Marie flipped it, saying, "No, no, no to war!" It's a promise, a life-affirming, thundering, electro-rock vow, propulsive and rhythmic, and it feels like a heartbeat taking over the listener's entire body.

Even the placement of the song on the album is genius. "Power in the Blood" follows the bold album opener, a risky and wild reinvention of Sainte-Marie's fifty-year-old classic, "It's My Way." But this isn't the stark, acoustic folk song it was on her 1964 album. It's steely and twangy, full of stomping, driving beats and electronic elements, and the texture of her voice brings a beautiful weight to the song's words. Kicking off the album with this one-two punch of one of her oldest songs and her newest is a brilliant juxtaposition, and it wasn't just fans who took notice. Critics were right there from the beginning too. NPR's Ann Powers wrote, "Those who know her mostly by reputation as a standout of the early sixties folk revival will be delighted to discover an artist who's more Bjork than Baez, more Kate Bush than Laurel Canyon. Sainte-Marie is a risk-taker, always chasing new sounds, and a plain talker when it comes to love and politics."[51] The *Telegraph* called it "one of her best."[52]

In 2015, *Power in the Blood* claimed the Polaris Music Prize, Canada's richest award for artistic achievement in music, which also carries serious cachet for its recipients. Modeled after the Mercury Prize, Polaris is awarded solely for artistic merit, has nothing to do with record sales, and has a reputation for being very hip. The win received international coverage, including in the *New York Times*, *Rolling Stone*, *Billboard*, and *The Guardian*, which ran the headline, "Buffy Sainte-Marie Beats Drake to Win Polaris Music Prize." The following year, *Power in the Blood* won two Junos, including Aboriginal Album of the Year and Contemporary Roots Album of the Year.

In many of the write-ups, there was an almost unflattering level of surprise that, at the age of seventy-four, Sainte-Marie had made a record that sounded so urgent and contemporary. The production is part of what gives *Power in the Blood* vitality, but it really does come back to her power as a songwriter. In a 2015 interview with *Indian Country Today*, it's easy to hear the bemusement in her words as she says, "Songwriting is a gift. I write at the same degree of excellence that I wrote in the sixties. It really surprised people—they asked 'How can you be so young and write with such wisdom?' Now, they ask 'How can you be the age you are and write with such freshness?'"[53]

As a songwriter, Sainte-Marie's purpose is to persuade, and that has guided her through more than five decades of offering gifts of knowledge instead of lectures. "If only you knew," her guiding principle, cushioned the sting of her message—not for her audience, but for herself, so that she could live with the crushing knowledge that most people knew but simply didn't care about Indigenous lives, that they were neither ignorant nor naïve, but careless and complicit.

Sainte-Marie credits her mother, who passed away in 2010, for keeping kindness and possibility alive in her heart and therefore in her songs. In her darkest moments, Winnie's unconditional love helped keep her going, and Winnie's constant encouragement became an integral component of Sainte-Marie's songwriting foundation.

She brought Winnie along on a few of her travels, and they went to both Hong Kong and Australia together. When Winnie and Smokey divorced, she left the East Coast and relocated to California. Winnie's life hadn't been easy either, which may have reinforced the bond between mother and daughter. "My mom was so sweet and so nice, and regardless of the shit that either one of us was going through in my childhood with some of the males in the family and just the fact that everything was so hushed up and laughed off, she was just personally so nice," Sainte-Marie says.

Winnie also imparted some very specific and instructive thoughts on domesticity to her daughter. "My mom told me, 'Don't ever get married. You'll just wind up chained to a sink,'" Sainte-Marie says with a laugh. "She hated housework. You know who changed my mind? Martha Stewart, because she makes homemaking so much fun, [you want to] take pride in it. I had never thought of that. When Martha Stewart came along, I started paying attention because my mom had never taught me anything—she just told me to try and escape it, which nobody can do."

But some of Winnie's advice stuck. Sainte-Marie has no interest in getting married again, though she absolutely adores her current partner, whom she prefers not to name. The sweetest song on *Power in the Blood* addresses the happiness she feels about their relationship. It's called "Farm in the Middle of Nowhere," and it's heart-melting and humble at once as she sings simply, "The one I love, he loves me." The thrice-divorced Sainte-Marie is now pretty strongly anti-marriage, particularly for women. "I didn't do well in marriage," she admits. "Somehow it would throw me back to my childhood days of oppression, and I would lose myself, like many other women have done." She also cautions against the implied promise of every woman's wedding-day dream, because the symbolism may not be enough to sustain the reality of ever-after. "I think a lot of women in the past couple hundred years have craved marriage because they finally have one occasion when they can be queen for a day," Sainte-Marie says. "It's the one day when everybody's eyes are on the bride, and she gets to wear a beautiful dress and be a star and get some attention."

She's also had to grapple with the gendered expectations of what qualifies as "good" at family life. Sainte-Marie admits that she has had a few second thoughts about the impact of both her career and her relationships on her child over the years. First, there was the touring when Cody was a little boy.

"Cody was a real homebody and he loved living in Hawai'i," she says. "Even years later, he preferred to stay home rather than to travel to the mainland. My relatives in Saskatchewan and my relatives in Massachusetts were always eager to see him, but he just didn't want to leave his friends or his stuff, or, later, his car. He came to Piapot's when he was younger but not nearly as much as he was invited."

But mother and son did enjoy hitting the road together on a few different occasions.

"We have had a lot of fun together," she says. "One of the best times for me was when Cody was about fourteen and the two of us went traveling for ten days. We spent four days in New Orleans, which was a total gas for us as musicians; then the next four days at Disney World... Then, since he was a pretty good keyboard player by age sixteen, I took him on the road as part of my band to a bunch of rocking hot concerts in England and Norway. He loved it and has continued to play music on his own."

Over the years, Sainte-Marie has loved watching Cody develop into an activist in his own right. "Now that he's grown up, I'm thrilled to see his activism come into its own, especially working with his dad, Sheldon, who has been involved not only in significant actions on behalf of the Mdewakanton people in his home state of Minnesota, but also as a filmmaker alongside Steven Newcomb, with whom he produced the excellent movie *The Doctrine of Discovery: Unmasking the Domination Code.* Cody scored the movie at home in his own studio."

Still, she can't deny that she has regrets, and it's hard not to hear the self-directed blame in her words, particularly when she's reflecting on her choices in male partners.

"I seem to have a blind spot when it comes to men," Sainte-Marie admits. "I just don't see it coming, the bad stuff. When I recall the way Jack treated me and the world and Cody, too, I'm ashamed I took so long to get out of there. It was borderline unsafe, but there I was continuing to make excuses for Jack's unforgivable rageaholic behavior. Years later, I had another boyfriend who turned out to be an intimidator—whom Cody could see more clearly than I did—and who was a con and an abuser of the support I provided to him and his family. I think I'm so afraid of male abuse that I don't even see it. My apologies to Cody will never be enough for exposing him to those two particular bozos."

Just like many women who have experienced violence and abuse, Sainte-Marie can be hard on herself. She has also always been the primary source of income in her relationships; she successfully raised her son as a single parent, and much later she left an abusive marriage to a musical genius. She's been a constant source of support and inspiration to her family, her band, other musicians, and her friends, particularly the women in her life. It wasn't at the forefront of her intentions, but simply by being herself and articulating her needs and her values, Sainte-Marie has disrupted the patriarchy over and over again. Creating something better—in spite of and beyond those hierarchal structures—is integral to decolonization, and it's at the heart of *Power in the Blood*.

The album revitalized Sainte-Marie's reputation as an activist, radical, and rabble-rouser. While she's held up as an activist hero by a lot of people and labeled an agitator and a threat by others, she's never thought of herself as a disruptor. It's a credible label, given Sainte-Marie's repeated challenges to systemic oppression and the threat she's posed to established power dynamics throughout her life, but Sainte-Marie just laughs at the suggestion. "That's pretty highfalutin. But I was not deliberately going up against a system and kicking at it. I was just trying to make the facts clearer. I didn't really have an agenda to disrupt the power agenda. That's giving me far too much credit."

She points to some of the people at Standing Rock as better examples of political disruptors. They are on the ground, putting their bodies where their beliefs are and facing down law-enforcement agencies, water cannons, and lawyers. "I'm right with them, yes, I am, but that's not what I was trying to do in my songs," Sainte-Marie says. "I was trying to do something else, and it was really pretty personal. I didn't look at Lyndon Johnson or Richard Nixon the way I do now, because I didn't even know they were blacklisting me." But, intentional or not, Sainte-Marie did change things through her music and activism by modeling Indigenous revolution in ways both big and small, loud and quiet, bold and humble. "I wasn't trying to disrupt the power agenda," Sainte-Marie says, "but I'm awfully glad I did."

CHAPTER 17

CARRY IT ON

WHILE ON TOUR in 2017, as America shuddered its way through the nightmarish first full year of Donald Trump's Republican administration, Sainte-Marie hung a red dress onstage in a spotlight at every concert, a symbol and reminder of the Missing and Murdered Women and Girls (the national emergency of gendered violence that targets Indigenous Canadian women and girls) and the crisis of human trafficking. Fifteen minutes before a massive summer outdoor show in a parking lot in downtown Vancouver, she realized that she'd left the red dress in her hotel room and raced back to get it. She returned to the backstage area with just three minutes to spare—long enough to gather with her band under the parking lot's lone tree for a brief pre-show smudge and blessing. It's a ritual they do before almost every show, led by Ojibwe drummer and grass dancer Michel Bruyere. Each night, he offers thanks to the Creator, the relations, and to every person in the circle, arms around one another, as they cleanse with the smoldering sweetgrass smoke. It's this sense of the sacred that Sainte-Marie carries in her songs.

At many of Sainte-Marie's shows in 2017, the most rapturous applause was for her most searing activist anthems, which feel more pressingly relevant than they have in years. Eager to "put her songs to work," she released a new collection in fall 2017 called *Medicine Songs*, which featured mostly new recordings of classics and forgotten or overlooked gems, as well as two new songs, "You Got to Run," a heart-racing collaboration with Inuk throat singing artist Tanya Tagaq, and the incisive and fiercely political protest song, "The War Racket," in which Sainte-Marie snarls, "And war is never, ever holy/It's just a greedy men's dream/And you two-faced crusaders/Both sides are obscene." When her manager, Gilles Paquin, first heard the song, he thought it was "too hard." Now, as the political climate continues its bleak descent, he can't help but marvel at Sainte-Marie's prescience. "Sometimes she sees things and they're not pretty," Paquin says, "but she sees them with compassion."

"Many times in my life, I have felt apologetic for loving the world, particularly in music," Sainte-Marie admits. "In show business, there's a sense of cynicism, like, 'We're here to outsmart the world and empty its pockets,' or 'We're here to get more fame than anybody else ever did.' It hasn't always been hip or fashionable to be in love with the world. It's a little dorky. And I'm okay with that."

It's that love and hope that fuel her song "Carry It On," a rousing, inspiring track with a sing-along chorus that rushes like a river in the midday sun. It's equal parts prayer and warning as Sainte-Marie sings, "Lift your heart to your own home planet/What do you see? What is your attitude?/Are you here to improve or damn it?/Look right now and you will see/we're only here/by the skin of our teeth as it is/so take heart and take care of your link with Life/Oh carry it on." It's not a lecture; it's always an invitation. Sainte-Marie has cultivated and perfected patience throughout her career. She's a philosopher; she can wait and find something to do in the meantime as the world ripens.

In April 2017, Sainte-Marie received the Allan Waters Humanitarian Award (for "exemplary dedication to social, environmental, and humanitarian causes") at the Juno Awards, and she also offered, as a guest, an official welcome to the Juno Awards ceremony before A Tribe Called Red and Tanya Tagaq opened the show. The performance was explosive, but Sainte-Marie ignited the spark with her speech, a necessary counterpoint to the celebration of Canada's sesquicentennial, "Canada 150"—which, in its very name, erases and denies the thousands of years of Indigenous existence before colonization.

This is the text of Sainte-Marie's welcome:

We are here in Ottawa on un-surrendered territory of the Algonquin and Anishinaabe nations. Tonight we want to thank and honor the land and the people of the Algonquin and Anishinaabe Nations, whose families have lived on this territory for thousands and thousands and thousands of years! And whose cultures and presence have nurtured and continue to nurture this land. We also acknowledge the enduring presence of all First Nations, Inuit, and Métis peoples. [54]

She had changed the text of what the Junos' organizers had handed her, phoning local First Nations elders and letting them know of her changes. Her use of the word "un-surrendered"—instead of the official government term "unceded"—was deliberate, she explained afterwards. Words such as "unceded" and "millennia" sound like "legal-ese" to her and disguise the truth of the situation. "Legal-ese words trip up the listener, distract you from the sense of the statement, which is important."

The morning after the Junos, Sainte-Marie was up early to meet with Canadian senators to discuss supporting the arts by making airfare more reasonable for touring musicians as well as ongoing challenges facing Indigenous people across the country.

"I got to speak at the Senate, in the chamber, to a whole bunch of senators and ministers—it is rare for them to get together, especially in that room," Sainte-Marie says. The invitation to address the Senate was a follow-up to conversations she'd had earlier in the week with Senators Murray Sinclair and Marilou McPhedran. Afterwards, she joined in a meeting of the Aboriginal Peoples Committee, when two prominent Indigenous Manitobans—Cree educator and activist Doris Young and John Morrisseau, former president of the Manitoba Métis Federation—testified about the trauma of the loss of Indigenous languages and land. "The senators were there to bear witness, and it was really informative, but heartbreaking," she says.

Medicine Songs' themes are ones Sainte-Marie's been singing about for decades; as a collection, it is proof that she's always been years, even decades, ahead of popular opinion. Others might doubt the efficacy of her songs or the importance of their messages, but not Sainte-Marie. She knows that sometimes the world stumbles forward slowly towards paths that are already laid out.

Being outspoken hasn't always made her popular; in fact, it's cost her a lot, over and over again, as she learned with the blacklist. "She always stood for her integrity and her truth, even though she could have sold out and probably become a bit more of a household name," her friend Denise Kaufman says with admiration. "Unfortunately, whatever those mechanisms of the industry are, she hasn't been in front of a lot of people who are craving her. In these terrible times, her music is more potent and appropriate and needed than ever."

Like so many Indigenous people, Sainte-Marie has sounded warning bells about greed, corruption, and the evils of colonialism, and she's suggested alternatives, only to be silenced or dismissed or ignored by the mostly white men in power. So how does she keep singing the same songs and writing new ones, sustaining hope, night after night, year after year, without just giving up? "You can't get discouraged just because the Academy Award people aren't noticing," Sainte-Marie says with a laugh. "You can't get discouraged just because the president isn't noticing. You have to realize that, because of your efforts, a lot of people do notice, and they come from a lot of different walks of life. You have to value and serve your own niche, count your blessings, and realize at the same time how much farther you have to go. It always helps, I think, to realize that although you're not impacting everybody, some people take your impact into directions that you, yourself, could not have done. I can't be discouraged," she says. "There are always new opportunities. And just like *Sesame Street* pointed out to me, there's always a new crop of five-year-olds who need to know the basics. It's beautiful, and you can't let it get you mad or you just burn up."

As an example, Sainte-Marie points to Lionel Bordeaux (Sicangu Lakota), one of the early Nihewan Foundation scholarship recipients. He not only founded and became president of Sinte Gleska College on the Rosebud Indian Reservation in South Dakota where he was born, but he also founded the American Indian Higher Education Consortium (the unifying community of America's thirty-six tribal colleges and universities).

Part of what keeps Sainte-Marie going are some guiding principles she's developed over her fifty-plus years of activism. She revisits these frequently when she's checking in with herself to stave off exhaustion. She has three "rules."

Rule number one: Don't burn out. "I'm always telling this to activists. You can't help anybody when you burn out. You have to know when you need a bath and a nap. If you don't take care of Brother Mule—your mind and your body—as Saint Francis said, then Brother Mule's not going to work anymore; you're gonna kill him. So I have taken care of my own Sister Mule, my body and my mind. When things get too crazy, I just leave. If I'm at a reception and everybody's starting to get drunk and I'm bored, I leave."

Rule number two: Don't misrepresent. "I've had corporations, political parties, even grassrootsers, try to give me a lot of money to come and be, [for example], the face of a fur company—as if!" she laughs. And related to this is knowing when to divert the spotlight. "Somebody recently wanted to give me an award related to climate change. I'm not an expert, but they didn't care; they just wanted me to show up and talk about myself. I referred them to Bill McKibben at 350.org who, like Naomi Klein, is the real deal. If I think there's somebody who can do it better, I take a pass, redirect the message. You have to know when to do that. It's part of educating and supporting each other.

"I know better than to show up like a shiny new vehicle, with all the bells and whistles and steal the spotlight," Sainte-Marie says. "I was invited to sing at Bobby Kennedy's funeral, and I said no. I've been invited to the White House many times, but I only went once and not to sing but to think and learn and share, when I was on Hillary Clinton's Committee to Save America's Treasures (such as Cahokia and Mesa Verde). You get to understand that just being window dressing is also a contribution. Know when to be invisible, when to share, and when to hand over the microphone.

"I was at the [2017] Women's March in Hawai'i. I didn't have to receive an invitation. Nobody had to fly me in, I didn't have to have my own sign, and I didn't have to have anybody announce me from the podium, 'Hey, guess who's here today!' No, I was just one face in a crowd, reflecting the light onto the issue, and that's the point of being effective. You don't want to block the light; you want to reflect it. Sometimes you just show up. Sometimes that's how you do it."

Sainte-Marie also knows the value of building connections on the ground because there's only so much that she, personally, can do. "I do what I can, and then I look around me and see who else is there and trying to fix it," Sainte-Marie says. "I keep it in mind that the locals are the real engine, and they are going to have to stay and deal with the repercussions of the issue and my visit."

Rule number three is simple, a side note to touring musicians: Don't fuck the band. "All my bandmates know this, the players and the backup singers," she laughs. "No romances on tour. It unbalances everything. The tour can't take it. If that's what's going to happen, you gotta wait till after the tour. Knowing that, the tour stays hot.

"So, don't burn out. Don't misrepresent, and do know when to divert the spotlight. And don't fuck the band."

She also encourages others to make something—a song, a painting, a petition—because they *need* to, not because "it's a favor to the world. You do it because it's in your head and you gotta turn it into something, see where it leads—that verse, that chord, that melody." Sainte-Marie's frank, matter-of-fact approach to life is as legendary as her relentless spirit and vitality, even amongst her friends.

"I think she's a superwoman," Elaine Bomberry says. "She's really led the way to give so many Indigenous musicians—male, female, young, and old—so much hope and aspirations to get into the music industry. She's our shining light; she's the one that everyone wants to be like. She's the one who opened up all those doors and all those gates. She's beaten down all those bushes to make that trail for all of us behind so we can say, 'Wow, we can do this. We're on this road together.'"

"She astounds me with her vitality," Steppenwolf's John Kay says. "We're neither one of us spring chickens at this point, and she just keeps soldiering on. This is another aspect of my admiration for her: not resting on your laurels, looking forward instead of over your shoulder as to where you've been all the time. You can probably surmise that I'm rather enamored with her on numerous levels."

Taj Mahal says, "She's one of my oldest and dearest friends, literally, since something like fifty-five years ago. The energy stayed incredible all these years and she hasn't lost her edge. It is a beacon of light to anyone, an inspiration. I was inspired by her work ethic—what it is that she does and how she does it. It's just incredible."

Sainte-Marie is still thinking about what's next. In 2018, she received two Juno nominations and one win—Indigenous Album of the Year—for *Medicine Songs*. She would like to bring the Cradleboard Teaching Project to Canada, create a Cradleboard Canada website, and expand it with Indigenous Canadian content provided by local educators and cultural experts.

She has also researched the five-hundred-year-old Indigenous slave trade in the Americas, and has been in research mode since reading Andrés Reséndez's 2016 book, *The Other Slavery: The Uncovered Story of Indian Enslavement in America*. The book has opened her eyes to the scope of the erasure of knowledge about Indigenous enslavement, as well as to how that slave trade continues to this day. Particularly vulnerable are Indigenous women and girls, many of whom, she believes, are among the Missing and Murdered Indigenous Women and Girls. "It's so disturbing," she says. "I thought I knew a thing or two before. I didn't know anything. The book is really illuminating. In many places, the business of selling Indigenous slaves to Europe, the Middle East, the Philippines, and South America was even bigger than the African slave trade, and it was mostly children and girls and women. We don't call it slavery now, we call it human trafficking, but in Canada, the majority of people who are trafficked are Indigenous, and most are women and girls."[55]

Sainte-Marie wants to shed light on the crisis and make people aware of what's happening. She knows only too well how difficult it is to hear stories like this. The first-person accounts that came out of Truth and Reconciliation were difficult to witness. A few weeks before the 2017 Junos, she performed at the 2017 Indspire Awards honoring Indigenous excellence in arts and in the community within Canada. Elder Tekatsi:tsia'kwa Katsi Cook was honored for her work in health; she, too, was a TRC witness. They spoke about how to make space for the devastating testimonies of survivors. "Katsi told me we're there to be a witness, not a container," Sainte-Marie says. It's something she's continued to keep in mind as she considers what she can do to stop the trafficking of young Indigenous women and girls.

Her friends are in awe of Sainte-Marie's continued tenacity and advocacy, but they're not surprised by it.

"Buffy brings the medicine," says Ulali vocalist Jennifer Kreisberg, a long-time friend and one of Sainte-Marie's backup singers. Kreisberg says it's not just about what Sainte-Marie inspires, but also what she models and what she has created for everyone. "It's not just Native musicians or female Aboriginal singers, but every one of us artists that are thriving. There are many who paved the way, but Buffy actually built the fucking road." And she's still building it.

"There's only a handful of artists that come along with that kind of feel and impact and repertoire and longevity," Jesse Green, her former bandmate, says. "She's got it all; she's a true musician and an artist."

"She's helped me in a lot of ways to look at myself and take care of myself and be healthier," her drummer, Michel Bruyere says. "I saw that I wasn't taking care of everything—my body, my spirituality—but when I met her, she always pushed that on me. I'm learning a lot and continuing to learn more. I used to be so strong about my First Nations messaging, but the message that she's spreading, it's spread through me now."

"She's had a huge impact in Indian country," Kreisberg says. "Her activism can be subtle, but it's there. She just does it without banging you over the head. She's so good at it because she means it, because it's real. Me and Charlie Hill's nickname for her used to be 'Buffy-motherfucking-Sainte-Marie,'" Kreisberg laughs. "We used to call her that behind her back. I don't know if she knows that."

Sainte-Marie will probably laugh at that nickname. Her brilliant sense of humor ranges from innocent to risqué. When she gleefully opens up a package of alfalfa sprouts in her dressing room, she exclaims, "It's nature's pubic hair!" before passing the container around the room. In the tour van, she jokes about the impossibility of reaching the electrical outlets behind hotel-room beds and how it's so much effort to plug in her vibrator that by the time she gets it working, she's barely in the mood. But also in the van, every time she spots a horse from the window she squeals and points. There is almost nothing in the world that makes her happier than animals. She says that when she's with her own animals on her farm, she'll just start to laugh in happiness, simply because of their sweetness.

Although not everyone is aware of just how funny she is, it's part of Sainte-Marie's artistry and work. With a song catalog like hers—ripe for rediscovery and unrivaled in the sprawling wilderness of its variety—as well as all of her activism and advocacy, Sainte-Marie's will be a name that echoes far into the future, well beyond seven generations. Hers is a generous, impressive, and positive legacy, and yet she doesn't take herself too seriously, nor does she spend time thinking about things like her "legacy." In fact, the word makes her roll her eyes a little. Even though she's one of the greatest living songwriters, she's utterly casual about her archival process. Which is to say, she doesn't really have one. Thirty or forty handwritten notebooks contain what she's managed to save of the bulk of the writing she's done over the decades. She also has drawers full of fragments, Post-Its, envelopes, and napkins, and she has iPhones and computers in which she has noted her thoughts so that she can revisit them someday. Maybe.

"One of these days, I might get around to them. Or I might not. It's only words, and the world keeps changing," she laughs. "We're all living on thin ice." One or two of Sainte-Marie's handwritten screenplays and three notebooks disappeared from Jack Nitzsche's car one night in the eighties when he and Robert Downey Sr. went out and failed to lock the doors to their vehicle. "One of the screenplays was about Pauline Johnson, which I never saw again," she says. "These were all handwritten, so once it was gone, it was gone."

Sainte-Marie is philosophical about letting things go, but she remembers the reaction of a friend who tended to put her on a pedestal, much to Sainte-Marie's chagrin. The friend was horrified about Sainte-Marie's drawers full of fragments and about what would happen if she—gasp—lost one. "God, you know, for a writer, this is kind of doo-doo, this is kind of like shit, this is what comes out of us," Sainte-Marie laughs. "We don't hang on to it and worship it forever more." She has the same perspective on emotions like bitterness and guilt. "Some things do not belong on your altar, and not everything is makeup for your face or a badge of how [adopts a raging voice] fucking bitter you are or how [adopts a crying, whining voice] insecure and guilty you are. Some things are doo-doo. The idea is to have a look and either repurpose it—either for fuel to make light and heat or as fertilizer to grow something new—or flush it. Don't turn it into your badge of identity."

Sainte-Marie feels her songs don't belong on the altar, either. "It's life—the life that we all share in songs and poetry and cries and whispers and moans and joys. Life itself is to be honored, not the freaking song that I wrote about it. Songs have a value and I love 'em and everything, but there's no way that I see them as more important than life itself. They're just my particular self-expression about life. They're only poetry, and there've been poets in the world before and hopefully there will be forever, and it's just wonderful. But poems don't take the place of life, or you didn't read them right."

Creation hums in her bones, and it's this vital, crucial spark that makes Sainte-Marie's contributions so tangible and specific, yet also broad and universal. There's an almost magical quality to Sainte-Marie's faith and joy—in herself and her center and her creativity—which inform her feelings about humanity as well and manifest as hope. An innate capacity for survival and to withstand trauma, but also a sacred joy and kindness which Sainte-Marie draws on to become whole, again and again and again. She has stayed true to the vision she so clearly declared in 1964: "It's my way."

"I'm still not even sure that I *am* a professional musician," Sainte-Marie jokes. "I think I'm just getting away with a lot. Hell, I can't even read music. But I love the world and I love people, I really do. My deep-down feeling is that the human race is young and ripening. After all, I've seen the almost impossible become possible in really big ways.

"I have two main prayers. One is 'thanks' and the other is 'wow.' I'm thrilled with so much of life. The miracle of being alive is the number-one big deal for me. Life knocked me on the ass with the first breath I took, and I've been going 'holy smokes' ever since."

BUFFY
AND ME

BUFFY SAINTE-MARIE'S MUSIC and words alter hearts and minds, and so, too, does the practical, messy, and tender work of collaborating with her to make something. At one point in this biography, I began a sentence with the words "Tearing down," and in the editing process, she crossed them out and provided this alternative: "Creating—in spite of and beyond." That simple re-framing blew my mind. I actually felt a seismic shift in my brain and in my body, and I know that I'll think about this forever and ever. My own language has a tendency to be rooted in destruction, I want to pull things apart and examine them, while her language is rooted in possibility, a desire to grow and explore and persuade. This is just one of the ways she models how to thrive.

The first time I interviewed Buffy was in April 2015 for a feature I wrote for CBC Music, my employer. It was a good week, personally and professionally. My first book on era-defining female musicians, *We Oughta Know: How Four Women Ruled the '90s and Changed Canadian Music*, had just come out, and now I was speaking with another musical icon about one of the most electrifying, radical albums I'd ever heard—a woman who should have been the subject of a million books, whose music and activism was revolutionary, who deserved to take up way more space in the music criticism and pop culture canons but whose legacy had been suppressed, minimized, and continually erased by media, other artists, and two presidential administrations.

It was surreal to call a phone number in Hawai'i and hear this friendly, bright, excited voice say, "Hi, it's Buffy!" The weight of her legacy—fifty years of amazing music and life-changing advocacy—was my burden, not hers. She's down-to-earth, friendly, positive, and suffers no fools, but she doesn't enjoy bleating deference the way that some of her celebrity peers do. She appreciates people who know their stuff, who have done their homework, and who get what she's trying to do. She's human, not a mythical creature, and she wants to be understood.

Our conversation about *Power in the Blood* was lively and we laughed a lot. At the end of the allotted twenty or thirty minutes, I didn't want to hang up, and my heart soared when she said exactly what I'd been thinking. We giggled over our quick bond, and later that day someone asked me whether I was already thinking about my next book. I was, I admitted. I wanted to write a biography of Buffy Sainte-Marie. But I put the idea in the back of my head and continued to write about *Power in the Blood* for the CBC and other outlets throughout 2015. The record wouldn't leave me; it was in my guts and bouncing around in my brain. I couldn't stop thinking about its vitality; not only how crucial it was at that time, but also that its next-level power would only reveal itself in the years to come. It would be a key, a foundation, perhaps, in making decolonization the new normal.

True North Records sent me a huge poster of *Power in the Blood* a few months after Buffy won the 2015 Polaris Music Prize with a note thanking me for writing about the record, and I hung the poster up in my cubicle at CBC. By early 2016, under the gaze of that poster, I was kicking around an idea for a book that was sort of anti–Canada 150—the government-marketed celebration of Canada's sesquicentennial—but would also capitalize on the 150 propaganda. It would be about the 150 best Canadian musicians who weren't the straight, white men who usually received all the attention, and Buffy Sainte-Marie was at the top of my list. Eventually, I emailed Jennifer Croll at Greystone Books and shared my idea. She advised that "list" books weren't usually their thing, but noted my interest in Buffy—and I let her know that my real dream was to write a biography of Sainte-Marie. I emailed Buffy's people to find out if there was any interest, and a few weeks later, I met Buffy in Richmond, B.C., to see how we hit it off in person before going any further.

She walked in wearing an all-black ensemble paired with high-heeled boots and bright blue nails, and she immediately told me she was a huge fan of my writing. I laughed out loud and said something like, "No, that's what I say to you!" and then we spent two hours talking and laughing and listening to each other. Buffy told me about how she had bought and read my book, and how much she loved it—and she meant it. She is a voracious reader who always has multiple books on the go, both audiobooks and print. She's also the kind of reader every writer longs for: engaged, critical, and who wants to talk with you about your work in a way that indicates how much time she has actually spent contemplating it. I talked with her about her music and her activism, told her about how it had changed me, and shared my frustrations at how little people seemed to know about her range and her innovation, the ways she'd experimented and didn't give a fuck about the status quo, and her leadership, strength, and vision. She appreciated my observations and then turned the conversation back to me and *We Oughta Know*. We compared reading lists and promised to send each other recommendations. We had both read and loved

Lindy West's *Shrill*. Eventually she told me that I seemed to actually get what she's spent her whole life trying to do, and not everybody does, and so the book was on. We hugged, and I floated out to my car and tried to scrawl down as many notes as I could about things she'd said, because I knew that, even if for some reason the book didn't happen, my life was never going to be the same.

Before the book contract was even signed, we started our interview process. We were on the phone twice a week, for two hours at a time, throughout January and February of 2017. I spent the hours I wasn't on the phone with her looking forward to the next interview, and at one point Buffy said, "Are you sure we're working on a book and not just building a really good friendship?" I laughed and said that we were doing both. For Valentine's Day, she introduced me to Cliteracy, artist Sophia Wallace's 2012 text-based project that "dismantle[s] the taboos associated with female and feminized genitals." I was delighted that she knew how much I would enjoy feminist, boundary-breaking art centered on female pleasure and that debunked myths and clichés about female anatomy. She told me about it over the phone and then sent me the link via email to make sure I had it. I honestly didn't know that I could love her more, and then: Cliteracy. It was great.

In late February, I met up with Buffy and her band in New York City and joined them on the road as they toured *Power in the Blood* and we did three days of interviews. In the small tour van, she ensured we sat next to each other. I didn't turn my recorder on, preferring to take notes in my notebook because I thought the recorder would interrupt the natural flow of the conversation. On the way from Manhattan to Woodstock, Buffy asked if anyone wanted to listen to an audiobook, and soon *The Lakota Way: Stories and Lessons for Living*, a gorgeously

written and narrated book by Joseph M. Marshall III, was fill-
ing everybody's heads and distracting us from the long miles
disappearing underneath us. Buffy motioned to her laptop.
"Wanna see some photos?" she asked, and began to show me
an impromptu slideshow of her photographs from a trip she'd
taken to Guatemala with her best friend, Kayle, a few years
previously.

Our bond deepened over some of our overlapping interests:
cats (even though I'm allergic), flowers, coffee, pinball, people,
books, music, and movies. (Sainte-Marie belongs to the Academy of Motion Picture Arts and Sciences and watches lots of
screeners.) We share an optimism that is almost relentless and
would probably be more annoying—I'm sure it is annoying to
some, but oh, well—if it weren't countered by an enthusiasm for
real talk. Buffy can cut through the bullshit faster than anybody
else I know. At one point, we discussed a contemporary singer
who held her album release at a famous prison, and Buffy said,
"Well, it's a good gimmick." I learned she has many laughs, and
all of them make me smile. We spent hours and hours laughing,
and even during the darkest and most difficult conversations, it
was her humor that buoyed us through the hard stuff and rooted
us on the other side.

After New York our phone interviews took on a less rigor-
ous schedule. By then I'd begun the hard work of transcribing
our more than forty hours of conversation, and then we met up
again in July when I joined her and the band on tour for a couple of shows on the West Coast. We went to a restaurant with
a small vineyard, and as we walked in together, we spotted a cat
sitting in the front seat of the car beside us. Buffy said it was a
good sign, since we had also met a cat as soon as we'd arrived in
Woodstock, the last time we'd seen each other. We tried to find
somewhere to go for karaoke on the first night—I was hoping

she would do Heart or something, and maybe I could just sing backup—but the small seaside town shuts down pretty early so the pressure was off. I spent the next few months writing all the time, nervous about what she'd think of the first draft, worried that she'd have regrets or take-backs, or that I hadn't taken enough care with her words and concepts, that I had misrepresented her somehow.

When I received an email from her saying that she loved the first draft, the relief hit me so hard I thought I might vomit. When I submitted the draft to Greystone, Buffy sent me the infamous GIF of Shaq shimmying his shoulders alternating with a cat shimmying its tail—her version of "You go, girl"—and I couldn't stop laughing, I loved it so much. Of course, there was still a ton of work to do on the book, changes and revisions, from both Buffy and my editor, to make it the best version it could be, one that lived up to and properly captured Buffy's life and spirit.

Before beginning to write this afterword on a cold winter Saturday in Vancouver, I worked through Buffy's suggestions and edits for the latest draft. That morning, six inches of snow blanketed the ground, but as the sun burned brightly and slowly across the sky, I listened to the vehicles going by. First, crunching through powder, then slogging through slush, and finally splashing through puddles as I went through the revisions. I cried on three separate occasions and lost track of the number of times I laughed out loud. Buffy has combed every inch of this book, every page bears her fingerprints, and I can hear her voice at every turn. The book is better for it. I'm better for it.

It still feels unreal that Buffy is now part of my life. It's such a privilege as a journalist and a writer to have people share their stories with you, but for someone like Buffy to share her whole life story with me—well, I'm basically going to spend forever hugging this feeling to myself, a little stunned and in perpetual gratitude that she said yes. I have learned to be a better listener, to be kinder, but to also stand up for my vision and trust my gut as well as my own expertise. She has given me so much perspective about what it means to be an activist and what people actually need from allies: it's doing the work, it's showing up, it's a lifetime commitment, it's not getting in the way. It's also vital to take time for yourself, to restore and revive and reconnect with whatever makes you whole. And of course, don't fuck the band, which I think is great advice for a lot of industries.

Buffy will be in Vancouver for the Juno Awards, and I'm finally going to take her to Catfe, the local cat café we've been talking about for months. We're making plans for when the book comes out, schemes that will get us into the same room. Eighteen months after Buffy and I first met in person, and almost three years since our first interview, we've built a lovely little friendship, and together we've made a book that needs to be in the world.

ANDREA WARNER, MARCH 2018

ACKNOWLEDGMENTS

THANKS, GRATITUDE, AND a giant chunk of my heart to Buffy Sainte-Marie, always and forever.

Thank you to Joni Mitchell for writing the foreword to this book. As a lifelong fan of your music, this is a dream come true. Thank you to Jennifer Croll for her tough editing love and her brilliant brain, and thank you to Rob Sanders and everybody at Greystone (particularly Alice Fleerackers, Jen Gauthier, and Nayeli Jimenez) for being excited about this book from the very beginning, as well as publicists Corina Eberle, Richard Nash, and Emily Cook for their work in helping launch the book out into the world. Thank you to my agent Kris Rothstein as well as Carolyn Swayze for your support, enthusiasm, and general awesomeness. Thanks to Gilles Paquin and the Paquin team; to Michel Bruyere, Anthony King, Mark Olexson, and Kimberly Glick for opening up your touring arms to me on the road; and to everybody else I interviewed for this book: Robbie Robertson, Elaine Bomberry, Jesse Green, Debra Piapot, Ntawnis Piapot, Denise Kaufman, Taj Mahal, John Kay, Randy Bachman, Kayle Higenbotham, and Jennifer Kreisberg. Thank you to my colleagues at CBC Music for your support, and for providing a place for some of my earliest writing about Buffy Sainte-Marie. Thank you also to *Exclaim!* for your invitation to write about Buffy Sainte-Marie's discography. Thank you to JB the First Lady, the First Ladies Crew, and Butterflies in Spirit for your music and art, sharing your lives with me, and trusting me with your stories. I have learned so much from you and will continue to appreciate and acknowledge your wisdom and leadership, and to do my best to assist in decolonizing music journalism and criticism.

The rest of my heart for Carlos Hernandez Fisher, who holds my hand and works through my freak-outs with me. Thank you for taking ownership of the basic maintenance of our shared lives the last two years, for editing and proofing and brainstorming. I love you. Thanks to my grandma, Lena Warner, for being interested always in everything that I do and your love and friendship, and to my sister, Jenn Warner, for your encouragement and for doing the heavy emotional lifting and literal showing up with family and shared friends while I was focused on interviewing and writing. Thank you to my mom, Elsie Warner, and my maternal grandma, Donna Allen, for your love and support. I am so grateful to Jackie Wong for your sensitive, thoughtful, careful feedback and edits, and your incredible glowing heart. Thank you to Michael Hogan for saving my bladder and sanity. And so much love to my ladies' assemblage—Julia Browning, Holly Gordon, Mette Bach, Florence Chee, Danica Longair, Ann-Marie Spicer, Andrea Gin, Zoe Grams, Lisa Christiansen, Samantha Smith, and Melanie Copple—for the support and hugs and high fives. I am very lucky to be surrounded by great women, and you make my life better in so many ways.

DISCOGRAPHY

It's My Way! (1964)

Vanguard (VSD-79142)

Sainte-Marie's groundbreaking debut has lost none of its power, thoughtfulness, or complexity since 1964, and its relevance isn't an echo so much as a scream. Everything she was singing about, telling us about, warning us about—the anti-war messaging ("Universal Soldier"), the plight of Indigenous people and the desperate need for decolonization ("Now That the Buffalo's Gone"), the dangers of addiction ("Cod'ine")—all of it persists to this day. The Library of Congress inducted *It's My Way!* into the National Recording Registry in 2015.

Many a Mile (1965)

Vanguard (VSD-79171)

Sainte-Marie added a few more traditional tunes into the mix of her sophomore follow-up, and two glorious covers—Bukka White's "Fixin' to Die" and Patrick Sky's "Many a Mile"—but she also recorded what would be her own most covered song of all time: "Until It's Time for You to Go." It quickly became a pop standard, and was a hit for everyone from the Four Pennies to Neil Diamond to Elvis Presley.

Little Wheel Spin and Spin (1966)

Vanguard (VSD-79211)

Sainte-Marie's third record reached the *Billboard* Top 100, an achievement made all the more meaningful considering the album included the almost seven-minute long epic detailing the plight of Indigenous people from colonization "My Country 'Tis of Thy People You're Dying."

Fire & Fleet & Candlelight (1967)

Vanguard (VSD-79250)

This is the record in which Sainte-Marie began to truly experiment with more rock, pop, and electronic sounds. She also recorded two songs by then-emerging and unknown singer-songwriter Joni Mitchell: "The Circle Game" and "Song to a Seagull."

I'm Gonna Be a Country Girl Again (1968)

Vanguard (VSD-79280)

Her fifth release was also Sainte-Marie's biggest departure creatively, a country album recorded in Nashville, secretly co-produced by country great Chet Atkins, who had to remain uncredited because of the conditions of his own recording contract.

Illuminations (1969)

Vanguard (VSD-79300)

Arguably Sainte-Marie's most polarizing record, this was largely an electronic album decades ahead of its time, made with synthesizers that contorted and layered her voice and acoustic guitar, and almost completely at odds with the image of her that many fans had, which was a guitar-playing folkie and protest singer. The record was wildly experimental, venturing into psychedelic rock and avant-garde territory, and was ignored by most people for a long time. More recently, *Illuminations* fans started to reclaim its legacy as an innovative and musically pioneering album. It's now hailed as one of the earliest electronic albums and was a big influence on Steve Hackett of Genesis.

She Used to Wanna Be a Ballerina (1971)

Vanguard (VSD-79311)

This was Sainte-Marie's first record not produced by Vanguard label co-owner Maynard Solomon. Instead, hotshot producer and film composer Jack Nitzsche, who'd just worked on albums for the Rolling Stones and Neil Young, approached Vanguard about producing a record for Sainte-Marie. The actual working relationship between the pair wasn't easy, but the music is good. It also features a few more covers than most Sainte-Marie albums, including Neil Young's "Helpless," Leonard Cohen's "Bells," and Carole King and Gerry Goffin's "Smackwater Jack."

Moonshot (1972)

Vanguard (VSD-79312)

Her eighth record kicked off a four-album working relationship with Norbert Putnam, a Nashville-based rock and pop producer and musician who co-owned his own studio. He recruited famed session musicians the Memphis Horns, and the resulting album pulses with life. The first track in particular, "Not the Lovin' Kind," is one of Sainte-Marie's most thrilling and underrated rock songs and it should have been a number-one hit.

Quiet Places (1973)

Vanguard (VSD-79330)

Sainte-Marie's final album for Vanguard was also her ninth record in ten years. It was again produced by Putnam and featured the Memphis Horns and David Briggs on the keyboards. It also featured another cover of a Joni Mitchell song, "For Free," as well as Randy Newman's "Have You Seen My Baby? (Hold On)."

Buffy (1974)

MCA (405)

It doesn't seem like a coincidence that, on her first record free from the confines of her lengthy and ultimately contentious contract with Vanguard, Sainte-Marie called the album *Buffy*. It was her first record for MCA.

Changing Woman (1975)

MCA (451)

Sainte-Marie's final album working with Putnam as her producer also marked her second and last record for MCA. It features the sweetly mournful ballad "Nobody Will Ever Know It's Real but You," which was co-written by Sainte-Marie and Putnam.

Sweet America (1976)

ABC (ABCD-929)

This thirteen-track album is most notable as Sainte-Marie's last LP before her sixteen-year hiatus from releasing studio albums, but even more importantly, it's home to "Starwalker," the first song to feature a sample of powwow music. Even in this first recording of the song, it's impossible to ignore the power and importance of Indigenizing rock music.

Coincidence and Likely Stories (1992)

Ensign/Chrysalis (F2-21920)

Sainte-Marie co-produced her first comeback album with Chris Birkett, and the two made the record largely over the internet using what was then cutting-edge technology. It was a political, provocative record (her first after she found out she'd been blacklisted), as if Sainte-Marie had been holding back for years and this showed her boiling over. She also continued to experiment sonically here, re-recording "Starwalker" to beef up the powwow sample. The album features a track she'd been writing off and on for fourteen years, "Bury My Heart at Wounded Knee."

Up Where We Belong (1996)

EMI (E4 35059)

This packaging of some of Sainte-Marie's greatest hits spans more than forty years and takes its title from her Academy Award–winning song. It's also one of her most comprehensive albums in terms of showcasing the depth and breadth of Sainte-Marie's genre-defying repertoire.

Running for the Drum (2008)

Appleseed Recordings (APR CD 1117)

Her second comeback album was again a co-production between Sainte-Marie and Birkett, and it starts off with three epic new songs packed with samples of traditional Indigenous music and beats: "No No Keshagesh," "Cho Cho Fire," and "Working for the Government." She won a Juno Award (Canada's Grammy) for Best Aboriginal Album.

Power in the Blood (2015)

True North Records (TND603)

Sainte-Marie's third comeback album was a revelation and was lauded by critics for its innovation, particularly the club-thumping reinvention of "It's My Way," the title track from her debut album more than five decades previously. Another standout was the electronic makeover and lyrical rewriting of Alabama 3's "Power in the Blood," transforming it from a violent rock song into an activist anthem and celebration of Indigenous resistance. The record won the 2015 Polaris Music Prize, Canada's biggest award for creative achievement in music, and two Juno Awards, one for Indigenous Music Album of the Year and one for Contemporary Roots Album of the Year.

Medicine Songs (2017)

True North Records (TND681)

This collection of Sainte-Marie's activist anthems also includes two new songs, "You Got to Run (Spirit of the Wind)" with award-winning Inuk throat singer Tanya Tagaq, and "The War Racket." It spans Sainte-Marie's entire career, and was nominated for two Juno Awards, one for Indigenous Music Album of the Year and one for Contemporary Roots Album of the Year, and won Indigenous Album of the Year.

NOTES

Unless cited here, all quotes come from interviews Andrea Warner conducted with Buffy Sainte-Marie between January 2017 and March 2018.

Chapter 1

1. âpihtawikosisân (Chelsea Vowel), "The Stolen Generation(s)," http://apihtawikosisan.com/2012/04/the-stolen-generations/.

Chapter 2

2. Marina Frolova-Walker, "Tchaikovsky A–Z, Letter H: Homosexuality," BBC 3, http://www.bbc.co.uk/radio3/classical/tchaikovsky/atoz/tchaik_h.shtml.

3. Aqukkasuk, "Federally Recognized Tribes Should Brace for Possible Termination Policy under Trump," *Alaska Indigenous*, January 21, 2017, https://alaskaindigenous.wordpress.com/2017/01/21/federally-recognized-tribes-should-brace-for-possible-termination-policy-under-trump/.

4. National Council of Urban Indian Health, "Relocation," https://www.ncuih.org/action/document/download?document_id=120.

Chapter 3

5. Frank Mastropolo, "Musicians Recall Dylan's First Big Gig and 25 Years of Music History at Gerde's Folk City," BedfordandBowery.com, September 29, 2017, http://bedfordandbowery.com/2017/09/musicians-recall-dylans-first-big-gig-and-25-years-of-music-history-at-gerdes-folk-city/.

6. Robert Shelton, "Old Music Taking On New Color: An Indian Girl Sings Her Compositions and Folk Songs," *New York Times*, August 17, 1963, 11.

7. [Author and title unknown], *BMI: The Many Worlds of Music*, 1966, 13.

8. "The Voices of Buffy Sainte-Marie," *Life*, December 1965, 53.

9. Robert Shelton, "Guthrie's Heirs," *New York Times*, June 14, 1964.

10. Robert Shelton, "Buffy Sainte-Marie Gives Park Concert," *New York Times*, September 5, 1966.

Chapter 4

11. John Einarson with Ian and Sylvia Tyson, *Four Strong Winds: Ian & Sylvia* (Toronto, ON: McClelland & Stewart, 2012).

12. Peter Ames Carlin, *Homeward Bound: The Life of Paul Simon* (New York, NY: Henry Holt and Company, 2016).

Chapter 5

13. "The Voices of Buffy Sainte-Marie, *Life*, December 1965, 53.

14. [Author and title unknown], *Status & Diplomat*, vol. 18, 1967.

15. Judy Klemesrud, "Fighting a War on Behalf of Indians," *New York Times*, October 24, 1970, 39.

Chapter 6

16. Christian Thompson, ed., *Saskatchewan First Nations: Lives Past and Present* (Regina, SK: Canadian Plains Research Center, University of Regina Press, 2004).

17. Kayla Webley, "Top 10 Most Historically Misleading Films," *Time*, January 25, 2011, http://entertainment.time.com/2011/01/26/top-10-historically-misleading-films/.

18. Daniel Schwartz, "Truth and Reconciliation Commission: By the Numbers," CBC News, June 2, 2015, http://www.cbc.ca/news/indigenous/truth-and-reconciliation-commission-by-the-numbers-1.3096185.

19. Bob Joseph, "Christopher Columbus and the Doctrine of Discovery: 5 Things to Know," https://www.ictinc.ca/blog/christopher-columbus-and-the-doctrine-of-discovery-5-things-to-know.

20. First Nations Education Steering Committee, "Indian Residential Schools and Reconciliation," http://www.fnesc.ca/wp/wp-content/uploads/2015/07/IRSRII-12-DE-1906-1910.pdf.

21. Judy Klemesrud, "Fighting a War on Behalf of Indians," *New York Times*, October 24, 1970, 39.

22. Kathryn Shattuck, "Leo Penn 77, Stage Actor and a Director for Television," *New York Times*, September 10, 1998, http://www.nytimes.com/1998/09/10/arts/leo-penn-77-stage-actor-and-a-director-for-television.html.

23. Scott Harrison, "From the Archives: Cree Folk Singer Buffy Sainte-Marie Gets Native Americans Hired for 'The Virginian,'" *Los Angeles Times*, November 16, 2017, http://www.latimes.com/visuals/photography/la-me-fw-archives-buffy-sainte-marie-gets-american-indians-hired-20170919-story.html.

Chapter 7

24. "Buffy Sainte-Marie in 1st Country Disk," *Billboard*, January 27, 1968.

25. "100 Records That Set the World On Fire [When No One Was Listening]," *The Wire*, September 1998, http://web.archive.org/web/20070613182618/http://www.rtxarchive.com/archive/articles/wire175.html.

26. Dan Sywala, "The Top 10 Albums of Steve Hackett," *Rock'n'Roll Journalist*, November 22, 2017, https://rocknrolljournalist.com/2017/11/the-top-10-albums-of-steve-hackett.html.

27. E. K. Caldwell, *Dreaming the Dawn: Conversations with Native Artists and Activists* (Lincoln, NB: University of Nebraska Press, 1999).

28. "My Lai Massacre," History.com, http://www.history.com/topics/vietnam-war/my-lai-massacre.

29. Dotson Rader, "Who Were the Bad Guys?" *New York Times,* September 20, 1970, 119, https://www.nytimes.com/1970/09/20/archives/who-were-the-bad-guys.html.

Chapter 10

30. Judy Klemesrud, "Fighting a War on Behalf of Indians," *New York Times*, October 24, 1970, 39.

31. "Benefit for the Indians on Alcatraz / Malvina Reynolds and Buffy Sainte-Marie," PacificRadioArchives.com, PRA Archive #: BB2375, https://pacificaradioarchives.org/recording/bb2375.

32. Alysa Landry, "Native History: AIM Occupation of Wounded Knee Begins," IndianCountryToday.com, February 27, 2017, https://indiancountrymedianetwork.com/history/events/native-history-aim-occupation-of-wounded-knee-begins/.

33. Alex Jacobs, "Remember Leonard Peltier, but also Remember Joe Stuntz," IndianCountryToday.com, June 28, 2016, https://indiancountrymedianetwork.com/history/events/remember-leonard-peltier-but-also-remember-joe-stuntz/.

34. Douglas O. Linder, "Famous Trials: The Leonard Peltier Trial," via WebArchive.org, https://web.archive.org/web/20071025005019/http://www.law.umkc.edu/faculty/projects/ftrials/peltier/peltieraccount.html.

35. Carson Walker, "Aquash Murder Gets New Grand Jury Hearing," IndianCountryNews.com, January 24, 2003, http://www.indiancountrynews.com/index.php/investigations/annie-mae-pictou-aquash/21-aquash-murder-gets-new-grand-jury-hearing-1-24-2003.

36. Dirk Lammers, "Denver Man's Sentence Reduced in 1975 AIM Slaying," CBS Denver/AP Writer, September 26, 2011, http://denver.cbslocal.com/2011/09/26/denver-mans-sentence-reduced-in-1975-aim-slaying/.

37. Carson Walker, "2 Charged in 1975 American Indian Movement Slaying," Native American Press/Ojibwe News (AP), September 1, 2009, http://stmedia.startribune.com/documents/billlawrence.pdf.

38. "Guilty Verdict in N.S. Native Activist's Death," CBC News, December 10, 2010, http://www.cbc.ca/news/world/guilty-verdict-in-n-s-native-activist-s-death-1.893680.

Chapter 11

39. Les Brown, "'Sesame Street' Dazzles In Television Premiere," *Variety*, December 24, 1969, http://variety.com/1969/tv/news/sesame-street-dazzles-in-television-premiere-1201342605/.

40. Michael Davis, *Street Gang: The Complete History of Sesame Street* (New York, NY: Penguin, 2008).

Chapter 12

41. April Chee, "The Longest Walk: Activism and Legislation in Indian Country," The National Museum of the American Indian, July 1, 2016, http://blog.nmai.si.edu/main/2016/07/the-longest-walk-activism-and-legislation-in-indian-country.html.

42. Linda Deutsch, "Actress Testifies about Assault; Rape Charge Dropped," *Free Lance-Star*/Associated Press, October 23, 1979, https://news.google.com/newspapers?nid=1298&dat=19791023&id=TPxNAAAAIBAJ&sjid=n4sDAAAAIBAJ&pg=3809,3075797&hl=en.

43. Louann Brizendine, *The Female Brain* (New York, NY: Harmony Books, 2007).

Chapter 13

44. Blair Stonechild, *Buffy Sainte-Marie: It's My Way* (Markham, ON: Fifth House, 2012).

45. Lindsay Zoladz, "Illuminations: A Biography of Buffy Sainte-Marie," *LA Review of Books*, December 2, 2012, https://lareviewofbooks.org/article/illuminations-a-biography-of-buffy-sainte-marie/.

46. Colin Irwin, "Buffy Sainte-Marie on a Rollercoaster Career That Even the FBI Kept an Eye on," *The Guardian*, July 31, 2009, https://www.theguardian.com/music/2009/jul/31/buffy-sainte-marie.

Chapter 14

47. Colin Irwin, "Buffy Sainte-Marie on a Rollercoaster Career That Even the FBI Kept an Eye on," *The Guardian*, July 31, 2009, https://www.theguardian.com/music/2009/jul/31/buffy-sainte-marie.

48. Steve Silberman, "Sharing the Fire Online," *Wired*, June 1998, https://www.wired.com/1998/06/sharing-the-fire-online/.

Chapter 15

49. Evan Schlansky, "The Triumphant Return of Buffy Sainte-Marie," *American Songwriter*, August 7, 2009, https://americansongwriter.com/2009/08/the-triumphant-return-of-buffy-st-marie/, and Colin Irwin, "Buffy Sainte-Marie at the Queen Elizabeth Hall: Review," *The Telegraph*, July 29, 2009, https://www.telegraph.co.uk/culture/music/rockandpopreviews/5933197/Buffy-Sainte-Marie-at-the-Queen-Elizabeth-Hall-review.html.

Chapter 16

50. Tim Groves, "#IdleNoMore Events in 2012: Events Spreading across Canada and the World," *The Media Co-op*, December 27, 2012, http://www.mediacoop.ca/story/idle-no-more-map-events-spreading-across-canada-an/15320.

51. Ann Powers, "Review: Buffy Sainte-Marie, 'Power in the Blood,'" NPR, May 3, 2015, https://www.npr.org/2015/05/03/403277165/first-listen-buffy-sainte-marie-power-in-the-blood.

52. Neil McCormick, "Buffy Sainte-Marie, Power in the Blood, Review: 'Every Track Counts,'" *The Telegraph*, May 10, 2015, https://www.telegraph.co.uk/

culture/music/cdreviews/11589710/Buffy-Sainte-Marie-Power-In-the-
Blood-review-every-track-counts.html.

53. Jason Morgan Edwards, "There's Power in Buffy Sainte-Marie's Blood:
First Album in 7 Years Released," *Indian Country Today*, May 12, 2015,
https://indiancountrymedianetwork.com/culture/arts-entertainment/
theres-power-in-buffy-sainte-maries-blood-first-album-in-7-years-released/.

Chapter 17

54. Holly Gordon, "Junos 2017: All the Best Moments," CBC Music,
November 10, 2017, http://www.cbc.ca/music/junos/archives/
junos-2017-all-the-best-moments-1.4391755.

55. Jacqueline Oxman-Martinez, Marie Lacroix, and Jill Hanley, "Victims of
Trafficking in Persons: Perspectives from the Canadian Community Sector,"
Department of Justice Canada, Research and Statistics Section, Rpt. No.
rr06-3e, August 2005, http://www.justice.gc.ca/eng/rp-pr/cj-jp/tp/rr06_3/
index.html.

BIBLIOGRAPHY

Books

Brizendine, Louann, *The Female Brain*. New York, NY: Harmony Books, 2007.

Caldwell, E. K. *Dreaming the Dawn: Conversations with Native Artists and Activists*. Lincoln, NB: University of Nebraska Press, 1999.

Carlin, Peter Ames. *Homeward Bound: The Life of Paul Simon*. New York, NY: Henry Holt and Company, 2016.

Davis, Michael. *Street Gang: The Complete History of Sesame Street*. New York, NY: Penguin, 2008.

Einarson, John with Ian and Sylvia Tyson. *Four Strong Winds: Ian & Sylvia*. Toronto, ON: McClelland & Stewart, 2011.

Stonechild, Blair. *Buffy Sainte-Marie: It's My Way*. Markham, ON: Fifth House, 2012.

Periodicals

The following magazines, journals, newspapers, wire services, and other periodicals were consulted or used as source material: Associated Press; *Billboard*; *BMI: The Many Worlds of Music*; *Free Lance-Star*; *The Guardian*; *Life*; *Los Angeles Times*; *New York Times*; *Status & Diplomat*; *Time*; *Variety*; and *Wired*.

Websites

www.alaskaindigenous.wordpress.com

www.apihtawikosisan.com

www.bbc.co.uk/radio3

www.bedfordandbowery.com

www.books.google.ca

www.buffysainte-marie.com

www.cbc.ca

www.cbcmusic.ca

www.denver.cbslocal.com

www.fnesc.ca

www.history.com

www.ictinc.ca

www.indiancountrymedianetwork.com

www.lareviewofbooks.org

www.mediacoop.ca

www.ncuih.org

http://blog.nmai.si.edu/main/2016/07/the-longest-walk-activism-and-
    legislation-in-indian-country.html

www.pacificaradioarchives.org

www.stmedia.startribune.com

www.theguardian.com

www.web.archive.org

INDEX

Aboriginal peoples. *See* Indigenous peoples

abuse: breaking cycle of, 236; childhood experiences, 21–23; colonial basis, 232–33, 236; common responses to, 184–85; by Nitzsche, 178–79, 179–80, 181–82, 183–85, 186–87; psychological impacts, 234; survival and recovery, 46, 233–34, 235

Academy Award, 179, plate 11

Ace of Cups, 70

activism: Alcatraz Island occupation, 147–48; anger and, 45, 96–97, 98–99; Boston Indian Council, 144; breaking abusive cycles, 236; Canadian Senate and, 257–58; decolonization, 76, 222, 230–31, 240, 251; effective, 260–61; government blacklist and, 195–97; Indigenous actors in Hollywood, 99–101; by Indigenous peoples, 90–91, 144–45, 146; Longest Walk, 173–74; marginalization from Indigenous territory, 145–46; National Indian Youth Council, 33–34, 90, 143, 144, 146; Nihewan Foundation for American Indian Education, 146–47, 209, 214, 220, 259; Outward Bound, 90, 91; protest songs, 45; Sainte-Marie and, 42, 44–45, 139, 143, 258–59, 263; in Sainte-Marie's music, 54–55, 67–68, 90, 92–94, 95, 97–98; sexism and

misogyny in, 149–50; violence during occupation of Gresham abbey, 151–52; Wounded Knee Incident, 151. *See also* American Indian Movement

addiction, drugs, 65–66, 186–87. *See also* alcohol; "Cod'ine" (Sainte-Marie)

adoption, 15–16, 43–44, 235–36

Akwesasne Freedom School, 217, 218

Alabama 3, 245, 246, 282

Alcatraz Island occupation, 147–48

alcohol, 76–77, 153

Ali, Muhammad, 174

Allan Waters Humanitarian Award, 257

Alvarez, Ramon Indius, 73–74

Amaya, Carmen, 9, 40, 138

American Indian Higher Education Consortium, 259

American Indian Movement (AIM): activism by, 144, 146; Aquash in, 149, 151; Longest Walk, 173–74; Pine Ridge shootings and Aquash murder, 155–57; Sainte-Marie and, 152–53, 154–55; sexism and misogyny, 149–50; "Starwalker" reference to, 154–55; Wounded Knee Incident, 151

American Indian Religious Freedom Act, 32

American Indian Tribal College movement, 217

Amram, David, 174

anger, 45, 96–97, 98–99

95–96, 231–32, 235; in show business, 9, 73, 80–82. *See also* activism
computers, 193, 194–95, 198–99, 203, 210–11, 216
Conroy-Rios, Thelma, 157
Constant, Leroy, plate 14
Cooder, Ry, 111, 114, 115
Cook, Tekatsi:tsia'kwa Katsi, 263
country music, 105–6
covers: "Cod'ine," 68, 75; "The Piney Wood Hills," 105; "Power in the Blood," 245, 246; by Sainte-Marie, 79, 92, 107, 114, 115–16, 124, 278, 280; "Universal Soldier," 68; "Until It's Time for You to Go," 83, 105, 121, 122–23, 124–27, 278
Cradleboard Teaching Project: attempted NASA partnership, 219–20; award, 219; development, 208–9, 210; funding, 214–15, 216, 220; future plans, 262; Grover and self-esteem, 169; Indigenous perspective and curriculum, 209, 210, 211–13, 215, 216; partnerships with educators, 217, 220–21; purpose and legacy, 207–8, 214, 221, 222; *Science Through Native American Eyes* (CD-ROMS), 221; teacher concerns about, 217–18; technological component, 210–11, 213, 216
creativity, 24, 36, 46
Cree, 15, 43–44, 165, 228, 237
"Cripple Creek" (Sainte-Marie), 58
Crow Dog, Mary, 149, 150
Crudup, Arthur, 124

Dalai Lama, 36
Darin, Bobby, 83, 122–23, 127
"Darling Don't Cry" (Sainte-Marie), 201, 202
Davis, Bette, 122
Davis, Clive, 83, 128
Davis, Michael, 161
decolonization, 76, 222, 230–31, 240, 251
Deer, Ada, 152
Diamond, Neil, 122, 278
"Disinformation" (Sainte-Marie), 200
Doctrine of Discovery, 94–95, 232
Donovan (Donovan Philips Leitch), 68–69
drug addiction, 65–66, 186–87. *See also* alcohol; "Cod'ine" (Sainte-Marie)

Duston, Pete, 28
"Dyed, Dead, Red" (Sainte-Marie), 111
Dylan, Bob, 41, 52–53, 77, 81, 82–83, 92, 134

education: American Indian Higher Education Consortium, 259; Nihewan Foundation for American Indian Education, 146–47, 208, 209, 214, 220, 259; teaching job, 41–42; typical experience for children, 207, 215–16; university experience, 30–32, 34–36, 37–38, 41–42, 50. *See also* Cradleboard Teaching Project
Einarson, John, 69
electronic music, 107–10, 111, 194, 198, 243
"Emma Lee" (Sainte-Marie), 200
emotions: dealing with from colonialism, 218–19; in music, 45, 59–60, 132
Ensign Records, 197–98, 199
environmentalism, 227–30

Falle, Daisy, 223
fame, 128
fans, 9–10, 56, 135–38
The Far Horizons (movie), 89
"Farm in the Middle of Nowhere" (Sainte-Marie), 248
fashion industry, 96
FBI, 137–38, 155, 156, 195–96
Felix, Julie, 69
film and television. *See* movie scores; *Sesame Street*; *The Virginian* (TV show)
Fire & Fleet & Candlelight (Sainte-Marie), 99, 109, 279
"Fixin' to Die" (Sainte-Marie), 278
Flack, Roberta, 122
flamenco, 40, 138–39
folk music, 41, 52–53, 76–77, 79–80, 84, 92
"For Free" (Sainte-Marie), 280
Four Pennies, 122, 278
Franklin, Aretha: "Respect," 122
Fraser, Jill, 178
Freed, Alan, 40
Friendship Centre (Toronto), 43
Funmaker, Walter, 33

Gandhi, Mahatma, 30
Gaslight (New York venue), 53